PENGUIN BOOKS

INSIDE OUTSIDER

Tony Gould was born in Devon in 1938, and grew up on a farm there. He did his National Service in the 7th Gurkha Rifles in Malaya, India and Hong Kong, and was invalided out of the army with polio. Later he read English at Cambridge, worked on and off for eight years at the BBC as a radio producer, and was a Lecturer at Leicester Polytechnic. He is also the author of *In Limbo: The Story of Stanley's Rear Column* (1979).

Tony Gould is Books Editor at *New Society*. He is married and has three children.

Inside Outsider won the 1984 PEN Silver Pen award.

D1353622

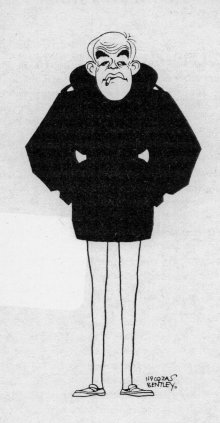

Inside Outsider

The Life and Times
of Colin MacInnes

Tony Gould

PENGUIN BOOKS

Penguin Books Ltd, Harmondsworth, Middlesex, England
Viking Penguin Inc., 40 West 23rd Street, New York, New York 10010, U.S.A.
Penguin Books Australia Ltd, Ringwood, Victoria, Australia
Penguin Books Canada Limited, 2801 John Street, Markham, Ontario, Canada L3R 1B4
Penguin Books (N.Z.) Ltd, 182–190 Wairau Road, Auckland 10, New Zealand

First published by Chatto & Windus · The Hogarth Press 1983
Published in Penguin Books 1986

Made and printed in Great Britain by
Richard Clay (The Chaucer Press) Ltd,
Bungay, Suffolk

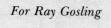

For Ray Gosling

Contents

List of illustrations

Frontispiece. Colin MacInnes by Nicolas Bentley.

Preface

It is impossible to recall what obscure impulse made me pick up the cheap and lurid Ace paperback edition of *City of Spades* during my national service at the end of the Fifties. Yet the book made a deep impression and I can still remember the amazement with which I read of the bizarre world of Africans and Caribbeans in London. That was the first time I came across the name of Colin MacInnes, though it meant nothing to me then.

Some years later, when I became a BBC radio producer, I heard the name again. Colin MacInnes was one of a select band – René Cutforth was another – of 'natural' broadcasters and radio 'personalities'. MacInnes, though, had a reputation for being 'difficult' and apparently did not broadcast any more. I never thought to ask why, but probably assumed that he had become too grand to do work for radio, which was by now very much the poor relation of television.

I also heard of Colin through a friend, Ray Gosling, who was himself rapidly making a name as a broadcaster. Ray spoke of Colin with affection but what he said had the effect of making me wary of him, though I did toy with the idea of approaching him with a view to getting him to broadcast again. But somehow my curiosity never quite overcame the reluctance I felt to set in motion something I might regret.

The first time I saw him (I must have noticed him because of his unusual height and recognised him from his photos) was at *New Society*'s ten-year anniversary party, which I attended as an occasional contributor. But I did not actually meet him until I became *New Society*'s Books Editor three years later, at the end of the summer of 1975, when he was sixty-one and had little more than six months left to live.

Our relationship was quite formal but friendly. By the time I knew him, Colin had retreated from the world somewhat. Not that he was ever a recluse; but he had alienated so many friends and well-wishers that he came to rely to some extent on professional contacts for friendship. Almost invariably, he would arrive early to mid-morning and stay till lunchtime. I don't know why I never asked him out to lunch – perhaps it was because he always chose when he would come and seldom gave me advance warning. Perhaps also he discouraged greater intimacy. Certainly I was still wary of him, though I liked him and enjoyed his visits.

Conversation with him was a very one-sided affair: one's own role was to be listener, though every so often he would punctuate his monologue with a challenging, 'Don't you agree?' If one were foolhardy enough to embark on an anecdote one needed strong nerves to complete it in the face of his ill-disguised impatience. He did not talk about himself – much – and was always ready to pounce when others did: 'Why are you always talking about yourself? This I . . . I . . . I . . . all the time . . .' Supremely ego-istical himself, mere egotism of the 'I . . . I . . . I . . .' sort irritated him.

If one's attention wandered, or thoughts of the work that lay on one's desk betrayed an anxiety to be rid of him, he would remark, 'I'm not boring you, am I?' or, more pointedly: 'I do think it's the duty of a literary editor to talk to his reviewers, don't you?' Yet he was obviously aware of the ambivalent feelings his marathon monologues could arouse; once he said, as he got up to leave the office, 'Well, either I'm an old bore, or you should have a tape-recorder. Perhaps it's a bit of both.' Perhaps it was, though his unusual personality ensured that he was never boring for long.

But he was cussed, and more than a bit of a bully – this in spite of an elaborate vein of old-world courtesy that he practised. 'You are kind,' he would say to a secretary who brought him a cup of coffee, for example. 'Is she always so thoughtful and con-siderate?' he would go on, turning to me for confirmation. But he was just as likely to blurt out, 'Don't ask me such a damnfool question!' to the most innocent inquiry. No doubt he was shield-ing his own sensibility, but he certainly wounded others.

If he was personally demanding, professionally he was both reliable and accommodating. He produced his reviews on time and to the length specified. On those occasions when lack of space or some other consideration obliged me to cut something he had written, he never raised the slightest objection. But if he thought an editor was acting unprofessionally he was quick to point it out. When one of my predecessors at *New Society* took over the job of Books Editor and wrote to say that he was unable to use a review

Colin had written, Colin replied: 'Dear Mr X, An editor has the right to reject a piece he has commissioned from a contributor. He can exercise this right in two ways, one courteous and professional, the other neither . . . to write, as you do, that since "you have already been paid for the work . . . we should be all square" is to misunderstand the situation. Let us suppose that, in your professional activities, you disagree with your employers, IPC. If they then told you that since they'd paid your wages, that made you and them "all square", would you agree to this proposition?' He was only half-mollified by a letter of apology. 'New editors,' he wrote back, determined to have the last word, 'are apt to want to wield new brooms, and there's nothing wrong with that. It may be best, though, not to do so clumsily.'

Just before Christmas he presented me with an inscribed copy of his *'No Novel Reader'*. But even this simple transaction was fraught with danger. He asked me if I had read Jane Austen's *Northanger Abbey*. I replied innocently that I had. 'Then you'll remember,' he said, 'her celebrated defence of the novel in that book?' Alas, I did not. So he attacked me for saying that I had read the novel when clearly I hadn't – because not remembering was the equivalent of not having read it. He was very scornful, but he gave me his book.

Early in 1976, when I heard that Colin had been operated on for cancer in St Pancras Hospital, I was not entirely surprised. He had the most appalling smoker's cough I've ever heard: it seemed to originate somewhere deep in his gut and well up obscenely through his body, leaving him gasping for breath. Word came that Colin wanted books to read in hospital, preferably paperbacks. I looked through the shelves of review copies and selected a couple of books I thought might amuse him and posted them off. A day or two later, when I went with a colleague to visit him, I made the mistake of asking him if he had received these books. 'What do you want,' he retorted, ' – gratitude?' And just in case I was deluded enough to imagine I had earned that, he added: 'Surely you don't expect me to read that stuff in hospital – paperbacks, I said I wanted *paperbacks*.' I explained that I had been unable to find a single suitable paperback on my shelves. 'You could've gone to Smith's and *bought* some, couldn't you?' he snorted, and then, as the idea took hold of him, went on: 'In fact, why don't you go to a bookshop when you leave here and get six paperbacks – three of them should be readable. Send them up by taxi,' he ordered, adding in a lordly manner, 'I'll pay for the cab.' He refused to offer any guidance on what he might like to read, so my colleague and I spent an uncomfortable hour in a bookshop trying to find six paperbacks that Colin MacInnes had not already read and might actually want to read. It was not an easy task. He did – much later – have the grace to thank us.

The last time I saw Colin he was plainly very sick indeed. He came to the office, but the effort of climbing stairs had left him exhausted. For much of the time he just sat there hunched in pain and when, after an uncharacteristically short visit, he prepared to leave, I spotted him standing irresolutely in a kind of no man's land in the centre of the office, outside the individual cubicles. I remember thinking how utterly solitary and out of place he looked, like some beached sea monster. He wrote at least one more review for me which he tried to deliver in person (he needed the money and insisted – as ever – on payment in cash); but the stairs defeated him and he had to send it up with the mini-cab driver. This driver, who knew him, reported that he looked dreadful. 'Six months ago,' he said, 'he would jump up and argue about anything. Now he just sits there . . .'

Yet, although I had been expecting it, the news of his death took me by surprise. More surprising still was how much I missed him. It would be less than honest not to admit that, mixed in with the other emotions his death aroused, there was an element of relief; but the sense of loss far outweighed it. Colin MacInnes was a bit larger than life. Whatever else he may have been, he was quite unique . . .

He was a good writer, but not a great one; certainly not a great novelist. Like George Orwell, with whom he invites comparison, he was a better essayist than novelist. Yet he could hardly have expressed the thoughts and feelings which give such vividness to *City of Spades* and *Absolute Beginners*, in particular, in any other form than in a novel; and though, to my mind, the volume of essays, *England, Half English*, contains the best of his writing, it has not been reprinted so often, or stayed in print so long, as the two above-mentioned novels and their companion piece, *Mr Love and Justice* – the tale of the ponce and the copper.

Absolute Beginners, indeed, was something of a cult book. It has been dubbed an English *Catcher in the Rye*, but it resembles its American forerunner only insofar as both novels have teenage heroes. Even then, Holden Caulfield and MacInnes's nameless teenager inhabit different worlds. But the impact of *Absolute Beginners* gives the clue to MacInnes's enduring interest. In that book and elsewhere he touched the nerve of his time – and his time was the Fifties. Before the Beatles, one might say. For the decade which was initiated by the Festival of Britain – that 'herbivorous' attempt to throw off the pall of post-war austerity – and ended with the downfall of the Macmillan 'You've never had it so good' Conservative administration in the wake of the Profumo scandal, MacInnes had his finger on the pulse of the nation. The reasons for this have to do with his psychological make-up. But MacInnes, who was already in his forties by the middle of the decade, was able to empathise to an almost uncanny degree with the younger generation; and his best writing accurately reflects the innocence and the optimism (however facile in retrospect) of the Macmillan era.

For three or four years at the end of the Fifties and beginning of the Sixties, he achieved near-celebrity status. But then he rather lost his touch in a world he found increasingly unsympathetic, first in its smug and strident materialism and then in its depressingly familiar return to harder times. MacInnes maintained, for the most part, a high standard of journalism but the chemistry which had transformed journalistic experience into contemporary fables was missing; and in his later fictions he retreated into a kind of historical make-believe, the ingenuity of which cannot conceal the barrenness, not of invention, but of purpose.

MacInnes was a solitary and a difficult man and not everyone, by any means, remembers him with affection. Colin Wilson, for example, who also made a name for himself in the Fifties with his book, *The Outsider*, and his much publicised bohemian life-style, only met MacInnes twice; but the memory of the second occasion still rankles after more than twenty years:

'. . . I saw him in Whitechapel at an art exhibition – it may have been Turner,' he writes, in a letter to me.

We talked for a minute or two, then he said he wanted to be alone for a while to look at the pictures. I saw William Saroyan there, and stood talking with him. When he heard that Colin MacInnes was there, he asked if I knew him and if I'd introduce him. Naturally, I said I'd be glad to, and took him over. I said: 'Colin, this is Bill Saroyan.' To my amazement, MacInnes turned on me viciously and snapped, 'I thought I told you I wanted to look at the pictures alone?' Naturally, both I and Saroyan walked away . . . as far as I was concerned the bastard could go and jump in the lake . . .

Yet the majority of people who knew MacInnes at all well, even if he tried them beyond endurance and they fell out with him eventually, do still recall him with some affection, as I discovered. The biography of a contemporary is inevitably a joint enterprise; and though the responsibility for what follows rests entirely with me, I could not have written it without considerable help – from Reg Davis-Poynter who, as MacInnes's literary executor, invited me to do it in the first place; from Paul Barker who, as Editor of *New Society*, allowed me time off both to research and to write the book; from Jacqueline Kavanagh and the staff at the BBC Written Archives in Reading, and from Peter Dzwonkoski and the staff of the Department of Rare Books, Manuscripts and Archives at the University of Rochester in New York State, who provided information and generally facilitated my research; from F.S. Crawford, Secretary of the Old Scotch Collegians' Association in Melbourne, who put me in touch with several of MacInnes's contemporaries at Scotch; and from my brother-in-law, Roger Cowell, who made the initial contacts in Australia on my behalf.

Of the many people who have given generously of their time either to talk to me or to correspond on the subject of Colin MacInnes, I would like to thank each and every one of them individually and at length but, at the risk of seeming ungrateful (and more so to any I may have inadvertently left out), I must content myself simply to list their names in gratitude. My thanks, then, to Elinor Bellingham Smith, John Berger, Ian Bevan, Edward Blishen, Victor Bonham Carter, Elaine Bromwich, Iain Campbell, James Campbell, Ross Campbell, Charles Causley, Michael Church, Sir Edward Cohen, Sir William Coldstream, Sue Crick, Frank Critchlow, Eric Dadson, the late Roy Edwards, A.P. Fleming, James Foston, Philip French, Ray Gosling, Kenny Graham, Fiona Green, Martin Green, Barney and Irene Green-man, Alfred Hall, Montague Haltrecht, David Harrison, Patrick

Harvey, Bryan Healing, Calvin Hernton, Eric Hobsbawm, R. Hudson Smith, Thelma Hulbert, Elspeth Huxley, Charles Jacobs, Douglas Johnson, Max and Betty Jones, Richard Keen, Frank Kermode, Roy Kerridge, Christopher Kininmonth, Bernard and Erica Kops, Jack Lambert, Melvin Lasky, Michael Law, W.A.J. Lawrence, Betty Lawson, Geoffrey Lawson, Denis Lemon, Eddie Linden, Peggy and Marcus Little, Joan McInnes, James MacGibbon, Norman Mailer, Alfred Maron, George Melly, Joy Melville, Beatrix Miller, J. Mourant, Rodrigo Moynihan, Victor Musgrave, the late Frank Norman, Tim O'Keeffe, John Osborne, Horace Ové, Tony Parker, Michael Portman, Paul Potts, Bryan Robertson, Sheila Sage, Edge Semmens, Maurice Shadbolt, Pamela Sharpe, Nancy Shepherdson, Clancy Sigal, David Sylvester, Terry Taylor, Lance and Kate Thirkell, Serena Thirkell, Julian Trevelyan, Sir Keith Waller, Robert Waller, Margot Walmsley, Nicolas Walter, Colin Ward, Maurice Wasterlain, Alexander Weatherson, Fred Weekes, John Weightman, Gillian Wilce, Richard Wollheim and Francis Wyndham.

Further thanks are due to two of the above, R. Hudson Smith and Robert Waller, for reading and commenting on particular chapters in typescript; to my friend Simon Gray for his most valuable comments on an early draft of the book; and to my wife Jenny who has not only read each chapter more than once, but has also had to live with the ghost of Colin MacInnes as house guest, so to speak, for more years than I care to number.

Finally, I am grateful to the following for permission to quote from published material in copyright: to the editors of *Encounter*, *Harpers & Queen*, *Jewish Chronicle*, *New Statesman*, *New Society*, the *Observer*, *Spectator*, the *Sunday Times* and *The Times Educational Supplement* for extracts from articles by Colin MacInnes and others; to Mrs Ann Graham Bell for extracts from the private letters of Graham Bell; to Robert Graves and A.P. Watt Ltd for extracts from the private letters of Robert Graves; to the estate of Graham McInnes and Hamish Hamilton Ltd for extracts from *The Road to Gundagai*, *Humping My Bluey* and *Finding a Father*; to the estate of Angela Thirkell and Hamish Hamilton Ltd for extracts from *Ankle Deep*, *O These Men, These Men!* and *Peace Breaks Out*; to Ruth Glass and George Allen & Unwin for extracts from

Newcomers: the West Indians in London. Full details of these and all other works quoted are given in the references at the end of the book.

Part one

Angela Thirkell's Son

1

A Victorian Cultural Dynasty

The remarkable Macdonald sisters had no wealth or social standing to recommend them; they had only their own merits and the intelligence to recognise merit in others. They were the off-spring of George Browne Macdonald, a Wesleyan preacher. Alice, the eldest, married John Lockwood Kipling and gave birth to Rudyard; Georgiana married Edward Burne-Jones when he was plain Mr Jones, a penniless and quite unknown young painter; Agnes married another painter, Edward Poynter, who later became President of the Royal Academy; and Louisa married an ironmaster, Alfred Baldwin, and was mother of the future Prime Minister, Stanley Baldwin. The preacher also had two sons and one other daughter who never married – to mention only those who survived infancy.

The family traces its origin to the Isle of Skye whence, some-time in the mid-eighteenth century, a Macdonald couple set sail for North America but got no further than Ireland. Their life there is shrouded in obscurity until their son, James, who was born near Enniskillen in 1761, grew up and – the family having joined the Methodist Society – was invited by John Wesley himself to become an itinerant preacher. That was in 1784. Eleven years later he came to England, where he spent the remaining thirty-nine years of his life.[1]

James's younger son, George, followed his father in becoming a Methodist minister. Having a Scottish father and an Irish mother, and living in England, he chose for himself a Welsh wife. She was called Hannah. In the 1830s and '40s, when Hannah was bearing their many children, the family never stayed more than three years in any one place. From Bristol they moved to Sheffield, from Sheffield to Birmingham, from Birmingham to Leeds, to Wakefield, to Huddersfield – and back to Birmingham again in 1850.

As they grew up the young Macdonald sisters all aspired to a larger and freer existence than that centred on a chapel; but Alice no doubt shocked the others when, packing in preparation for one of their innumerable moves, she discovered a yellowed envelope marked 'A lock of Mr Wesley's hair', removed the revered memento and threw it on the fire, saying: 'See! A hair of the dog that bit us!'[2]

Though they eventually succeeded in escaping the chapel confines, the sisters inevitably retained something of the sternness of their upbringing. 'If there was a flaw common to all their characters,' a descendant wrote, 'it could be said, and doubtless was said in the broader-minded world that acknowledged their enchanting virtues, that, while they were slow to bless, they were often incontinently swift to chide.'[3]

Georgiana was not quite sixteen when Edward Burne-Jones asked to marry her. Her parents left the decision entirely to her and she remained grateful to them for refraining from discussion of his 'prospects' – 'my father asked Edward no questions about his "position", but, so far as my judgment goes, acted as a minister of the Christian religion should do, seeking nothing but character and leaving the question of fortune altogether on one side.'[4]

When Georgie entered the world of Burne-Jones, William Morris and Rossetti, it was startlingly new to her, for she was 'a young girl whose experience so far had been quite remote from art'. Yet in a way it was also familiar. She felt, as she described it many years later, 'in the presence of a new religion. Their love of beauty did not seem to me unbalanced, but as if it included the whole world and raised the point from which they regarded everything.' There was uplift in art just as there was in religion; and women, to these second-wave Pre-Raphaelites, were 'holy things'.[5]

Burne-Jones's origins were no grander than Georgie's. His father was an artisan – a carver and gilder. His mother had died when Burne-Jones was born and it was some time before his father became reconciled to the son whose birth had caused his wife's death. But Burne-Jones's childhood, though a solitary one, was not unduly miserable. He grew up above his father's picture shop in Birmingham and went on occasional excursions to visit country cousins. He was destined for the church when he went up to Oxford; there he met his lifelong friend, William Morris, who also intended to take holy orders. But for both of them religion was displaced by art. Morris came from a prosperous background and when Burne-Jones first visited his friend's home he was astonished at its vastness. Later in life, when he flirted with the fashionable world in such gathering places as Little Holland House (home of the Prinseps), Morris disapproved. Reading between the lines of Georgiana's *Memorials of Edward Burne-Jones*, it is plain that she too frowned on these ventures into 'society': '*I could not then realise as I do now* what this visit to Little Holland House must have been to him . . .' (my italics).[6]

Burne-Jones might take pleasure in the world but, as his paintings show only too clearly for most people's taste, he was essentially other-worldly. Birmingham was his birthplace, but he took refuge from all nineteenth-century Coketowns in dreams of Dante and the Arthurian legends. His need to escape, though, was psychological as much as social: the uncompromising naturalism of the greatest nineteenth-century art was unacceptable to him. When Tolstoy's *Anna Karenina* was recommended to him, he demurred, saying:

I don't mind being harrowed, but then it must be in lofty rhyme or verse heroical – great kings and queens – and then I like it very much; but I can't bear a tale that has in it a woman who is knocked about and made miserable and mad, and thrown away on a wretch, and is altogether heart-breaking . . . I know how good they are . . . that the Russians can make splendid women in their books – but I do really suffer when I read them and get demoralised with miserable reflections.[7]

Burne-Jones idealised women just as he idealised the medieval past. Women were his inspiration; he was always falling in love, but it seems that, as with his representation of them in paintings, it was in a very ethereal way – a way even their husbands might tolerate. Art, of course, had to be noble, but in contrast to what? The only answer can be: life. Expression in art was 'decadent', which was why the Pre-Raphaelites looked to those who came before Raphael and abominated the 'passions' and 'emotions' that others admired in that painter's work.

A recent biographer of Burne-Jones has suggested that he was the model for the lama in Kipling's *Kim*. He certainly had something of the lama's other-worldliness; and just as Kim must in the end reject that in favour of a life of action, so Kipling himself had to reject his Uncle Ned's life-denying vision in order to become the greater artist that he undoubtedly was.[8]

Of course there was more to Burne-Jones than an enchanted dreamer. By all accounts he was a wonderful talker, funny if not witty. He did not value wit very highly, saying that 'the books I most worship are as devoid of it as the paintings I worship. None in Homer, none in Aeschylus or Dante, none in the *Morte d'Arthur*.'[9] He was a true Victorian in his enjoyment of practical jokes, and he had a rare talent for comic drawing. But it was his pictures of languid knights and attenuated maidens that brought him renown and riches in late Victorian England.

He espoused a vision of art so distanced from life, so far above and beyond it, that it is not surprising he 'failed' his friend Morris, as he saw it, in the latter's more earthly grail, the quest for socialism. In this, Morris found a readier disciple in Georgiana, with whom he was more than a little in love at the time. Georgie was of a far more practical turn of mind than her husband, and her sympathy with Morris's aims meant that he confided in her. This lovely, tiny woman, whose beautiful and guileless eyes impressed all who knew her, made up for her lack of inches with her daunting moral stature. Yet she was modest and unaffected, content to play a secondary role while her husband lived and then, when he died, to devote five years of her life to writing his *Memorials*. Her discretion is absolute and there are no intimate revelations in her book, though a pithy sentence she quotes from one of Burne-Jones's letters, written late in his life, gives an indication of what she had to put up with in relation to his susceptibility to damsels in distress: 'There's a self-contradiction in pitying a woman though – the worst of it is that as soon as you've taken pity on her she's no longer to be pitied. You're the one to be pitied then – so beware!'[10]

Georgie's virtues, her loyalty (which Burne-Jones tested to the full), her honesty and courage, inspired awe as well as love. Even her great-grandson Colin, who was only an infant when she died, knew that 'although she was infinitely just and kind, one must not, as with other benevolent seniors, take any liberties with her';[11] while her granddaughter Angela, though she admired her 'self-possession and dignity and . . . power of accepting everyone – no matter what their social position – entirely for what they were in themselves', was herself 'ready to cry with confusion' when as a child she was taken along to visit working people in their cottages and forced to listen to her grandmother bringing 'tidings of comfort from *Fors Clavigera*' to 'some gnarled and unlettered old woman'.[12]

Of the generation between, Philip and Margaret Burne-Jones were the only children to survive infancy (a third, Christopher, died very young). Philip grew up morbidly sensitive; it did not help that his parents sent him to William Morris's old school, Marlborough. Eventually he had to be taken away and privately tutored before he went up to Oxford. Like many another son of a famous man, he never really got out of his father's shadow. He had the Burne-Jones facility for comic drawing, but his father made him promise never to turn that to commercial advantage. Instead, he had to be a serious painter. He did succeed in painting one or two excellent portraits – of his father and of his cousin, Kipling, for example – but he lacked his father's application. His ambitions were social rather than artistic and the story goes that Burne-Jones accepted the baronetcy Gladstone pressed upon him largely to please his son, who would then inherit the title and retain a place in society.[13]

Angela Thirkell's description of her Uncle Phil shows that there was a remarkable temperamental affinity between him and his great-nephew Colin. His friends found him an 'incalculable quantity' and his niece remembered his visits to the nursery as a 'fearful joy'. These visits either promised some delightful outing or resulted in a speedy removal from the room in order to avoid a scene: 'His kindness of heart was unbounded and yet he could wound most cruelly and deliberately.'[14]

Overshadowed by his father, not needing to work for a living, Philip – according to his niece – had another temperamental disadvantage: 'There was on his mother's side, coming from her mother's family, a strain of deep melancholy and self-distrust which in some of the family was almost a disease.' Another sufferer was Kipling's sister, Trix, who for a long period of her life teetered on the brink of insanity and would not allow her poor husband, Colonel Fleming, anywhere near her. With Philip it was not so extreme, though he never married; but 'he was quick to suspect an imagined slight or insult and would say or write something which would bring the unsuspecting offender to bewildered tears.'[15]

Margaret Burne-Jones was also prone to melancholy, though her grandson attributes that more to her Burne-Jones inheritance than to the Macdonald family disease (Sir William Rothenstein once asked him, 'Colin, why was your great-grandfather so sad a man? He had a wife and children who adored him, devoted friends, material success and fairly early recognition – then why is it that he always spoke of himself as such a sad man?').[16] She was a pretty child – 'unfairly pretty', one friend of the family found her at the age of fourteen.[17] Her parents, particularly her father, spoiled her. Burne-Jones wrote: '. . . Margaret came home from school – the brightest of bright things is that damsel, half a head taller than her mother, and I sit and chuckle at the sight of her, and nudge my neighbour: also I praise her to her face that she may be used to flattery and be sick of it, and not astonished or touched when it is used by others – that is my way with her . . .'[18]

Margaret grew up on terms of easy familiarity with the great. Apart from artists and politicians, such as Tennyson, Ruskin, Morris, Wilde and Gladstone, who were a part of her early life, there were her lifelong friendships with the likes of Lady Wemyss and Lady Glenconner which gave her daughter Angela an entrée into the world she was to make it her artistic business to reproduce in countless novels. Unlike her mother Georgiana, whose midlands and northern Methodist background gave her an affinity with the novelist George Eliot, Margaret grew up in the fashionable world; she sat for G.F. Watts as well as, of course, for her father.

According to family legend, Burne-Jones invented a type in his paintings which his descendants came to resemble (Colin's half-brother, Lance Thirkell, sees an uncanny physical resemblance to Colin in Burne-Jones's depiction of the eponymous hero in the painting, *The Beguiling of Merlin*)[19] and he was painting Margaret even before she was born. A prosaic explanation would be that Georgie was the prototype and that Burne-Jones gave her in paintings the inches she lacked in life, so that he arrived at a type with a small head and elongated body which his descendants actually grew up like (though Margaret herself was not much taller than her mother).[20]

As she grew up, Margaret also shouldered her mother's role as Burne-Jones's companion, going for walks with him and reading to him in his studio. Georgiana writes, '. . . as soon as Margaret was old enough she began to share then almost entirely to take over my post as reader-aloud in the studio. Beside many other books she went through the whole of Thackeray twice in this way; Dickens was my special province . . .'[21]

Unsurprisingly, in view of the father-daughter intimacy, Burne-Jones was frantically jealous when Margaret got married. He had even expressed the hope 'that she might never know love, and stay with me.'[22] It took him some time to be reconciled to the marriage, though it must have helped that his son-in-law was writing the biography of his closest friend, William Morris, and had come to him in the first place for his help. J.W. Mackail was a scholar-poet; he married Margaret just seven years after Burne-Jones had gone to Oxford to receive an honorary doctorate and stayed on to listen to the winner of the Newdigate Prize read out his prizewinning poem, little realising that the budding poet was his future son-in-law.

Mackail was a son of the manse. His father had been Chaplain to the Black Watch in Malta, and then to the Free Church in Calcutta. When he returned to Scotland he became a minister in Ayr. John William Mackail was born on the island of Arran and educated at Ayr Academy. He went to Edinburgh University with a bursary and from there he got a scholarship to Balliol. He almost never went back to Scotland, but in London he made a name for himself both as a conscientious civil servant and as a tireless writer and translator.[23] He became Professor of Poetry at Oxford and was awarded the OM. Yet for all his genuine distinction he remained something of a pedant. Lady Cynthia Asquith called him 'the most complete walking encyclopaedia I've ever met'.[24]

Margaret Mackail – according to Colin MacInnes – was 'a far more complex and dominating character' than her husband, who was 'a good and gentle, even timorous man'; and their Kensington home (6 Pembroke Gardens), so full of the flavour of Morris & Co., 'was more, one felt, her house than my grandfather's, for despite his own high achievement, he had been somewhat absorbed into the Pre-Raphaelite heritage of his wife.' Yet 'whereas her father and husband had done great things – as had even her mother, Lady Burne-Jones, whose *Memorials* of her husband are a minor, and reticent, masterpiece – the only work of art she herself had created was her own considerable personality.'[25]

In an essay on cultural dynasties, MacInnes tries to draw up a balance sheet of the defects and virtues of his particular clan. Among the defects he lists the fact that 'they had, to a man and woman, an excellent opinion of themselves'; that 'they were not particularly loving people' (or rather, that 'their love seemed, however intense, to be rather chill and demanding' – witness Kipling's 'boyhood martyrdom' at Southsea); and that they were less tolerant than they imagined, that there was 'something almost provincial' in their outlook.[26]

Their chief virtue, on the other hand, was 'a real, total and quite unquestioning respect for art and learning'. Their attitude to money, too – 'a lack of respect for it' but no 'snobbish contempt for commerce' – was admirable (out of loyalty, perhaps, Mac-Innes refrains from mentioning their parsimoniousness). They were also patriotic, though not at all jingoistic: when the Boer War ended, Georgiana hung a banner from the window of her house in Rottingdean proclaiming, 'We have killed and also taken possession.' It was only the timely intervention of her nephew and near-neighbour, Rudyard Kipling, which prevented a riot in the village.[27]

Towards Kipling – 'incontestably a radical (albeit a Tory one)' – MacInnes's feelings were reverential: 'If one is entitled to be "proud" of distant relatives at all, I most certainly, and most respectfully, am of him.'[28] But as for the others, 'if they were inspiring people, they were also appallingly demanding. They were, in fact, the sort of family that one would perhaps rather read about, than belong to . . .'[29]

Angela was the eldest of the three Mackail children: she was born in 1890, her brother Denis (who was also to make a name as a popular novelist) in 1892 and her sister Clare in 1896. In the first year of her life her doting grandfather Burne-Jones wrote: '. . . Miss Angela Mackail [is] the principal comfort at present. She is a haughty-looking person, with an expression mostly of indignant surprise.'[30] Before she was three, she was bossing the cook around and her mother noted: 'What am I to do with a Baby of 2¼ who gives her own orders in the house?' And by the time she was seven, she could look at a family portrait and say: 'Mother, why in Mr Graham Robertson's picture do I look so defiant? & Clare so hopeless? & Den like a cowering stag? & you like a noble king? We all look like something except Ba [her father]. He's not there.'[31]

Angela's childhood was made up of 'long warm summers': there were not only her adoring parents and grandparents, her generous – if unpredictable – Uncle Phil; there was also Cousin Ruddy, who would try out his newly-written *Just So Stories* on a nursery audience consisting of her and of his own daughter Josephine (whose early death would shatter him). J.M. Barrie was Angela's godfather, and Beatrix Potter a London neighbour.

The 'Three Houses' that Angela remembered with such nostalgia when she came to write her memoir of them in the gloomy 1930s were her parents' first home together, a terraced house in Young Street, opposite Kensington Square and next to a pub called the Greyhound, and her grandparents' two houses: one, the Grange in North End Road in Fulham, was once the home of the eighteenth-century novelist, Samuel Richardson, and is now demolished; the other, North End House in Rottingdean, was Georgiana's discovery. On a walk over the Sussex downs she found a cottage for sale on the village green and Burne-Jones bought it to please her. They enlarged it considerably over the years, until it came to be twice its original size. It was a rather inconvenient house, but that only added to its appeal for children. Among the objects it contained, Colin MacInnes would remember a 'rather unexpected device my great-grandmother had in her bedroom: . . . an electrical arrangement whereby the face of a clock appeared, reflected from somewhere or other, in lights upon a darkened ceiling: a strangely modern invention in 1918 or thereabouts in a house otherwise notable for beautiful but very austere William Morris furniture.'[32]

The Grange went out of the family when Burne-Jones died in 1898; and the Mackails then moved from Young Street to No. 6 Pembroke Gardens, which remained their home for the rest of their life together. Only North End House remained; Georgiana went to live there permanently after her husband's death and Rottingdean became a kind of family centre for the Macdonald sisters and their descendants. Kipling bought 'The Elms' across the green and wrote *Kim* there; and Stanley Baldwin went there to woo Cissy Ridsdale, who lived in 'The Dene'. Angela Mackail and her contemporaries ran on the downs or played on the beach under the watchful eyes of their nannies, just as her sons, Graham and Colin, would do a generation later – only by then, just across the Channel, the war that was to end all wars was ending, instead, this sheltered and highly privileged middle class way of life.

Angela went to St Paul's School, where she won several prizes for literature. Second only to literature was her love of music and she learned to play the piano at school. Yet she was no blue-stocking; she enjoyed games and, in spite of – or perhaps because of – her father's intellectual standing, had no academic ambitions.[33]

Physically, she was tall, taking after her father rather than her mother. She had a pretty face, and she wore her hair up to reveal her long neck, but her waist was not as slender as she would have liked and her legs were large and somewhat shapeless. She was, perhaps, more striking than beautiful.

When she left school, beyond vague yearnings to write, which her parents did not encourage, she had little idea what she would do – or be, since there was no immediate need for her to *do* anything. It was expected that she would make a good marriage. In fact, she did what her second son would do more than twenty years later: she spent six months in Paris improving her French and then, the following year, went to Germany to do the same for her German. Both languages she had originally learnt from governesses, then studied at school.[34]

Spirited and independent though she was, Angela Mackail was no feminist. Her attitude to men was as romantic and idealistic as her grandfather's had been towards women, and though she is inclined to mock Anne Fielding in this passage from her novel, *Peace Breaks Out* (1946), it is with all the indulgence of an older self recalling the innocent folly of her youth:

Anne stood on the landing and gazed at the upward curve of the stairs, which she had often tried to draw, though she had never obtained a result to her own liking. From her nursery days the barley-sugar curve of the staircase had held a secret romance for her. Up and down it had passed in her mind every fairy prince, mythological hero, long-locked Cavalier, dashing and heartless rake, romantic ne'er-do-well, scholar, poet, lover, of her omniverous appetite for reading, a passion born of a solitary childhood, quickened and fostered by the elderly governess Miss Bunting who had crowned her life's work by implanting in Anne Fielding some of her own uncompromising rectitude and love of literature. Each figure had kissed her hand, bowed low with the sweep of a plumed hat, held a sword aloft in salute; cast a look of dark adoration from the mantle enshrouding his face; and more than once had a gallant (period unspecified) ridden up the front door steps, down the flagged hall to the foot of the stairs, and reined in his foam-flecked steed at the foot of the staircase. Sometimes he had swung her to his saddle and ridden away with her . . . sometimes, the blood welling from between the fingers pressed to his side, he had fallen dead at her feet in a most attractive way . . .[35]

It is a vision entirely appropriate to the granddaughter of Burne-Jones. Angela Mackail at twenty-one was a bookish young lady whose intellectual attainments far outstripped her emotional development. Therein lay her vulnerability. She was proud, too, and sensed that her parents' relationship with their several friends among the landed gentry was not without an element of deference on one side and patronage on the other. She might aspire to the condition of the landed families, but she would not stoop to ingratiate herself. Perhaps it was her sharp tongue that frightened off prospective suitors among the gentry, or it could have been that she found the young upper-class Edwardians too insipid for her taste. Either way, romance, when it came into her life, came not in the shape of some scion of the nobility but in the form of a total outsider, a six foot four, swarthy and handsome lieder singer called James Campbell McInnes. If he did not quite swing her on to his saddle and ride away with her, he certainly swept her off her feet.

They met at a country-house party in the spring of 1911, and in less than two months they were married.

2

A Family at War

'I also had – somewhat surprisingly, it would almost seem – a father,' Colin MacInnes writes.

His personal life left much to be desired, and let those judge him who are able. But as an artist, he was a very great one. He was born in Lancashire, of Scottish emigrant parents . . . who were very poor and, politically, active radicals. Endowed by nature with a 'prodigy' voice, my father studied in London and Europe on scholarships and in penury, and rose to be, in the late Victorian and Edwardian eras, the foremost British lieder singer of his generation.[1]

James Campbell McInnes – spelt thus: Colin adopted the 'Mac' spelling to make it easier for the French to understand his surname – was sixteen years older than Angela Mackail. His father was an engraver and he grew up among Lancashire mill-workers. His talent for singing was spotted early on by the local lady of the manor, a Mrs Aitken, who paid for him to have singing lessons once a week in the nearby town of Bury. He walked there and back, a journey of five miles each way.[2] If Colin MacInnes's incomplete and unpublished novel, *Angus Bard*, which follows closely the contours of his father's life, is anything to go by, there was something of a tug-of-war between father and patroness over the young James. The father, Archibald McInnes, was an alcoholic; his behaviour was alternately brutal and maudlin, and always terrifying – occasionally he would chase his entire family out of the house on to the rooftops.[3] In the battle over James, however, it was Mrs Aitken who won – in the short run, at least. She continued to pay his fees when he won a place, though not the scholarship he had tried for, at the Royal College of Music in London.

After further study in Paris under the Belgian baritone, Jacques Bouhy, McInnes made his debut in London in 1899. From then on he was much in demand in drawing rooms and country houses, as well as on concert platforms. He sang solos in the first performance of Vaughan Williams's *A Sea Symphony* in 1910, and when George Butterworth set Housman's *A Shropshire*

Lad to music, McInnes was the obvious choice of singer – obvious because he was known for his renderings of the country ballads he had learnt as a child. When he married Angela he was at the height of his popularity as a singer; and part of his appeal for her – if not for her parents, who disapproved of the match – was his romantically working-class background.

As for McInnes himself, nothing could be more flattering than to make a conquest of this haughty girl, so very much younger than him. It was a sign that he had truly arrived. Up until then he had been living with the composer, Graham Peel – a relationship which, if truer to his sexual nature, lacked the glamour of marriage to a society beauty. Peel was the son of a wealthy north country businessman and McInnes lived off, as well as with, him. It was a mutually advantageous relationship, though, since McInnes both inspired and sang Peel's songs and, in his performances, gave them a life and resonance they otherwise lacked. Peel's was a fragile talent; indeed, when McInnes left him to marry Angela Mackail, he gave up writing music and retired to Bournemouth.

The first three years of their married life – until the beginning of the First World War, in fact – seem to have been happy ones for the McInnes's. They lived at 108 Church Street in Kensington, a short walk away from Angela's parents, and in February 1912 their first son, Graham, was born there. In 1914 they moved to 20 The Grove, Boltons (now the Little Boltons) in South Kensington, where Colin was born on 20 August – his birth certificate gives the 'rank or profession of father' as 'professor of music'. No. 20 The Grove, Boltons, was a bigger house than 108 Church Street, and it was in a quieter street; but it was still within walking distance of the Mackails.

Only a few days before the war broke out, James McInnes had been invited to sing at a party at Lady Glenconner's, where one of the guests was Sir Edward Grey. McInnes noticed the Foreign Secretary's fatigue and pallor and, with characteristic impulsiveness, wrote him a letter: 'Dear Sir Edward – I am so glad you liked the music, and if the world is going to become a howling wilderness, won't you let me sing to you again?'

Grey was too preoccupied to answer immediately; when he did get round to replying the war had already begun. He wrote: 'Dear Mr McInnes – I am touched by your letter and will keep it by me in case there is a time when I can come. I love Handel's music and it does me good. Europe is in the most terrible trouble it has ever known in civilised times, and no one can say what will be left at the end. But Handel's music will survive.'

Grey's biographer, G.M. Trevelyan, goes on: 'And several times during the war Grey went to Mr McInnes who sang to him Handel and Bach and the old Italian songs.'⁴ Grey's visits were also recorded in Angela McInnes's diary of the war years. But according to Graham McInnes, as his father grew older he embellished the story to such an extent that Grey did not merely come to hear him sing, but eagerly sought his advice on the conduct of the war and appreciatively relayed his *bons mots* to his cabinet colleagues, who all happened to be sitting round the dinner table along with the editor of *The Times*, etc, etc – rather in the manner of that supreme romancer of the era, Ford Madox Ford, who, by his own account, was also prominent in the nation's councils of war.

In fact, the war affected James McInnes's career adversely. As early as September 1914 Angela was writing to the children's nanny, Barbara Parson, from a hotel in Hindhead, where she had gone with James to convalesce after Colin's birth: '. . . I cannot give you the extra help for the nursery as I had hoped. The war will make a great deal of difference to us, and we shall have to live as carefully as we can.'⁵ Although there were fewer singing engagements, and McInnes was eventually reduced to supplementing their income by teaching, to begin with the war hardly seems to have affected their social life at all. James was now forty, too old to enlist, at least in the early stages of the war; so he became a special constable, which meant that he might be called out in the event of an air raid. Otherwise it was the usual round of children, family, friends, social and musical engagements, and visits to Rottingdean that Angela noted in her diary.

On 7 December 1915, for instance, in the morning she sat for John Singer Sargent, who made a charcoal drawing of her which she treasured ever afterwards; she lunched with Jim and in the afternoon they went to a 'stupid' charity concert at South Lodge where, she writes, 'Princess Louise was very nice to us both.' Jim was always hopping off to Bournemouth to see Graham Peel on one pretext or another (Graham McInnes was named after Peel, who was also his godfather) and every so often he would spend a day with his sister-in-law Clare, who seems to have been more than a little in love with him herself. Angela does not comment on these matters; her diary is for the most part strictly factual.[6]

The first entry to hint that anything is wrong with the marriage is dated 30 January 1916, a Sunday. As ever, it is a cryptic note: 'My 26th birthday – not much remembered . . .' Yet given the restraint that characterises the diary, these three words convey a wealth of meaning. Superficially, things go on as before: in March Jim sings for a party of wounded soldiers at the Duchess of Wellington's, '. . . and then we had tea in a sitting room, Jim and I with the Duke and Duchess, Queen Alexandra and Princess Victoria, and the other performers separately'; in July the family goes, with Nanny, to Rottingdean and Angela becomes pregnant for the third time; in September she goes with Jim to Edinburgh for a concert, and Graham Peel joins them . . . But under the surface the love of husband and wife is transformed into rage and violence on one side, and fear and hatred on the other.

The crisis came when a daughter, Mary, was born at the end of March 1917. The diary ceases a week before this event and is not taken up again until August; even then there are only a couple of entries before it is abandoned once more, not to be resumed until the end of November. The intervening months, which were so fateful for Angela McInnes, are summed up with a few strokes of the pen: 'Mary was born on March 30. On 1 May I came to Pembroke Gardens and have never seen Jim again.' Then comes a catalogue of houses visited – North End House in Rottingdean, of course, but also Clouds, the family home of the Wyndhams, and two other houses belonging to Wyndhams: Stanway (Lady Wemyss) and Wilsford (Lady Glenconner). Lady Cynthia Asquith, daughter of the Countess of Wemyss, records in *her* diary for 18 May: '. . . lunched at Cadogan Square. Conversation with Mamma afterwards. She told me of the terrible Campbell McInnes melodrama. He has become a raving drunkard and she is going to divorce him. She has just been packed off to Clouds with her new baby. Fancy he and poor, tiny, little Phil had a ghastly struggle at Rottingdean and Phil actually downed him!'[7] McInnes, surprised to find his house deserted when he returned after one of his periodic absences, sought his wife in Rottingdean and, not finding her there, demanded to know her whereabouts. Philip – now Sir Philip – Burne-Jones staunchly refused to tell him and in the ensuing scuffle succeeded in flooring his much larger opponent.

Angela fled still further, to Lady Wemyss's at Stanway in Gloucestershire, where she was, according to Cynthia Asquith, 'a pathetic refugee'. She only had Graham with her; Colin and Mary were with Nanny.

By early August she was back in London, but only briefly, in order to let the house in The Grove; then she was off on her travels again, this time taking both boys, to Wilsford on Salisbury Plain. (Because of a missed connection Colin's third birthday was celebrated in the waiting room at Salisbury station.) At Wilsford she 'saw a good many Australians', among them a Captain Thirkell who 'came over a good deal and brought friends'. 'Thirk', a third generation Australian, got his B.Sc. at the University of Tasmania shortly before the war and was among the first Australians to respond to the patriotic call from 'home' and enlist in the forces after the war broke out (in fact, he joined up on the day Colin MacInnes was born, 20 August 1914). He was commissioned in the engineers and sailed to Egypt two months later. He was also one of the first Australians to see action, when the Turks attacked the Suez Canal at the beginning of 1915. He shared the formative ANZAC experience of Gallipoli, having led a section of engineers in the raid on Gaba Tepe in which they were lucky to escape annihilation. Later in the war he served on the Western Front and in between, on leave in Britain, along with many other Australian officers he was petted and fêted by the upper classes, becoming particularly friendly with the Countess of Strathmore and her daughters, one of whom, Lady Elizabeth Bowes-Lyon, would later become Queen.[8]

In mid-October Angela returned to London, settling back into life at her parents' home in Pembroke Gardens and preparing – though she makes no mention of this in her diary – for her divorce.

The case, which opened in court on 19 November 1917, was undefended. The grounds for divorce were 'cruelty and adultery', and the newspapers made the most of the sensational details. McInnes, it appeared, had raped the nursemaid – she was called Lily – in the dining room and then boasted of his conquest to Angela.[9] A friend, writing to the children's nanny some months before the divorce, had admitted her inability 'to sum Lily up':

'Really I don't think she can be quite normal, [though] all through it appeared to me that she was filled with flattery.'[10] At the time Lily was dismissed instantly with a month's wages; later she was persuaded to give evidence in court. The judge said McInnes had behaved 'like a drunken beast' and granted Angela a decree nisi and custody of the children.[11]

Angela's own feelings about the divorce are made plain in this passage from her novel, *O, These Men, These Men!*: '. . . there was a difference between a divorce which took place because one or other had fallen in love elsewhere, and a divorce which was bound up with days and nights of terror . . . Where the man was possessed by the beast, divorce was simply a human being striking out wildly and savagely in self-defence.'[12]

James McInnes had certainly behaved diabolically. His drunken outbursts, violence to his pregnant wife, seduction and/or rape of the nursemaid in their own house – followed not by repentance, but by exultation – were not his only aberrations. He was apparently in the throes of a love affair with one of his students, who was a promising singer, and there was also some sort of involvement with Angela's younger sister, Clare. Either she was in love with him and he encouraged her, or he simply forced his attentions upon her. Among Colin MacInnes's pencilled notes for an unwritten section of *Angus Bard* are these cryptic references to an attempt on Clare's virtue: 'Tries to rape C.'; 'Assault on – at R'dean'; and 'Attack on C. on cliff'.

Whatever James felt for Clare, and vice-versa, he did not get on with his other in-laws (another source of distress to Angela). The Mackails must have viewed the break-up of the marriage with mixed feelings: relief at the removal of the ill-bred McInnes had to be set against the added responsibility of housing and supporting not only their daughter, but her three young children and their nanny as well. To ease the burden and enable Angela to undergo the ordeal of the divorce unencumbered, Nanny Parson took the six-month-old Mary up to her mother's house in Whaplode, near Spalding in Lincolnshire. On 20 October 1917 Angela wrote to her, saying there had been 'a further postponement' of her case and would her mother be prepared to have Mary for a little longer.[13] Nanny and her mother were happy to oblige; they were both devoted to the baby.

As soon as the divorce was over Angela's life came to be centred on the Australian Officers' Club in Piccadilly, where she spent several days in the company of Captain Thirkell, who was about to be posted abroad again. Even after he had gone she continued to haunt the Australian club; indeed her enthusiasm for these colonial heroes who had come to Britain's aid in her hour of need was so great that she volunteered to work at the club – as a parlourmaid. This arrangement lasted four or five months, between January and May 1918, during which time Captain Thirkell was temporarily supplanted by a Major Roos. Roos was a Boer; he had fought in the Boer War and had been General Smuts's private secretary for two years. So Angela also went to dances at the South African Officers' Club . . . In the midst of all this, Mary was taken into Great Ormond Street Hospital to have her tonsils and adenoids removed. A week later she was dead – a month before her first birthday.[14]

Angela would have nothing to do with the funeral. Her mother went to the hospital and made all the arrangements; her mother, her sister and Nanny went to Golders Green for the cremation; and her mother, her father and Nanny travelled to Rottingdean to bury Mary's ashes. The evening before, Angela had dined with Major Roos at the Royal Automobile Club.[15]

Margaret Mackail wrote to Barbara Parson's mother in praise of Nanny: 'Barbara . . . came first with Mary, for she cared for her and loved her all those months that her poor young mother was too ill and unhappy to be able to.'[16] However, by the time Mary died Angela was no longer ill; nor was she so unhappy that she could not respond to the admiration of Australian and South African army officers. No, the explanation for her detachment must be sought in the circumstances surrounding Mary's birth, her conception even. When Mary was conceived, the love that Angela had originally felt for James Campbell McInnes had evaporated, to be replaced by fear and loathing. In hardening her heart against him, consciously or unconsciously she came to reject his child within her. And when Mary was born, she thrust her into Nanny's arms and more or less washed her hands of the child. At that time, at least, she was still numb with shock.

'There are natures,' she wrote years later,

that can be generous and forgiving under slights, neglect, privation, but if once terrified, physically or mentally, the wound to their inner self, the degradation of the immortal being, is such that they will be cold and implacable to the offender for ever. They will never seek revenge, nor speak bitter words, but their lives will run frozen over black depths where past cruelties lie.[17]

These lines might serve as an epitaph for Angela's first marriage.

James McInnes did not, of course, simply disappear after the divorce; Angela heard that he had a commission in the Royal Flying Corps and had become Equipment Officer at Regent's Park – 'one of the most coveted funk-holes in the army', her brother, Denis Mackail, told his mother. She also learned that he had been thrown out of a teaching job at a girls' school in Wimbledon when the ladies who ran it found out about the divorce. Through her lawyer, she set about trying to get some maintenance out of him, or at least the government allowance for children which he had neglected to put in for.[18] She did not want to be entirely dependent on her parents, especially now that the boys were going to school at the Froebel Institute in Baron's Court.

In the summer of 1918, when Nanny left to get married herself (she was to name her own four children, and her house in Lincolnshire, after various members of the family she had been with in what she would always describe as the happiest time of her life), Angela took the boys to stay for a month at the Old Mill in Stourport, a house belonging to an aunt. They went for walks together, played in a barn, paddled in the River Severn, and Angela gave the children their first French lesson. It was an idyllic month, the first time the boys had had their mother to themselves. But it did not last. The end of August was idyllic in another sense for Angela, less so for the boys. Angela notes succinctly in her diary: 'George Thirkell asked me to marry him the night after he came here and we are both perfectly happy.'[19] The boys, when Angela asked them whom they would like her to marry, should she choose to marry again, unanimously voted for Uncle Denis, her brother, which was not the answer she had hoped for.[20]

This time she was determined to be practical in her approach: through October and November she took cookery lessons at the Gloucester Road Cookery School. She arranged about the marriage licence and, on 13 December, she and George Lancelot Allnut (the boys inevitably dubbed him 'Walnut') Thirkell were married in Kensington registry office. A month earlier, on 11

21

November, the armistice had been signed. The war was finally over and in 6 Pembroke Gardens the young Colin MacInnes was ushered into his grandparents' Pre-Raphaelite drawing room, which was full of expectant adults:

Tremulously, my four-year-old lips uttered the words I had been taught outside. 'Austria-Hungary has surrendered,' I said to the assembly, half afraid I'd got it wrong, with no notion of my meaning, yet hopeful the adults, in their mysterious way, would applaud my borrowed infant sagacity. This they did: they beamed, they cooed, huge scented furs suffocatingly embraced me, and I was given some milk in a saucer (all the tea-cups being in use) like a cherished cat.[21]

The war years had only the dimmest reality in Colin's memory: there were mysterious nighttime evacuations of the nursery for the safety of the kitchen, and equally mysterious daytime sightings of 'sausage' balloons, with men in baskets hanging from them, up in the sky. The disappearance of his father and the death of his baby sister meant less to him than to his brother Graham, who was a vital two years older. Colin's infancy was centred on his nanny, Barbara Parson. She it was who took the boys to Kensington Gardens or, better still, Brompton Cemetery, where giants in khaki would ingratiate themselves with the boys as a way of chatting her up, and once, Colin remembered, they saw 'some forlorn figures in blue-grey, with little circular caps'.[22] Nanny said they were German prisoners. The boys also went on visits to Nanny's home in Lincolnshire. There they had their first taste of fizzy lemonade, and Barbara Parson's father took them for rides on a pony called Taffy.[23]

When Nanny left, her loss – coming on top of the loss of their father and their sister – was a serious blow to her young charges. This would account for Angela's unusual solicitude towards them during their month together at Stourport. Generally during his infancy Colin found his mother 'a remote, ineffable figure . . . who appeared in the nursery, like a celestial stranger, sometimes summoned my elder brother and myself downstairs to hear the piano or be exhibited like trophies . . . and occasionally took us . . . for rather constricted, unloquacious walks.' His relationship with Nanny, by contrast, he remembered as 'personal in the extreme – severe, intimate and generously affectionate'. He traced his lifelong love of Music Hall to her early influence.[24]

Next to Nanny, in order of popularity, came the boys' grandmother, Margaret Mackail or 'Maany', as she was universally known. Her chief contribution to infant jollity was to institute so-called Bad Behaviour meals, in which Graham and Colin were encouraged to do 'all the greedy, messy ill-mannered things children naturally do with food and drink and which we had otherwise been punctiliously trained not to.' (Later, when the boys tried to persuade their mother to adopt this tradition, they were told sharply that if they once succeeded in behaving well at a meal she might consider it, but not otherwise.) Another of Maany's attributes was reading aloud 'in character'. In this she scored over her own mother, Georgiana Burne-Jones or 'Maam', who – though she too was popular with the boys – when reading aloud 'did not differentiate, to our infant satisfaction, between villain and hero'.[25]

The boys' grandfather, Jack Mackail, was a remote figure, but he would take them on occasional outings and show them historic London. A visit to the Tower of London in June 1919 made a deep impression on Colin: 'As for the Tower itself, with its Traitors' Gate and execution block and instruments of torture, it filled me with a horror from which I have never since quite recovered; and, no doubt by sympathetic magic, this edifying visit was followed by the fevers and nightmares of a sharp attack of measles.'[26]

Margaret Mackail, writing to Nanny on 18 June to congratulate her on the birth of her first child, reported that both the boys had measles, 'Colin quite sharply'.[27] Georgiana Burne-Jones also wrote, telling Nanny that the brothers were still good companions and 'as happy as can be'. They had been good patients too. 'None of the changes in their young lives have thrown them out of the regular order of their days, and they are punctual and obedient, and are very dear to us.'[28]

None of the changes in their young lives, however, compared with the one they were about to experience: a seven-week voyage to the other side of the world on a troopship requisitioned from the Germans and filled with Australian soldiers, a large proportion of whom were prisoners – deserters and the like – returning to their homeland in disgrace.

'I can't write of it,' Georgiana Burne-Jones admitted to her younger sister, Louisa, in the last letter she wrote her. Ten days later she was dead.[29]

3
Mother versus Australia

The long voyage to Australia started badly. With the Thirkells went Mabel Baden, a children's nurse or, as she preferred, 'Lady Help' – a title which, Graham McInnes writes, 'reflected with paralysing accuracy her mode of speech and outlook on life'. On the boat which took the Thirkell party out to the ship she vomited all over Angela's coat. And on board the *Friedrichsruh* it was discovered that the Germans, before handing over the ship as part of war reparations, had amused themselves by tinkering with the plumbing and electrical wiring: the lavatories flushed boiling water; the effluent was channelled into the laundry tanks, turning the washing into 'a nauseating red-hot swill'; salt water flowed from fresh-water taps and vice versa; and the bell-push gave you a nasty shock. Graham and Colin added their own mite of mischief, when the ship got under way, by locking all the lavatories on the inside and wriggling out under the doors.[1]

These pranks were as nothing, however, compared to the threat of mutiny from the hard core of disgraced diggers who were imprisoned on the lower decks. These deserters and common criminals soon found they had nothing to fear from their guards and they openly flouted their authority.

The *Friedrichsruh*, which was – perhaps fortunately – a dry ship, only docked twice for re-fuelling on its long, slow journey to Australia and both times – at Port Said and again at Colombo – the diggers ran riot in what would now be described as true 'okker' fashion. At Colombo George Thirkell was one of the officers who helped to get them back on board ship but only after a brawl in which a Singhalese official in a rickshaw was tipped into the water and had to be fished out of the harbour. Finally, a company of Gurkhas was called out to restore order.

The boys playing on the promenade deck were unaware of the danger and saw only a sweaty mass of soldiery below them. Sometimes the diggers would tease them and Graham McInnes records an occasion when Colin, taunted with the question, 'Hey, Snowy, have your balls dropped yet?', responded by throwing down his large rubber ball – to the huge delight of the soldiers, who thought him 'a bonzer kid'. Graham found himself envying his brother's more extrovert temperament. His own experiences with the diggers were painful and embarrassing: he could not respond to their ribaldry in the right spirit; he inevitably revealed himself as stuck-up, toffee-nosed, a true son of his fiercely superior English mother.[2]

Yet when Angela Thirkell came to write (under a male pseudonym), her own fictionalised account of this nightmare voyage to Australia, *Trooper to the Southern Cross*, she did it with humour and affection. It was the only book of hers that Colin MacInnes liked, because it was the only book in which, he felt, she was true to her own experience. 'It is funny, quite realistic, and agreeably malicious,' he wrote. He thought it contained 'some excellent satire on Anglo-Australian *mores*'[3] –a quality which has also endeared it to the Australian satirist, Barry Humphries.

For the McInnes boys, their Australian childhood profoundly influenced their lives and both wrote copiously about it. Graham's four volumes of autobiography are very largely about Australia in the Twenties; Colin wrote innumerable essays and articles on Australian subjects, as well as a Time/Life book on Australasia, two published and two unpublished novels with Australian settings.

Both brothers, in their very different ways, wrote extremely well about 'the old grey, cryptic continent', as Graham calls it.[4] Graham's writing is personal and anecdotal; he seems to have almost total recall and he paints a portrait not only of himself as a young man (and boy), but also of the land in which he grew up. Many Australians, like the poet Peter Porter, find the evocation of their homeland 'accurate to the point of pain'.[5] Colin, who eschewed the autobiographical mode of writing unless it were to point a moral or illustrate a theme, is more concerned with a timeless, 'romantic' Australia, the Australia – and Australians – of myth and legend.

The new continent meant a new identity for the two boys. In Tasmania, where they first went to stay with Thirk's parents before settling in Melbourne, Angela summoned Graham and simply told him that he and Colin would be going to their new school under the name of Thirkell, not their own – which,

Graham says, she could not even bring herself to pronounce. She asserted that since Thirk was now in effect their 'dad', they should take his name.[6] In later life both boys would come to resent her high-handed action in depriving them of their own name; they did not resent their stepfather: they recognised that his was only a secondary role in their lives. He was, as Colin remembers him, tough, generous, kindly and unimaginative: 'though he acted justly to me, there was no point of human contact whatsoever.'[7]

It was their mother's selfishness they could not forgive; the change of name was purely for her own convenience. She did not wish to be reminded of her former marriage, nor did she wish to be bothered with explanations. If she did not acknowledge a problem, for her it did not exist. But, as Graham points out, by taking away the boys' name she only succeeded 'in transferring from herself to me and my brother the burden of explanation and embarrassment which she herself was unwilling to assume.' She did not even take the trouble to do it officially, by deed-poll. This made it easier, later on, for them to revert to their real name but hardly justifies the years of uncertain identity that went before, the doubts and questions that haunted them throughout their schooldays. All mention of their father was forbidden; yet Angela's diaries and photograph albums covering the years of her first marriage were openly displayed for all to see, so that 'though [he was] banished from the house as unclean,' as Graham writes, 'James Campbell McInnes continued to lead a shadowy Plutonian existence.[8]

The Melbourne that was to be the Thirkell family home for a decade was an imposing city; Graham called it 'one of the stately cities of the world . . . Turin in the antipodes with an Anglo-Saxon flavour.'[9] It was a city, too, that had undergone – as the historian, Asa Briggs, puts it – 'a change of urban personality'.[10] Its meteoric rise in the nineteenth century from primitive settlement in the 1830s through Gold Rush town in the 1850s to boom city of the 1880s earned it the sobriquet of 'most American of Australian cities'. But its subsequent slump in the 1890s meant that Sydney, which up to that point had been considered the abode of 'quieter, less assertive, more civilised' people, overtook it both in terms of population and as the Australian metropolis. The two cities reversed roles: Sydney became the jazzy, lawless and glamorous place, while Melbourne acquired the reputation of being staid and straitlaced, now 'the most British of Australian cities'.[11]

Its Victorian heyday provided Melbourne with wide streets and stately mansions; and if its grandeur occasionally slipped over into grandiloquence, there was still 'a sense of spaciousness and of public occasion about the city'.[12] It might lack Sydney's magnificent natural harbour setting but, ringed with hills to the north and with the beaches of Port Phillip Bay to the south, it had its own physical splendour. Colin MacInnes, however, remains sceptical about Melbourne's grandeur. Melbourne consists, he says, 'of a gridiron of large, dull thoroughfares down which the north wind howls amid the clanking of obsolete electric trams'; and the River Yarra, 'to the impartial eye, is a small, turgid, murky stream'.[13]

With a population in 1920 of 750,000 out of an Australian total of five million, Melbourne was – as it still is – a low-density city with suburbs that stretched for miles. 'These immense deserts of brick and terra-cotta, or wood and galvanised iron' induced in Graham 'a sense of overpowering dullness, of stupefying sameness, a worthy, plodding, pedestrian, middle-class, low church conformity'; and it was in the middle of one such desert, a suburb called Malvern 'that was neither affluent nor disreputable, but very middle-class and excessively suburban', built in the first decade of the twentieth century and full of the sort of houses Osbert Lancaster has immortalised in the phrase 'bypass variegated', that the Thirkells made their abode. No. 4 Grace Street was an eight-room bungalow which differed little from its neighbours: set back from the road, 'red brick with yellow roughcast above and with the usual terra-cotta roof', it had gables to the front and side and a red-tiled porch with the front door off it next to 'a window in the shape of a porthole with local stained glass'. It was, however, the only house in the immediate vicinity without a name: in contrast to *Ti-Tree Lodge* and *Hiawatha*, *Doonside* and *Mon Repos*, it announced itself, starkly, as No. 4.[14]

It was bought with the aid both of a loan, which Angela's cousin, Stanley Baldwin (who became Prime Minister of England in 1923), had made to her at the time of her divorce, and of a mortgage financed through Thirk's demobilisation gratuity. When they arrived in Grace Street in June 1920, in the middle of winter, Thirk was acting as agent for Brown, Firth of Sheffield, a steel company he had worked for briefly in England. But eventually he found work as a metallurgical engineer with a firm called Gregory's in the Collingwood district of Melbourne. He worked there for two years before starting his own business, manufacturing car parts. The firm he helped to found had the grandiose name of The Australian Metal Equipment Company (TAMECO for short), and he was its general manager. He had a company car he was very proud of (which his fellow directors would later use as a pretext to get rid of him, claiming that he had misused it for family outings). But the business was never very prosperous, so his earnings were proportionately low. And by the summer of 1921 there was an additional mouth to feed. Lancelot George Thirkell, Angela's fourth and last child, was born on 9 January.

An annual ritual at 4 Grace Street was the family photograph taken in the garden. Preparations for this event were such as to attract the attention of curious neighbours. As Angela was a few inches taller as well as a few years older than her second husband, she would announce – to the amazement of onlookers and the embarrassment of her children (it was Colin who used to tell this story) – in her ringing Kensington tones: 'George, stand over there. That way you'll have the *avantage du terrain*.'[15]

Graham recalls another excruciating incident, when Thirk made the mistake of bringing a friend home to dinner both late and without any warning – they probably stopped on the way, as was Thirk's custom, at the Naval and Military Club. Angela presided at the head of the table, icily polite. When the 'all too familiar spotted-dog' was brought in by the Lady Help, Angela asked the guest if he would care for some suet pudding, as she called it. He replied in all innocence, 'Well, I don't mind if I do.'

'In that case,' she said, 'you don't mind if you don't.'

The hiatus which followed this remark was so painful that Graham deliberately drew his mother's fire on his own head by leaving the table without permission; anything was better than that awful silence.[16]

Graham gives instances when Angela's wit was more than matched by the Australian opposition. But it made little difference which side won any particular skirmish; her extravagant superciliousness was a source of agonising embarrassment to her offspring. The tradesmen she had insulted, for instance, would take their revenge on the boys who were inevitably tarred with the same brush and labelled 'high-and-mighty'. Graham writes that 'broadly speaking Mother looked on Australians, with few exceptions, as members of the Lower Classes. She agreed heartily with an English visitor who once told her (within our incredulous hearing) that Australia was "a wonderful country for Warrant Officers".[17] It was all very well for her to take on Australia, or affect an easy superiority; the boys had no such option. They had to come to terms with their adoptive land; otherwise they were in for a miserable time, particularly at school. Wisely they adapted – as children will – or at any rate learned to live a double life.

Nevertheless, both Graham and Colin retain a grudging admiration for their mother. Colin, despite himself, sees the positive side of her cultural pretensions, the fact that they earned her a reputation as a 'character' which, in turn, transformed her unprepossessing house, with its outside lavatory masked by carpets hanging on the washing-line, into a place of pilgrimage. She made, he writes, 'countless Australian friends who almost wept when the family departed.'[18] Celebrities like Dame Nellie Melba and General Sir John Monash came and went, and Angela became something of a local celebrity herself, serving her literary apprenticeship by contributing 'neo-Beerbohmian' essays to English and Australian periodicals 'to pay for the laundry', and conducting 'a truly ghastly "literate" radio programme for kids in which she introduced herself to the amazed Australian young as Mother Elder' (from Hans Christian Andersen).[19] In those early days of radio she also gave talks on the ABC about celebrated people she was supposed to have known, though more often, in fact, they were people she had met perhaps once if at all; some – Keats, for example – had died a good many years before she was born.[20] She behaved, according to Colin, 'in this colonial decor, like a suave settler in darkest Africa. Beneath a torrid sun, and often in circumstances of great material distress, she resolutely maintained the values – and the accent – of her Kensingtonian culture in London, much to the astonishment of the natives.'[21]

One Kensingtonian custom which astonished the natives was Reading Aloud. 'The ritual was that, after supper, the kids had to drop everything else and appear in the drawing-room, more or less spick and span, for the evening reading – rarely reluctantly, I may add,' Colin writes. 'We thus, over the years, worked through much of Dickens, Thackeray and Scott, with odds and ends of Mark Twain and Dumas.'[22]

Graham tells of an occasion when he was out in the garden playing football with an Australian mate and Reading Aloud was announced; his mother brushed aside his protests and his friend, whose curiosity was aroused – 'And who's Little Dorritt?' – stayed to find out. They listened to an instalment and the Aussie lad returned the next night to hear another chapter; but after that 'he said he'd rather play football with the other fellows: reading aloud was a bit "queeny".'[23]

Although they were read Dickens and Thackeray, they supplemented this traditional fare with a vast quantity of popular rubbish, both English and Australian. Colin maintains that this was 'a pleasant corrective to the moralisings of the Victorian classics'.[24] (Comics were officially forbidden at 4 Grace Street, but the boys smuggled them in.) For Graham, it was his mother's too exclusive attention to the Victorian classics that was responsible for her 'essentially literary conception of life', from which she derived a 'code of conduct' thoroughly inappropriate to the business of daily living.[25]

'Reading Aloud' came after 'Play QUIETLY during grown-ups' dinner' and before 'Prepare for bed. Bath on bath nights' in the 'Programme of work and play for Graham and Colin during the holidays' dreamed up by Angela Thirkell to keep the boys fully occupied and out of her way.[26] Their duties included: preparing breakfast; washing up; doing shopping errands; hosing the back yard; sweeping the woodshed or washhouse (alternate days); and chopping chips for the chipheater. These jobs were not particularly onerous; what the boys objected to was being time-tabled, as if home were simply another version of school and every minute of the day had to be accounted for.

How far removed this was from the archetypal Australia dreamed up in Norman Lindsay's popular children's fable, *The Magic Pudding*, which Colin must have first read about this time. 'What a happy world this is of bush and endless summer,' he writes forty years later, during a visit to Australia, 'a perpetual diet of meat, suet, jam and billy tea, a sockdolager on the snout to solve every problem . . . In his final tableau of sloth and bliss we have Lindsay's vision of the Australian Dream. There they all are, in their home in the tree with its corrugated iron water tank and the Southern Cross fluttering at the masthead, in an idyllic rural setting with a charming township on the skyline . . . doing *absolutely nothing* . . .'[27]

At 4 Grace Street, sloth was a sin and idleness was punished. Graham tells how the boys fell behind with their allotted tasks and Mother announced that 'Dad' would beat them. Colin, who was only half dressed, lashed out bravely with his shorts, which happened to be in his hand. One of the buttons caught in his mother's hair and pulled it loose, so that it fell about her shoulders. The boys made the mistake of laughing. Angela furiously ordered them out into the garden, where an initially reluctant Thirk awaited them. She read out the charges and he administered the punishment, rapidly warming to the task.[28] Once again, it was not the thrashing itself which galled the boys but the ritualistic element in its imposition.

According to Sir Keith Waller, an Australian contemporary of Colin's, now a retired diplomat, 4 Grace Street was 'quite as horrible' as Graham depicts it: 'I went there many times to play with Colin, although never without some feeling of terror of Mrs Thirkell, who in spite of her charm was a somewhat intimidating woman and the small boys were always on their best behaviour.'[29]

Yet the young inmates of No. 4 were far from unhappy. As Colin puts it, 'Youth has such energy, and in Australia such licence, that its elders fight a perpetually losing battle.'[30] He had a happy childhood; he got on well with Graham and though – like all elder brothers – he often teased Lance, he was generally kindly disposed towards his young half-brother, who worshipped him in return. If at this stage he felt any jealousy towards Lance, who had replaced him as the baby of the family and was, on his own admission, spoiled, he did not show it. Lance was anyway so much younger that for him 'it was like being an only child'.[31]

It was by chance that the boys went to Scotch College; they were originally intended for Melbourne Grammar, which was properly establishment and C of E in its orientation, but Angela was so horrified by the headmaster's Aussie accent that she had second thoughts. Remembering her own father's Presbyterian education she settled for Scotch (the boys going first to its prep school, Grimwade House). This was not from religious conviction: neither she nor her sons were baptised and, though she had taught them to say their prayers, she never took them to church.

Religious instruction at Scotch was anyway minimal, consisting of the Shorter Catechism, daily morning prayers and one period of scripture a week. Scotch was – according to Colin – 'what one might call the Rugby of Australia, specialising in the production of state (not federal) prime ministers, captains of industry, and prosperous pastoralists'.[32] Sir Keith Waller describes the college as being traditionally strongly represented in business, less so in politics.

Scotch College is one of six public schools in Melbourne: its head is a member of the British Headmasters' Conference. Unlike the majority of English public schools, however, the six Melbourne schools are predominantly day-schools. In those days Scotch had about 1,200 boys – 300 in the prep school, 900 in the public school. It 'differed most from the other five,' Sir Keith writes, 'in its deeply ingrained Scottish tradition that education was a privilege which must not be treated lightly . . . we were never allowed to forget that the getting of wisdom was our aim in life.'[33]

Colin remembered his school with affection: '. . . writers are supposed to loathe their school days, whereas I found this Australian–Presbyterian academy delightful: one where the "games ethic" was kept in bounds, and scholarship not despised.'[34]

Colin MacInnes once asked, 'What have Paul McCartney, Lord Hill of Luton, Cary Grant, Ken Dodd, the Prime Minister [then Harold Wilson] – and, for that matter, the writer of these lines – in common?' The answer was: 'They were all once boy scouts.'[35]

Graham and Colin both joined the 1st Toorak Troop. This was acceptable to their mother because of the name: Graham describes Toorak as 'the Belgravia of Melbourne'. But in fact, 'the First Toorak Troop drew the bulk of its boys from the poorer area down near the railroad tracks and the adjacent industrial Prahran. The great mansions perched among flowering gum-trees and curving streets on the heights above the Yarra sent no boys to the First Toorak Troop,' which was 'a little democracy in the heart of snobdom'.[36]

The scoutmaster, known as 'the Boss' or, as he preferred, 'the Baas', was a kind of midget, who had a massive head and wore pince-nez with pebble lenses. He was 'a man possessed, eaten up by a mysterious fire'. His welcoming speech, when Graham joined the troop, was 'an amazing hodge-podge of half developed social theories, religious-cum-sexual mumbo-jumbo and patriotic scoundrelisms. But it made a tremendous impression . . . what this queer bony little man had was the power of leadership.'[37] Queer he probably was in more senses than one, 'but highly sublimated', as Colin puts it. In real life he was a clerk at Dorman Long's; and the assistant scoutmaster was a garage mechanic.[38]

The appeal for Colin – 'I can't be objective about the scouts, since I enjoyed myself so much for so many years among them' – was that 'here was an organisation that got you out of the womb of your family and flung you among kids of your own age, but different backgrounds, to sink or swim.' It also took you out of the suburbs into real country: 'I think what it most did for me was to banish my fear of working class boys, and of the country. When I was inducted into the army, I found the 1st Toorak experience extremely useful.'[39]

Colin always defended the scouts against leftish accusations of incipient fascism and the like. How could he not be loyal when the 'prophetic book' was none other than Cousin Ruddy's *Kim*? He describes the ideology of the movement as 'the weirdest blend of Old Tory militarism, Arthurian mysticism, masonic secrecy and ritual, non-sectarian religiosity, nature and beast worship, and a passion for peoples (Red Indian, Australian aborigines, African tribesmen) whom Christian imperialism had tried for centuries to destroy.' He makes a distinction between militarism – useless to deny, he argues, what it is for which the scout should chiefly 'be prepared' – and the para-militarism of the Boys' Brigade. The true military heir to Baden-Powell (he writes in 1961) is Dayan. Fascist and Communist countries alike usually end up suppressing the scouts.[40]

In his boyhood, though, Colin was less interested in the message of the movement than in the exhilarating freedom it offered:

How beautiful the wild, untutored, hot, untidy Australian bush can be, so unlike the laundered countrysides of Europe, so welcoming, by its very indifference, to a fervent youthful spirit! We camped and swam and sang and built trestle bridges and cooked truly revolting food around fires whose smoke chased the myriads of mosquitoes . . . we indulged to the full in a brash outdoor hedonism which was the perfect antidote to urban gloom.[41]

When Colin first became a writer he kept a notebook of 'Australiana' and under the heading, 'Scout camps', he listed several items, one of which reads 'Platypus (June)'. The parenthetical 'June' refers to *June in Her Spring* (1952), the first novel MacInnes wrote with an Australian setting. It opens with a description of the sighting of a platypus in the river where the eponymous heroine has been swimming. Such sightings are so rare that June takes it as an omen. Full of youthful confidence she is sure it will bring her luck. The irony is that luck can be either good or bad, and the fact that it is to her father – a deeply, and mysteriously, gloomy figure – that she brings news of the platypus underlines the ambiguity and sets the tone of the book.

In fiction and in other writings, MacInnes returns again and again to Australia. For him it was synonymous with childhood and youth: the Australian bush was his 'lost domain'. So it comes as no surprise to discover that in the early Fifties he undertook a translation of Alain-Fournier's *Le Grand Meaulnes* (which he never completed).

'Adults have vivid memories of childhood,' he begins an essay called 'Through the Looking Glass to Adolescence',

and no less vivid of their adolescence when they falteringly grow into men and women. For me the brief period between these two, that moment when the young human creature is neither child nor nubile, remains plunged in the deepest recesses of our memories, as if we wished to hide these recollections from ourselves. Can this be because they were so painful – and yet so splendidly entrancing? Do we forget them because this was, in some sense, the most vital moment of our lives, and thus one we dare not fully remember because the sense of their loss would be so poignant?[42]

Even before they joined the scouts the boys had had a taste of the Australian countryside. One holiday – the first of many – they were invited by a couple called Basil and Nell Hall to their orchard on Panton Hill, some thirty miles north of Melbourne. 'With dim memories of England,' Graham writes, 'I imagined a high wall of plum-coloured brick with perhaps some peaches and pears espaliered along it. The reality when it came opened a dramatic door through which we walked out of 4 Grace Street and into Australia.'[43]

'Up on the river Murray,' Colin writes, 'there is a garden area of the State of Victoria where fruit is grown in endless acres with row upon row of plums, apricots and peaches extending over hill and dale for miles . . .'[44]

This was where the Halls had their orchard. Later, when they moved from Panton Hill to Greendale, near Ballarat, the boys continued to visit them virtually every holiday. Graham worked out that over ten years he must have stayed with the Halls for a total of eighteen months. At one time he thought his mother must have paid the Halls to have him and Colin during the holidays, but when he asked her about it she said she had never offered them a penny. He concludes, for want of any other explanation, that the relationship 'was one of those wonderful accidents which sometimes seem to be the only predictable features of life . . . sheer kindness on the part of the older people, and simple enthusiasm and prankishness on the part of two boys . . .' Basil and Nell Hall, who had younger children of their own, became honorary uncle and aunt.[45]

The boys did all the things that youngsters do on farms: they learned to ride horses, kill chickens – Graham reports that Colin was the less squeamish of the two over this – hunt rabbits and, of course, pick fruit. During one fruit-picking season, when Colin was in what he describes as 'the brief pre-adolescent stage', he met 'a half-caste aboriginal of indeed repellent aspect'.

Among the white fruit-pickers this aboriginal was a figure of fun. As a result, perhaps, he kept his distance. Colin initially was frightened of him; his strange appearance, the tales that were told of aboriginal 'fecklessness, dishonesty and sudden treacherous malice . . . ("You can't trust the abo, son")' made him wary. But he was also attracted, for the aboriginal – unlike his brother and those friends of his who had already entered the mysterious world of adolescence and left him behind – accepted his company without question and even shared his cigarettes with him.

One evening, after the fruit had been weighed and the pickers had gone to their tents, the aboriginal invited Colin to go for a swim in the river with him. Colin knew the Halls would disapprove; he did not dare risk being seen with the aboriginal, but agreed to meet him down by the river. He was still afraid, but his curiosity got the better of him and so he went. At the riverside his companion stripped off and jumped into the water, Colin timidly following suit. When Colin got in he could not see his companion anywhere; he was searching anxiously for him when he suddenly

felt himself lifted into the air and flipped over on to his back.
Before he could recover the aboriginal had leapt on top of him
and pushed him under. He surfaced breathless and enraged. But
the aboriginal only smiled, patting his cheek and wiping the hair
out of his eyes. Then they swam to the shore:

There, while we had a cigarette, he gazed at me craftily, then rose and, to
my great surprise, stood knee-deep in the stream and bedaubed his whole
body with its ochred mud. As soon as it had partly hardened, he began to
trace patterns on his body which I recognised, from photographs I had
seen, as being those appropriate to an initiation. He stood proudly before
me in the rising moonlight, flashed his teeth grinning, then advanced,
pulled me to my feet, and led me to the water. There he anointed me
fondly with the slime, told me to lie down, and traced similar patterns on
both sides of my body. While he did this, he examined me minutely, his
hands wandering promiscuously, familiarly, but without violation. As I
lay next to this boy-man by the river, I felt an exaltation – he was
promising me that the strength he possessed would soon be mine as well. I
reached up and kissed his muddy face, but he laughed, rose briskly to his
feet, dived in the stream and disappeared towards the further shore.[46]

MacInnes follows this account of his assignation with
the aboriginal with a description of his first 'pre-adolescent'
encounter with a girl. She was one of a succession of 'girl helps' to
follow Mabel Baden, the original Lady Help, who had not lasted
long in Australia: her name was Oenone; she was about seventeen; and she worked part-time at 4 Grace Street. She was wary of
the elder boy, Graham, but chatted happily to Colin about the
boys who took her to the local dance-hall.

'About this time,' Colin writes,

though as yet no untoward hair had appeared upon my body, I had
joined the school cadet corps, which had a dazzling uniform like that
worn by Latin American officers. When I first wore this, the sight of my
youthful body in the mirror convinced me I was now a *man* and, trembling with daring, I invited Oenone, after I'd helped her with the washing-
up, to come and gather fruit with me in the back garden. She smiled to
herself, then laughed and agreed, and we made for the hammock that
was strung, beneath the Southern Cross, between a peach tree and a
nectarine. Reaching up for fruit, and being flung together by the extreme
discomfort of the hammock, I began to fondle her, at which she giggled,
slapped me, but didn't stop me. ('Hands off the model, son,' she said. And
'Don't try anything I might forgive, but couldn't forget.') Even if I had
known what to do, and even if I had been capable of doing it, I believe
Oenone's prudence, if not virtue, would have halted my endeavours; but
as it was, I had a melancholy gnawing sense of inadequacy. Clearly, I no

longer felt towards her as a boy – the uniform no doubt encouraging this sensation – but equally, I was as yet unable to act towards her as a man. Sensing this, she was indulgent, and yet slightly mocking: I realised with a pang she did not feel I was dangerous, yet also with excitement that she felt I might become so before long.[47]

This description lacks the magic of the passage about the aboriginal. Whereas that encounter seemed natural and unforced, this one seems more than a trifle *voulu* – a *machismo* donned along with the Latin American-style uniform.

Both of Colin MacInnes's published novels with Australian settings, *June in Her Spring* and *All Day Saturday*, share a locale – not the fruit-growing country of Panton Hill, not Melbourne itself, and certainly not the suburb of Malvern with the street named Grace Street which 'hadn't got much grace about it'.[48] What awed and enchanted the boy from the suburbs and appealed to the later novelist's imagination was 'the Bush':

It is the sheep and cattle stations, and the wild Bush beyond them, that everyone feels to be the 'real' Australia – the repository of the virtues of an older way of life, and still the fountain of prosperity. A sheep or cattle station is a self-contained community where work is play, and man is nature: a place where what has to be done, and what is necessary, and what is agreeable, are all identical. As for the Bush itself, those who know only the new, man-manufactured landscapes of the 'old world' can scarcely conceive of the sense of awe and mystery with which the prospect of the vast, untidy, ancient inland country of Australia strikes the beholder.[49]

'Everyone knows what the true Australia is,' a reviewer once remarked in the Melbourne *Age*. 'It is the Bush – where most Australians don't live.'[50] It is a nice paradox that one of the most intensely urbanised societies in the world should cherish a rural myth: but the 'real' Australia is real enough to some; and for the rest (as with the European myth of the Noble Savage) the Bush has a powerful imaginative hold. It is myth *as opposed to* reality, a kind of yearning for a lost innocence. This is what it represented for Colin MacInnes, whose prototype Arcadia, 'a kind of paradise before the Fall',[51] was the sheep country round Ballan on the edge of the Western District of the State of Victoria, home of the squattocracy. It was here that the Halls settled after leaving Panton Hill; they had 700 acres of land – a mere smallholding by Western District standards. The really big properties measured

20,000 – even 40,000 – acres. 'Ballan lay just on the border line between the sheep country and the farm country,' Graham McInnes explains,

and the stations were of more modest acreage. But there was nevertheless a subtle change in the status and bearing of the neighbours, and one quickly discovered, even in democratic rural Australia, that two classes existed. On the one hand, were the station owners and their town guests, the professional men from Ballan, the doctor, the lawyer, the engineers of the local wireless transmitting station and one or two marginal farmers who went in for mixed sheep and wheat or fruit, and were therefore considered on the verge of being respectable. On the other hand were the roustabouts and boundary riders from the sheep stations, the railway folk, the workers in the little town and the local phenomenon known as the 'cocky' farmer. This really meant, in European terms, a peasant yeoman, although no Australian would ever admit it.[52]

For the sons of Angela Thirkell, life on a sheep station combined the excitement of the new world with the reassuring characteristics of the old. Bungeeltap and Yaloak, Darra and Ballark have a harsher, less mellow sound than Clouds, Stanway and Wilsford, it is true, but these were the 'hospitable homes' where, as Graham puts it, 'the minor Australian squattocracy rode out the roaring Twenties on the sheep's back'.[53] The gymkhanas, tennis parties and cricket matches created a wonderfully genial and harmonious atmosphere.

Colin MacInnes peoples his novels with the real inhabitants of the district of Ballan (which he calls 'Ballantyne'). The Westley family in *June in Her Spring*, for instance, is readily identifiable as the family of Mr and Mrs William Rhodes, who lived at Bungeeltap.

Nathan Westley's prototype, Bill Rhodes, was – according to Graham McInnes – 'a lean, knuckle-nosed and melancholy man . . . highly respected by the squatters on the rich sheep-to-the-acre country around Ballan, for Bill Rhodes had "beaten the drought".' He had previously owned a station in the semi-desert of western Queensland, where he had survived six consecutive summers without rain. His children were seven and five before they had their first sight of rain. He had a small artesian bore which saved him, while all around his neighbours went under. Rhodes sold up at a profit and came south to the kinder climate of Ballan. While his wife and his daughter, Jean, 'were not simply the life of the party, they *were* the party and the party was endless',

Bill himself 'remained moody and introspective'. Graham says that he 'held within himself suppressed thunders of appalling dimensions'.[54]

Of Jean, who is transformed into the heroine of Colin's *June*, Graham writes:

She summed up for most of us the Roaring Twenties and Our Dancing Daughters. She was a firefly will-o'-the-wisp utterly and entirely fastidious; no breath of gossip ever touched her yet she was always in the middle of whatever shenanigans were in progress. Like many Australian country girls she unleashed a terrific forehand drive, just casually thrown away as if there were nothing to it, and a line of tough sardonic humour in delightful contrast to her showy dress and make-up. Her Homeric cackle floated across the valley of the Moorabool and when they were whooping it up at Bungeeltap she was the wildest and gayest of them all.[55]

The real power in the district was J.M. Molesworth of Ballark (E.W. Canterbury in *June*), 'a genial latter-day Squire Trelawny in moleskin breeks', as Graham remembers him.

Everyone knew that J.M. Molesworth was the boss, that he lived in an enormous homestead and that he was worth a hundred thousand pounds or so. He himself did not pretend that any of this was untrue, but to see him burning a break, dipping sheep or leaning over a wire fence talking to a stockrider, was to recognise a grazier's hierarchy in which everyone was equal because everyone had his place. In the land of the freeborn, Molesworth and the boundary rider conversed as equals, not monetarily of course, but as men engaged in a co-operative activity. The bulk of the profits went to the boss, but he provided the men with a hard, free, open life in which they acknowledged few equals and no superiors and out of which came the extraordinary Australian sense of 'mateship'.[56]

But Ballan was only on the fringe of the Western District proper, and there were even more fabulous estates than Molesworth's to be seen on the great plain – like Mount Hesse, where Angela Thirkell once, by sheer effrontery, managed to inflict the boys on the Kininmonths, who had invited the Halls to stay with them without realising – why should they? – that in doing so they were depriving the 'Thirkell' boys of their regular summer holiday. This was more than Angela could tolerate: the thought of having two energetic, growing boys cooped up with her in Grace Street all summer was too much for her. She phoned the Halls at Mount Hesse and, blithely ignoring the fact that they were guests there themselves, virtually demanded that her offspring be invited up there too. Nell Hall was spared some embarrassment when one of the Kininmonth sisters, who had been listening all the time on another extension, joined in the conversation and generously invited the two unknown boys just as Angela wished. So for one glorious holiday Graham and Colin lived the life of the Western District.

And it was probably there more than anywhere – as they enjoyed the freedom of the open spaces; went swimming in the nearby dam, or riding the horses provided for them – that the boys from suburbia experienced most profoundly the romance of their adoptive land and its people.

'There is indubitably a greatness about the Australian people,' Colin writes: 'a bigness, a wideness, an inborn capacity for the large, the heroic gesture. If peoples are born serfs or princes – as they are – the Aussies are a kingly race.'[57]

Yet even the Western District was not entirely free of that lawless and destructive element in Australian society known as 'larrikinism'. In the nineteenth century the larrikin was considered primarily an urban phenomenon but by the 1880s he was already a familiar, if unwelcome, figure in the District, especially evident at such social events as race week and show week. Wanton damage to property and an exaggerated contempt for authority were the hallmarks of larrikinism. Historians have speculated about its origins. To some extent it may simply have been a reaction to 'wowserism', the excessively churchy, non-smoking, non-drinking puritanism of many early colonial settlers. It could also be seen as the unacceptable face of egalitarianism, an aggressive attitude not so much of 'Jack's as good as his master' as 'Jack has no master – and you'd better believe it.' It might even be a legacy of transportation which spread to those parts of the country which were not originally peopled by convicts. But the most interesting theory – when one considers, say, the condition of the children of West Indian parents who have made their home in Britain – is one advanced by the historian of the Western District in the nineteenth century, Margaret Kiddle: the larrikin, she suggests,

was a native Australian who was born lacking his immigrant parents' interests and traditions. The fact that Caledonian games and the folk songs of the Old World were still such an important part of the life of the District is significant. The immigrant generation enjoyed them and drew spiritual strength from them, but their children must often have found them unreal.[58]

According to Margaret Kiddle, 'Education helped to quell larrikinism, but for a time it remained an ugly element in the life of the community, and the outbreak of bushranging in the seventies and eighties culminated in the exploits of the Kelly gang as its most spectacular expression.'[59]

In contrast to earlier bushrangers, though, the Kelly gang robbed only banks, never individuals; and if Ned Kelly is to be seen as the supreme larrikin, then his mythological status shows the ambivalence of Australian attitudes towards larrikinism. Colin MacInnes, who writes about the Kelly myth in relation to the paintings of Sidney Nolan, remarks: '. . . think what one will of bushrangers, banks, and hangmen, Kelly was not only a remarkable figure in himself, but even the prototype (however much they may deny him) of the Australian's own idea about himself: a noble tough, a violent champion, whose example has potently helped to mould the national character.'[60] And in *June in Her Spring* and *All Day Saturday* MacInnes offers two contrasting portraits of larrikins: with Arthur Westley in *June* the emphasis is on the negative and (self-)destructive aspects of the type; Norman Culley in *All Day Saturday*, on the other hand, is 'the characteristic male Aussie figure carried to the edge of its particular potential of perfection: lithe, tough, mindless and delinquent,'[61] the very type, in fact, of the heroes who forged the other formative Australian myth – that of Gallipoli.

For the squattocracy the ride through the Twenties on the sheep's back ended thousands of miles away in the Wall Street crash. The bottom dropped out of the wool market and only the wealthiest of squatters escaped unscathed; others, mere farmers like the Halls, suffered just as self-employed businessmen in Melbourne like George Thirkell did.

It was not, however, the crash that ended the boys' summer visits to Ballan, but the Halls' departure in 1929 on their trip 'home' – which, fortunately for them, narrowly preceded it. In 1928 Angela Thirkell had taken *her* trip home, along with the young Lance. She was gone for the best part of a year, leaving her husband and two elder sons to be looked after by a Lady Help called Eileen McBride. It seemed strange to Graham that she left them in the care of a single girl of twenty-six: 'It was a gesture either of supreme innocence or supreme indifference.'[62]

41

More likely she had simply wearied of married life with a man as undemanding as Thirk was in every respect but one. In her autobiographical first novel, *Ankle Deep* (1933), Angela Thirkell, in the person of 'Aurea', expresses her distaste for her husband's – she calls him 'Ned' – 'adoration' of her:

Aurea shut her eyes quickly and tightly, trying to escape remembrances of the many times when adoration had taken the one hated shape, of her own efforts to stave off the adoration, of the humiliating scene that always followed, of Ned whimpering, actually whimpering because she was not what he called 'kind', of the utter contempt with which she finally gave in. A spasm of pain contracted her face alone in the dark. I suppose, she thought, I am a pretty bad wife. A person who, not to mince words, dislikes and despises her husband, can't be much of a success. And seeing his good side only makes it worse . . .'[63]

His good points, in the novel as in life, were his kindness, his good temper, his honesty, his affection for his children, even his adoration of his wife which she so dreaded:

But could one really respect a man who was never angry with one? If one had been silly, or stupid, one needed pulling up, one needed a master. That was it; a master. And that was what Ned had never been. Honesty; yes, though it didn't seem much praise for a man to say he wasn't dishonest. As for the children, so long as he was not troubled about them, and Aurea spent her own allowance on their clothing and education, he was quite fond of them, and would keep them up much too late for his own amusement. Luckily they were getting to an age when they could go their own way.[64]

This description coincides too precisely with Graham's recollections of his step-father to be dismissed as fiction:
'Five eighths of an inch of whisky,' Graham recalls,

usually in the middle of a wet Sunday afternoon when he was poring over his wonderful stamp collection, I shall take as the essence, psyche or anima of my stepfather, Thirk, Dad. There you have – in one nip, as it were – his engineering training, his happy-go-lucky geniality, and yet again (since it is not the kind of errand on which one might normally send a boy) his lethargy. With Mother everything was sharp and tight and on schedule. Bells rang, cannons boomed, gongs clanged, flags were run up and the form was more important than the substance. With Dad it was a world of laisser faire, sudden impulses, tuneless cheerful whistling, odd tasks begun and never finished. I think Mother gave him up fairly early, and in the end she left him: but the sons of the first marriage felt towards him a wary affection, and in small things he was always generous. Dad never paid a school bill of mine in his life and never kept an appointment on time; but if you wanted ten bob suddenly, or if you were in a jam with the cops, or if you simply *had* to have that striped tie, well . . . He was unkind only when forced by insistent browbeating to be Mother's instrument. Normally he was a lackadaisical believer in live-and-let-live except where his passions were concerned: stamp collecting, standard roses and the Works.[65]

Unfortunately for Thirk, he was in the process of being rejected not only by his wife but also by his fellow directors at TAMECO. The Works was the mainstay of his existence – along with the Naval and Military Club, where the sharing of ANZAC memories and opinions, even more than the five-eighths of an inch of whisky, was balm to his troubled soul. And now his old friends ganged up on him and succeeded in ousting him when the crash came. So poor old Thirk – not so old, either – who was the real father of only one of his three children, was no longer even the breadwinner of the family.

The tragedy of George Thirkell was both a collective and an individual one: on the one hand there was the failure of the ANZAC dream, the fact that post-war life – culminating in the Depression, which hit the middle classes hard in Australia – called for other qualities than the casual heroics of Gallipoli; on the other, there was his personal mistake in choosing as his life's partner a woman as unsuitable as Angela.

Yet the end, when it came, was curiously ambiguous. In leaving Thirk, Angela behaved with uncharacteristic evasiveness. She admitted to no one, not even to herself perhaps, that she was going for good; yet to take another trip home, so soon after the last one and with George out of work, was surely out of the question. (Angela's godfather, J.M. Barrie, paid her fare: she exchanged the return fare he sent her for two single passages for herself and her son, Lance; Colin was to follow after he had finished his School Leaving Certificate Honours exams.)

Graham was already independent, having won scholarships to Melbourne University; he was in residence there at Ormond College. At weekends he would drop in at 4 Grace Street 'to parade my new-found sophistication before my sometimes admiring brothers'. One day he sensed that something was up – the rented piano, he noticed, was no longer in the drawing room. He approached Colin, who was now fifteen and swotting for his exams. Colin told him that he had overheard their mother on the phone arranging travel insurance for her most treasured possession, Sargent's portrait of her. This could only mean one thing and Graham taxed her with it:

'Mother.'
'Try not to interrupt when I'm working.'
'Mother, I *have* to talk to you.'
She swung round and faced me over her half moon glasses.
'Well, what is it, love?' she added with a judicious mixture of affection and exasperation.
'Are you going to England?'
'Yes, I am. Dad's not earning any money and it will be easier for him if I remove the family burden. Not you, darling, of course,' she added looking at me quizzically. 'You've been a *great* help.'
'You mean I'm self-supporting?'
She gave me an enamelled smile but didn't answer directly.
'I shall take Lance with me, and Colin will follow.' She turned round to her desk again, but I wasn't to be put off.
'When are you coming back?' I said to the back of her head. She whirled on me this time, pushing the hair out of her eyes.
'When your stepfather can earn some money to support us all!' she said with the teary edge to her voice which always intruded when she felt herself crossed. My stepfather, I thought? You mean your husband, don't you? But all I said was
'Are you taking the Sargent?'
'Yes,' she said shortly.
'Why?' I persisted ponderously.
'Don't ask silly questions,' she snapped.
'I'm sorry, Mother.'
She did an unexpected thing; she to whom any show of emotion or affection was so hard. She rose quickly from her desk, gave me a brief hug and a peck and said 'You're a great comfort. Now I *must* get the tea.'[66]

Graham calls his mother's 'the tragedy of the inarticulate heart':

The one she had was warm but it was deeply buried and it was terribly difficult for it to come out. It was like a small animal crouched in a burrow peering with frightened beady eyes at the intruder; and when it put out its tongue, as you thought in affection, woe betide the hand that reached for it. Instead there would be a snap and a raising of lizardly hackles. She could 'give' on paper. I have wonderfully amusing, witty and loving letters from her; but to be demonstrative, in person, ah! that was different.

He likens her predicament to that of the princess in the fairy tale whose heart is stolen by the wicked witch. In the fairy tale, of course, a prince comes to the rescue and restores the princess's heart. In life, things work out differently: 'Princess Joan was my mother; it was her ill luck that two marriages failed to bring her the fairy prince.'[67]

Graham here writes of his mother with an understanding and objectivity that Colin would never achieve. Love her or hate her, Colin remained too close to make that kind of assessment; the central chapters of his novel, *Angus Bard*, which were to describe his parents' marriage, were never written. And if Colin's, too, was to some extent 'the tragedy of the inarticulate heart', it requires no great perspicacity to identify the 'wicked witch' who stole *his* heart at birth . . .

Colin experienced the usual gamut of adolescent emotion, from deepest gloom to wildest exhilaration. In early adolescence he 'became a prodigious liar and thief, and failed in critical school examinations'. He read Keats and studied reproductions of Botticelli – 'but art, alas, though it certainly explains life and enhances it, is of no help to those whose own grip on life is insecure.' He 'became entangled with religion . . . I did not of course then understand what part of this impulse was genuine, and what larger part of it emotive and unreal, as I sat out services in church and read holy works seeking for impossible consolations. What I sought, but did not know it, were love and reassurance . . .' He became 'afflicted by curious snobberies', and began telling his friends (who were not at all impressed) that he was not *Australian*, but *English*. He affected an attitude of 'nonchalant indifference' and 'took to visiting, in my one good suit, older friends of my mother's and sought to impress them by the brilliant maturity of my uncouth observations.' In other words, he became 'a show-off (Australian, "skite")'. But as he was also 'a cute kid', he found he could make some headway with the girls he met at the homes of 'the more pretentious of my mother's friends'. There were theatricals, at which he shone – 'or at any rate, thought I did sufficiently to give me the courage, or effrontery, to talk to these girls without fear of their claws or, worse, indifference.' Occasionally, too, he picked up the crumbs that fell from his brother's table: some of Graham's 'sirens' would sometimes kiss him surreptitiously, filling him with 'shock, ardour, and frustration'.[68]

In the right mood even school became glamorous:

The masters seemed benevolent and full of consideration for my pretensions, the sportsmen young heroes out of legends, my comrades worthy companions before whom my undoubted gifts might shine . . . and I wandered among the gums along the river in the evening, long after I should have returned home, watching the oarsmen and the swimmers, and feeling part of a splendid and devoted confraternity of like-minded young.[69]

Colin took part to the full in school activities. In his last year at Scotch he was a probationer (Graham had been a prefect but Colin, who left school younger, did not quite achieve that eminence); he was on the editorial board of the school magazine, the *Scotch Collegian*; he was treasurer of the Christian Union; he was an NCO in the school Cadet Corps; and he was a member of the Debating Club, the Literary Club, the Amateur Dramatic Society – not to mention the newly-formed French Circle.

In a school debate on the subject of the 'White Australia' policy, Colin won a prize for attacking this policy; but later in life he took the opposite line:

The Australians are the only people of European stock in the entire world who, living in a torrid climate, have resolutely refused to batten on coolie labour. To realise this is to see the 'White Australia' policy, so shocking to liberal inclination, in an entirely different light. To bar the way to Asians was to reject the pleasures of a parasite existence, and to decide that all the manual labour in Australia would be performed by Australian hands.[70]

At school, though, it would have been hard to see it this way: high-minded imperialism was in the very air they breathed. For Graham McInnes, 'the mingling of war and religion and Empire – the three seem in my memory to have been indistinguishable – gives the era in retrospect a certain fierce and formidable pride.'[71] And Colin wrote a poem called *The Empire* in which the sentiments – if not the prosody – would have pleased Cousin Ruddy.

As to Colin's appearance, one of his contemporaries writes: 'I have a clear recollection of the way he looked – round face with (strange to remember) generous sensitive lips, tall and lolloping, big feet and long, thick, but non-athletic looking legs. He was no sissy, and could hold his own in trouble, but as far as I can remember, had no talent for sport.'[72] He was no dandy either. According to another contemporary, Sir Keith Waller, 'in his late teens he had a quite dreadful Harris Tweed greatcoat, cut in the Raglan style, which made him look like a Teddy Bear. He was never dapper. Graham was, but not Colin whose clothes tended to have a slept-in appearance.'[73]

In 1952 there was a Scotch College Old Boys' dinner in London to celebrate the school's centenary. Waller, who was in London at the time, was invited but refused, 'as I have a congenital dislike of the heartiness inseparable from such occasions.' Shortly afterwards, however, he met Colin at Angela Thirkell's house in Chelsea and Colin asked why he had not attended the dinner: 'He had and claimed to have enjoyed it. It was a rather hilarious evening with lots of singing of the school songs which he claimed was great fun. I was, to say the least, astonished. I begin to wonder whether there was not a good deal more nostalgia for Australia than I had thought likely or possible.'[74]

At the age of sixteen Colin won a senior scholarship to the University of Melbourne and the Victoria State exhibiton on the subject of economics, about which he claims to have known nothing, then or ever. His excellent exam results 'were entirely the consequence of swotting up facts that drove me mad with boredom and resentment'.[75] He maintains that the anxiety of exams nearly 'wrecked' him: 'An instinct for self-preservation prompted me to take a job rather than walk the treadmill of examinations for a further spell of university years. Of course I lost by this as a scholar, but I also survived psychologically as I believe I would not have done had I been processed in the examination machinery much longer.'[76]

In this account Colin makes it look like a straightforward choice between university and work. It was not as simple as that. By the time he took his final exams he was living in a house that had been transformed following the departure of Angela and Lance. Of the family, only Colin and Thirk were still at 4 Grace Street; and the house was being taken over by a Colonel and Mrs Biggs from Sydney who, in exchange for free lodging, were supposed to take care of them. In fact, as soon as Colin left to follow his mother to England on the SS *Mooltan*, the Biggs' imported two children of their own and were extremely reluctant to let Graham come and stay even for a holiday in what was, after all, his home.[77]

As with his mother, when Colin left Australia nothing was settled. He could return to Melbourne and go to the university to study, of all things, law; or he might stay on in Europe. The uncertainty of his mother's intentions crucially affected his own prospects. As he sailed out of Melbourne at the end of 1930 he was still only sixteen years old.

4
Family Reunions

The forty-day voyage to England, Colin later told a friend, was one long nightmare: he suffered so badly from seasickness that he spent most of the journey prone on the floor of his cabin.[1] But eventually the *Mooltan* docked at Tilbury and there followed, for Colin, 'in the first months of 1931, one of the most exciting moments of my life'.[2]

However he came to regard Australia retrospectively, at the time he had felt an alien there. He boasted he was English; he admits he was a snob. He was 'homesick for a country I hardly even remembered'.[3] In after-school games of cricket on Grace Street, when the ball crashed past his bat into the petrol can which served as a wicket, Colin went into the house and consoled himself by gazing at the objects which reminded him of home and family: pictures by his great-grandfather; books by his grandfather.

England was 'the promised land'; and the home of his grandparents, 6 Pembroke Gardens, 'an earthly paradise'. All through his childhood, they sent him letters and parcels – clothes, books and postal orders. His grandfather wrote wise and kindly letters, advising him on his studies and solemnly reminding him that bad spelling is a form of bad manners; while his grandmother's letters were magical, full of 'such fancy and invention, such tenderness, and such a rare understanding of what a boy of seven, or ten, or fifteen, would think and feel.'[4]

The Mackails did in fact visit Australia in 1924. J.W. Mackail gave lectures and 'Maany' registered her disapproval of the Australian accents her grandsons had inevitably acquired. But apart from this one short visit, Colin had not seen his grandparents since he sailed away to Australia at the age of five.

Now he was back in the marvellous home, full of Pre-Raphaelite memorabilia, dimly remembered from infancy.

At first all went well. Colin was touched by his grandmother's admission that she had worried he might remember how she had spoken to him crossly in the flurry of departure from 6 Pembroke Gardens eleven years before. He appreciated his grandfather's generosity in giving him pound notes to spend on clothes, in taking him to the theatre to see *Measure for Measure* (at the same time warning him, 'in tones appropriate to the son of a Calvinist minister', that it was not a pleasant play) and offering him, man to man, a cigar.[5] The house might have shrunk in the decade he had not seen it, but the treasures it contained in the way of pictures, furniture (however uncomfortable), wallpaper, books lovingly inscribed by their authors, were enhanced in value. As his grandmother read out to him the letters her cousin Kipling had written her from India (in the days when he worked for the *Civil and Military Gazette*) or his grandfather read aloud to his wife after their ritual post-prandial game of backgammon, Colin could feel the magic of the past come into the present.[6]

Not that the present lacked excitement. He had breakfast with another cousin of his grandmother, Stanley Baldwin, just then out of office but soon to be Prime Minister again, and was impressed by his first sight of an English butler. (He was less impressed, though, by Baldwin himself, who showed him an H.M. Bateman drawing of a cinema audience in which seated next to an excitable young couple, there was an emotionless, bowler-hatted and walrus-moustachioed gentleman. 'That's the man whose vote I've got to get,' the once and future Prime Minister remarked. 'Those other two are easy enough.')[7] He was whisked off to tea by Mrs Patrick Campbell 'amid an odious flurry of cherished Pekinese'. His mother took him to the Adelphi to visit Sir James Barrie who, after politely asking Colin how he was, retreated to the fireside and did not speak again for the rest of the visit, so that Angela Thirkell both had to ask him questions and answer them herself. He was taken – by his grandmother – to stay 'with a real countess in an authentically historic stately home', where he was embarrassed to have to seek the footman's aid in tying his 'first evening tie'. He visited the House of Commons, where another political cousin, the socialist Oliver Baldwin, tempted him to sit on the throne.[8]

It was Oliver Baldwin who took him to a Music Hall revival at the Victoria Palace, where he saw Harry Champion and Vesta Victoria perform. This, rather than infant memories of Nanny's rendering of Music Hall songs, was perhaps the true beginning of Colin's lifelong enthusiasm for the Halls.

He also sought out Yvette Guilbert, who – like the Music Hall artists – was by the Thirties 'performing her own legend'. The skinny creature of the Nineties, immortalised by Toulouse Lautrec, was now large and matronly. In a volume of memoirs she had expressed regret that she had turned down Burne-Jones's offer to paint her portrait. So Colin, 'with the effrontery of youth', took one of his great-grandfather's drawings to the Wigmore Hall, where she was appearing, and gave it to her. In return, she invited him to tea. 'Truth to tell,' he writes, 'I found her a disappointment off the stage . . . But I continued to admire her art immensely.'[9]

Another old lady Colin now met for the first time was his so-called 'Aunt Trix', though Alice Fleming, née Kipling, was in fact his first cousin twice removed – a relationship which she herself expressed rather more fancifully: 'Dear and amiable White Knight twice Removed, or any other move on the chess board which suggests the two-step of our complex cousinship . . .' Aunt Trix, or 'Auntrix', even 'Ancestrix', as he sometimes called her, became a favourite of Colin's. He journeyed to Edinburgh to see her. There they visited the zoo, where, in the memorable opening sentence of MacInnes's essay about her, 'My Aunt Trix, like St Francis, spoke to the birds' – to the astonishment of the worthy burghers of Edinburgh. He once told her, 'You know, if that had happened 500 years ago those people would have burned you as a witch.' 'I know they would have, my dear,' she answered with a glint in her eye. Though she was some fifty years older than him and 'rather a ruthless talker', her attraction for Colin was that she was 'so utterly ageless . . . that I was able to talk and behave far more freely with her than with any other relative of her generation.'[10]

As this remark suggests, the honeymoon period of Colin's relationship with his grandparents, following his homecoming, did not last. They had hardly seen one another for eleven years and the expectations on both sides were impossibly high. As they grew to know each other better there was a mutual sense of let-down. Perhaps the Mackails, already burdened with Angela and her son Lance for an indefinite period, resented having another mouth to feed; or if they did not resent it, thought it gave them the right to criticise. Certainly Colin felt that his grandmother set impossible, even undesirable, standards: 'She wanted me, I think, to be good, obedient and pure, and as I am none of these, she disapproved.'[11]

He began to suspect, too, that his grandfather's erudition was rather too exclusive. For instance, when Colin enthused over an early poem by W.H. Auden, Mackail 'listened magisterially while I read the lyric, then roundly declared – of the work of an artist who was to be a successor in the Oxford Chair – "That is *not* poetry." ' What was particularly galling was that on the rare occasions when Mackail did express a literary opinion he wouldn't give any reasons for it; his were *ex cathedra* utterances, assertions rather than arguments. But the rigid exclusiveness of his professional opinions – 'he gave . . . the impression that everything worth writing had been written long before 1910' – was in marked contrast to his personal benignity. He was a good and gentle man and he did not lack humour. He had in his study (the only room in the house that was truly his, and not a part of the Morris/Burne-Jones legacy) a photograph of an African chieftain surrounded by naked wives and warriors; underneath it ran the legend, 'Macmillan & Co'. Kipling had begged him to hand over this group portrait, as he declared it to be, of the directors of his publishers; but Mackail would not part with it.[12]

On his side, Colin became critical of his artistic heritage: 'I began to feel that these sad artists of the Pre-Raphaelite tradition had turned their backs on a happy animal side of life for which I hankered. I began to feel that I was living among another generation's ghosts; realities of my grandparents' own past but, to me, ghosts.'[13]

He could not, in any case, stay indefinitely at 6 Pembroke Gardens. Originally he had pleaded for a year in England before taking up his scholarships at Melbourne University. Now the notion was that he should spend some months in Europe (as his mother had done when she left school) 'scanning the scene and learning languages' before he went back to study law in Australia.[14]

He already spoke some French. At school he had made friends with a French-speaking Alsatian boy and had been a founder member of the French Circle, where the boys practised their spoken French. He also had a 'highly Francophile' mother, who never missed an opportunity to show off her French which, according to her son, 'was not as good as she supposed'.[15]

He spent three months with a French family (who, he claimed, starved him) at Sceaux-Robinson outside Paris; then he spent another month attending lectures on Flemish painting at Frei-burg University in order to learn some German as painlessly as possible. This was in pre-Hitler Germany, during the last days of the Weimar Republic. Colin stayed with a Jewish family and met some of their friends. 'In my ignorance,' he wrote later, 'I would not believe their fears.'[16]

Back in London, he startled his family by announcing that he was not returning to Melbourne.

When they asked me why, I said I wanted to go into business. I knew absolutely nothing about business, and had no real ambitions in that direction, but on two things I was totally determined. I was never again going to sit for an examination . . . and I wanted to stay in Europe. And if I stayed in Europe, I knew I couldn't attend an English university because they wouldn't accept my Australian matriculation (I had checked on this), and there wasn't any money anyway.[17]

Whether the seventeen-year-old Colin really wanted to go into business, as he retrospectively maintains, or was more or less pushed into it by a family eager to get him off their hands, is not clear. Surviving members of the family reckon that though there may not have been enough money to see him through Oxford or Cambridge — even if these had been open to him — his grand-parents could have financed him at art college had they wanted to; and Colin himself would have liked to have gone to the Slade.[18]

Whoever first mooted the idea of his going into business, the family was soon busy pulling strings. They began by trying to get him into Thomas Cook and Sons, 'but my mother patronised the contact there so much that he was unhelpful.' Next they tried Bryant and May's, but that too came to nothing. In the end it was through the offices of a former Chancellor of the Exchequer, Reginald McKenna, that Colin was taken on by the grandly named Imperial Continental Gas Association with a salary of £52 per annum.[19]

To get any sort of job in the early Thirties was something to be grateful for, but to get a job where the salary was instantly trebled — due to a generous overseas 'living allowance' — was rare good fortune. Colin was only going to Antwerp but 'when the Associ-ation posted anyone abroad it was, in their minds, as if they were sending him to darkest Africa.'[20]

Colin was fortunate, too, in his manager at the *Antwerpsche*

Gasmaatschappij: his name was Eric Dadson, and he was destined to become Managing-Director of the Association. He was then in his late twenties and Colin recalls that he was 'kind and ruthless to me. "I don't like favourites," was his greeting to me when we met at Antwerp docks – the reference being to my employment by influence rather than merit.'[21] But the two men rapidly came to like and respect one another and remained on friendly terms long after their ways parted.

After some months Colin was transferred to Brussels. In the Belgian capital there were several subsidiary companies. He began by working for a company which manufactured gas and was put in the department which sold off its byproduct, coke. The manager believed in throwing him in the deep end and after he had only been there a few weeks instructed him to draft the company's monthly report to London. Colin was proud of the fact that, though the manager had to rewrite most of it, some of his original paragraphs survived. 'Then I moved on to other companies, worked in the contracts department, sold land, and even, after a fashion (and helped out by kindly colleagues), juggled with accounts.'[22]

According to the company history of the Imperial Continental Gas Association, 'The most significant pattern that appeared during the 1930s was the gradual shift in emphasis from France to Belgium.'[23] So from a professional point of view Colin seems to have been in the right place at the right time. From a personal point of view, too, it was a good choice: 'I made many friends in Belgium, and they were all painters, writers and musicians. Most fortunately, I came under the influence of several who made me read a lot and who, I can say, educated me in so far as I am educated at all.'[24]

Chief of these influential friends was the painter Mayou Iserentant, who was married to a lawyer, Victor, several years older than herself. When they met, Colin cannot have been more than eighteen; Mayou was in her late twenties and already had two children.

With both the principals now dead, it is impossible to ascertain the precise nature of the relationship between Colin and Mayou, but there can be little doubt that they were lovers and that she also fulfilled the role of surrogate mother to him. Mayou was, according to Lance Thirkell, the perfect antithesis to his mother who, because of two contrasting but equally disastrous marriages, rejected the entire male sex – including her sons. Whereas Angela was icy, Mayou exuded warmth and Colin blossomed as a result.

For Mayou was also a part of the 'in set of Brussels, the NW1, so to speak', as Lance puts it.[25] She was a friend of the painter Spiriot, and of many other artists and musicians. She provided Colin with an entrée into the world to which he aspired to belong, a world far removed from the office and thoughts of 'kilowatt-hours and cubic metres'.[26]

On 27 March 1933, Colin wrote his mother a long account of a weekend in Paris, the high spot of which was a visit to the Casino de Paris to see Josephine Baker. Then he described how, on the train coming back, there was a Spaniard in his compartment who 'held forth politically for almost four hours'. Colin noted his arguments: that disarmament was really armament; disarmament was just an *histoire*, the League of Nations was just an *histoire*; the Pope was a *farceur*; and so on. Whether it was the man's politics or boorishness, or both, that riled Colin, he began a loud conversation with his companion in which he sang the praises of Alfonso XIII, Primo de Rivera, Prince Juan Bourbon and General Sanjurjo. But, he admits, 'we didn't draw him; he buried his face in his nasty socialist newspaper.'[27]

By the time of the Spanish Civil War Colin had changed sides. His attitude changed no less dramatically in respect of another issue on which he argued with a Belgian colleague called Maurice Wasterlain – namely, the inferiority of blacks. Negrophile though he became, MacInnes never pretended that it was easy for the races to love one another, and perhaps a part of the intensity of his feeling for racial equality stemmed from guilt: he too had travelled the road to Damascus.

But it was his attack on the Treaty of Versailles which most disturbed his Belgian friends in the early 1930s. Colin took the line that the Allies had treated Germany unfairly. He knew the treaty by heart and never missed an opportunity to criticise Lloyd George, Clemenceau and Woodrow Wilson. At first the Belgians attributed this to the fact that he was too young to remember the Great War and had never been through the experience of occupation. Later Wasterlain, in particular, thought that perhaps he had come under the influence of the Hitler Youth when he was, first, a student and then a visitor to Germany.[28]

I was seventeen when I first went there [says the narrator of MacInnes's first novel, *To the Victors the Spoils*] just the right age. I fell in love with Germany then, because I found everything I wanted.

I got there at the beginning of the spring, the sort of lad you can imagine. My instincts were sensual and my real feelings were tender and melancholy, but they hadn't had an outlet up till then. So to lessen my despair, I had smothered my longing, which bubbled up in the form of a perpetual flow of heady and tiresome chatter.

But as soon as I came to Germany, I found it was all right to have sensual instincts and all right to feel tender and melancholy. I wasn't there long before I met a girl who came walking with me in the woods to exchange German conversation for English, and we'd lie on the side of the sunny slope overlooking a lovely vista of the river valley. And boys of my age would be ready to start off in the middle of the night, stopping on a hilltop to sing songs in parts, and tell their troubles to one another very seriously. We all used to go camping up by the lakes in the mountains, sleeping in barns in the forest villages, or down to swim in the river, travelling in railway carriages that smelt of varnish and the sweat of both sexes. The landscape was poetic and smiling, or else romantic and rather gloomy, and it perfectly suited the mood of exaltation we lived in . . .[29]

By the late 1940s, when he came to write *To the Victors*, MacInnes had had plenty of time to analyse the attraction/repulsion he felt towards the Germans. He had seen where all that youthful exhilaration, all that communing with nature led – how the magic and violence ended in brutality, war and humiliation. He could be wise after the event. But in September 1933, when he set out on a strenuous sightseeing tour of Venice and Florence, he was sufficiently curious and open-minded about Germany and its new Chancellor to make a detour to take in the Nuremberg rally en route.

The early Thirties was the period in Colin's life when he tried hardest to please his mother and his maternal grandparents. Though still under twenty, he was financially independent; he had a respectable job and he worked hard at it; he spent his leisure hours constructively, visiting art galleries and museums; and he was not yet in open conflict with their social and political attitudes. But what was he to do if one of *them* stepped out of line and behaved uncharacteristically? This was the situation that faced him when his beloved grandmother joined the Oxford

Group (the movement which later became Moral Rearmament, or MRA).

On the surface, nothing could have seemed more unlikely than that this Victorian, reticent, traditionalist – not to say, snobbish – daughter of Burne-Jones should be attracted to the brash new Anglo-American gospel of the Buchmanites: she should surely have agreed with an old friend who told her, 'Margaret, I can't get my religion at Woolworth's.' But she didn't. However unlikely it was, 'Maany' had found a spiritual home after a lifetime of religious searching. It wouldn't have mattered if she had kept her 'quiet times' to herself and left others in their pagan or Anglican peace. But with the zeal of a convert she wanted to spread the good word; and among those whom she proselytised was her young and – she no doubt hoped – impressionable grandson.[30]

Colin was still 'enraptured' by his grandmother. True, when he was in London there had been 'brief, occasional, sharp hints of a total later estrangement, then hidden suspended in futurity; but so few, it didn't seem to matter.' The sight of her handwriting on an envelope still filled him with a delicious sense of anticipation. Even so, he had doubts about the Oxford Group, doubts which were fanned by his mother's caustic words on the subject. 'But I must try to be faithful to my young distant self,' he writes in maturity, 'and remember the lad I was then had also religious questionings and hopes.'[31]

He complied with his grandmother's wishes to the extent of agreeing to attend an international 'house party' organised by the Group at St Germain-en-Laye, near Paris, where the founder, Frank Buchman himself, was to be present. But he wrote to her to say he would only go on certain conditions:

I suggested that if I went to St Germain, my grandmother should pay for everything. If I was there converted to the faith, I'd pay her back; if not, not. I don't think she admired the proposition much; and when, after a silence longer than was usual, she answered accepting this peculiar spiritual-financial transaction, she did so in terms somewhat terse, and of notably diminished cordiality. I sensed this, of course; yet could not but feel that as I didn't really want to go (or wasn't sure whether I did), and as nothing had been said about the cost of the expedition, and as she had more money than I had, and it was *her* idea anyway . . .[32]

MacInnes has some fun at the expense of the earnest and stupid Groupers, who include an English Colonel and two young men he insists on calling 'salesmen'. He christens them 'Pasture' and 'Meadow', professes himself unable to tell them apart and deliberately confuses their names. In the session known as 'Sharing' – which he describes as 'do-it-yourself spiritual strip-tease' – the Colonel 'prefaced a rambling account of his un-regenerate pre-Grouping days by telling the perplexed assembly, '*Autrefois, j'avais des squelettes dans mon armoire . . .*'

Earlier, at supper, Buchman had sat at Colin's table. His appearance was 'that of an inwardly – if faintly – illuminated pumpkin'. Colin took an instant dislike to him and told the Colonel he thought the Founder unimpressive. The Colonel professed delight, 'Exactly so! It's by his being unimpressive people are impressed.' But by then Colin had begun to under-stand that the Group's technique was to agree with everything one said.

'The only illumination I received,' he writes, 'was to get out of St Germain immediately' and seek out the fleshpots of Paris. His settled attitude to the movement was 'to wonder how anyone with any moral instinct whatsoever [could] be other than revolted by the notion of combining, as in those much publicised initials, the utterly contrasting concepts of morality and of re-armament.'[33]

As far as his relationship with his grandmother was concerned, this was the beginning of the end:

I wrote [her] a full account, probably unjust in many respects, and certainly, in all that mattered, wounding to her. I also claimed my pound of flesh (the promised expenses), and I got them. As is often the case when, between two human persons, there exist large areas of difference and dispute which are hidden from them by happier shared memories, by the illusion all is still well, and by the reluctance to 'speak out' and break the spell – one disagreement on a particular event can release a whole chain-reaction of disillusionment and sorrow. This was what happened. My grandmother withdrew further within her faith – and further away from others besides myself; and I do not believe she found fulfilment there.[34]

Colin's fault, perhaps, was to speak his mind. His mother, whose attitude to the Oxford Group was, if anything, even more scathing, simply avoided the subject: 'Face to face with the older woman, the younger said not a word other than was "correct" (for my mother had a due and fit respect for *any* mother).'[35]

But Angela could not afford to break with her mother even if she had wanted to: she was dependent on her parents for the roof over her head. Her decision to leave George Thirkell and never to return to Melbourne meant that she needed to earn a living even more than when she had started writing articles and broadcasting in Australia. Her broadcasting experience encouraged her to try the BBC, but when she submitted a script to them – called 'A London Childhood in the Nineties' – they managed to offend her in some way so that she would have nothing more to do with them.[36] In later life she affected to despise the 'wireless' and her snooty attitude may well have been the long-term effect of this early rebuff.

She began to write fiction, but her first book was the volume of childhood reminiscences called *Three Houses*. Though this enjoyed a modest *succès d'estime*, it marked the end of her amateur phase as a writer of occasional pieces rather than the beginning of her professional career as a novelist. That started with *Ankle Deep* (1933) and continued on the crest of a wave of creative energy which lasted throughout the Thirties, producing some two novels a year up to the outbreak of the Second World War; after that she settled down to a more sedate one novel a year for the rest of her life. Angela was lucky perhaps in her literary advisers, E.V. Lucas and W. Graham Robertson, both older men who gave her confidence, and luckier still to find such an enthusiastic and enterprising publisher as the young Hamish Hamilton, who published all her fiction with the solitary exception of the pseudonymous *Trooper to the Southern Cross*.

Like her fictional *alter ego*, Mrs Morland, Angela Thirkell wrote 'good bad books . . . not very good books, you know, but good of a second-rate kind.'[37] Her early novels, at least, have plenty of wit and sparkle; the 'Barchester' locale which she borrowed from Trollope and first used in *The Demon in the House* (1934) may be a place of fantasy, an escape from the real world, but it is also a piece of enchantment. After her death, MacInnes wrote that he found her 'productions' – he could not bring himself to dignify them with the title of novels – 'able in execution . . . and in content totally revolting'. He continued, 'I shudder to think that millions of copies of her sterile, life-denying vision of our land should have persuaded and delighted so many hundreds of thousands in our country and the US.'[38] But when he first read *Ankle Deep* as a young man he reacted very differently, writing enthusiastically to his mother:

I must say, I found the book 5,673,942 times better than I thought I would

– without offence. I mean that it was cleverer and deeper and less autobiographic than I had expected . . . In fact, I think you are extremely clever to have turned it out so competently and professionally; it lacks the amateur 'This is my first novel' touch altogether. I don't see what should stop you going on and on – what, evidently, does a plot matter?[39]

Although he admired Angela's portraits of her father and mother, it was her self-portrait as 'Aurea' which earned her this backhanded compliment from her eighteen-year-old son:

Your Aurea is so good that she becomes too good for the book at times. In fact, although Mr and Mrs H, Valentine, and the Turners could be written as well by a man or a woman, Aurea is so strongly and vigorously alive and competently analysed that only a man writer could present her so dominantly. And yet you, who I have always believed to be a woman, have done her even better; this is most surprising . . .[40]

The letter ends with a drawing of an elongated and bespectacled Colin, book in one hand and handkerchief in the other, standing, his trousers rolled up, 'ankle deep' in a pool of his own tears.

While Colin 'Thirkell' was undergoing his commercial apprenticeship in Belgium, his brother Graham was finishing his degree in English and History at Melbourne University. He graduated with first-class honours at the end of 1933 and then, instead of following the rest of the family to England, went to Canada to look for his father. After seventeen years' separation this dimly remembered figure had acquired legendary proportions: he was a 'bardic-king'; Graham imagined him as director of an opera company, conductor of an orchestra, a singer much sought after by Canadian millionaires; he saw him 'moving in the glitter of great social occasions'.[41] In order, as he puts it, not to mar the image he had so assiduously built up, he didn't take the trouble either to find out exactly where his father lived or to let him know that he was coming to visit him.

Predictably, the reality fell some way short of Graham's expectations. He found his father in Toronto – by the simple expedient of looking him up in the phone book – but though his appearance and manner did not lack theatricality, his life-style was disappointingly mundane. At sixty-three, he was long past his prime and, though he might still be an asset to the musical society of Toronto, his great days as a performer were now distant memories.

Initially bewildered by his elder son's totally unexpected arrival, Campbell McInnes rapidly adjusted to the role of deprived and ever-loving parent. There was a tricky moment when he was so carried away by the emotionality of the occasion that he claimed once to have written Graham a letter, only to become irritable and evasive when cross-examined about where he'd sent it. But for the most part he proudly showed off his full-grown son to a circle of admiring friends.

As he was responsible for releasing this gust of feeling, Graham felt obliged to play his part in the charade. But he noticed, with the critical objectivity of youth, that his father overdid the reminiscences of his days of triumph and tended to repeat himself, prefacing some often-told tale with the words, 'Did I ever tell ye about the time . . .' And out would come a familiar story about Bouhy, de Reszke, Santley, or 'me old friend Donald Tovey'. Graham also noticed that he drank endless cups of tea and practically chain-smoked home-rolled cigarettes. A Cockney fellow-expatriate explained that 'Campbell', as he now called himself, was a reformed alcoholic: '. . . he's surrounded himself with a bunch of blue-ribboners. The Holy Camp I call 'em. But he's safe.'[42]

After about a week, Graham – 'unreasonably fed up with my father's sentimental possessiveness' – fled from Toronto, promising to return shortly. In parting he suggested that perhaps his father should think of revisiting England; then he would be able to meet Colin and they could have a grand reunion. Graham was himself going to England, but first he would pay a visit to New York; perhaps he would return to Toronto before crossing the Atlantic. In the event he had such a good time in New York that he omitted to go back to Toronto to say goodbye to his father. Instead he wrote him an effusive letter, repeating his suggestion that he come over to Europe in the summer to renew their acquaintance and to meet Colin.

This, to Graham's great surprise, his father did. Just as Graham was about to go off to Paris and hit the high spots with an Australian mate, Ross Campbell, he received word that his father was due to arrive in England the following week on the *Empress of Canada*. He sent him a postcard 'to await arrival', suggesting he go straight to Colin in Brussels and he would meet him there.

So James Campbell McInnes was reunited with his two sons in

Brussels in the summer of 1934. Ross Campbell was present; he remembers Colin then as 'pleasant, well-mannered and keenly intelligent. He had a number of pictures in his flat, and seemed to know about art.' Campbell was impressed by Colin's linguistic ability and amused by his story that the motto of the company he worked for was *Suicidez-vous par le gaz*. He found the father 'an amiable man . . . much affected by the first meeting with both his sons together for a long time. While they were out of the room he said, "Ross – I think I may call you Ross – those boys are my love children." Being young and heartless, and also acquainted with their mother, the arctic Angela, I privately considered this comical.'[43]

The high point of the visit was a performance by Campbell McInnes at the home of the Iserentants. This is Graham's description of it:

We listened to my father sing *The Self Banished* and the *Twa Sisters of Binnorie* and *Der Doppelgänger* in a tremulous full-throated deep-chested bay. His rich treacherous voice had not lost its power to grab your intestines and tie them in knots against your will. Listening to him breached social fortresses, made castles crumble and found you alone on the darkling plain filled with a nameless dread. It was a voice that unmanned you: the rich gritty bray of the authentic bard.

The Iserentants . . . regarded him as a man from Mars, though his communication with them and their Belgian guests was, being wordless, instantaneous and deep.[44]

The father and two sons returned to London together. McInnes senior stayed at the Russell Hotel, saw musical friends, gave a performance at the Wigmore Hall and – or so Colin later told more than one friend – made a pass at his second son in a taxi. He also terrified his ex-wife by telephoning her. Angela put the phone down on him but was so shaken by the thought of his renewed proximity (even if only for a week or two) that she shut herself up and wrote the novel, *O These Men, These Men!* which is a fictional approximation of her first marriage and its aftermath, only set in her present rather than her past.

When James Campbell McInnes left on the *Empress of Britain* for Canada, the boys sent him a telegram – it was Colin's idea – saying: 'Best wishes for voyage and the next hundred years'.[45] But they had no intention of letting time pass without seeing him again. It was agreed, in fact, that Colin would visit Canada the next year. As for Graham, he was already considering making Canada his home: 'I preferred the Canada of my father to the England of my mother and the Australia of my stepfather.'[46] And from that moment they both resumed the name of McInnes and 'Thirkell vanished into oblivion.'[47] (Colin did not immediately adopt the 'Mac' spelling: he used that first about a year later.)

W. Graham Robertson, who was an old family friend, describes Colin at this time as 'a pure throwback to Burne-Jones and a charming creature, devoted to pictures and art of all sorts'.[48] But following his father's dramatic re-entry into his life Colin was turning against his mother's entire family, including herself. In a note dated 1935 and written in French, he subjects her character to critical analysis:

My mother is an unhappy woman. She has two dreadful faults:
– She wants to know; but she doesn't begin to know how to feel;
– She wants to bring everything down to her level.

She has a stock of knowledge but what she adds to it is only what happens to stick.

In conversation she is incapable of being other than egoistical. She kills emotion and restricts herself to ideas.

She doesn't take in what you have to say, only how you answer her. So she only gets to know what relates to what she already knows or is curious to discover.

But this is not what she wants – hence this unhappiness. She admires and desires simplicity, but is incapable of it.

With her an emotion is transformed into an idea, never into feeling.

To begin to understand life you must be prepared to descend into the depths in order to climb the higher. She is also incapable of that. If she asks a question it is so that she can comment on the reply.

The eternal truths escape her, because they are too grand and too simple and are not subject to explanation.

Her philosophy is no use to her because it is based on self – not on our common humanity.[49]

This amounts to a declaration of independence, if not of war. As early as 1935 MacInnes was already contemplating a plan of action – a descent 'into the depths' – which would not only startle and amaze his mother, but also put her to rout. But try as he might to escape her domination, in the long run he would only succeed in proving how like her he was, even in opposition.

Colin celebrated his twenty-first birthday on board the *Empress of Britain* en route to Canada for a second 'grand reunion', as Graham calls it – this one to be staged by his father.

Campbell McInnes met Colin off the ship in Montreal and together they went by train to Toronto, where Graham awaited them. The next week belonged to James Campbell McInnes. He could hardly have expected, when he was divorced for cruelty back in 1917, that the sons he left behind – whom he never subsequently attempted to contact (except, perhaps, in fantasy) – would seek him out and, better still, be proud to bear his name. He who had contributed nothing to their upbringing, was more than happy to bask in the glory of having sired two such fine upstanding young men – more especially as he had, in his Canadian incarnation, settled into an enduring homosexual relationship (something which Graham only hints at, but which helps to explain his antipathy to 'the adoring camp' surrounding his father).

The big event, to which 'the elite of the Toronto musical and social world' was invited, was a reception on the roof garden of the Royal York Hotel. Graham and Colin knew nobody there but did their best not to spoil the occasion; their father was so evidently enjoying it. 'He looked very handsome and majestic,' Graham writes, 'and his deep resonant voice, pausing just this side of the fruity, conveyed a wonderful impression of plenitude and graciousness.'[50]

What bothered the younger McInnes's was the absence of alcohol. Whether this was due to the Ontario Temperance Act or to their father's express desire, they could not be sure; but Graham remembered what he had been told about his father's alcoholism. Whatever the reason, the party ended soberly and, as far as Campbell McInnes was concerned, triumphantly.

After a week, during which Campbell McInnes paraded his sons around, showing them 'his Canada', Colin suggested to Graham that the two of them take a trip to Montreal and New York – he would pay for it. By this time they were both anxious to get away from 'the adoring camp'. Their father raised no objections and the thought occurred to Graham that perhaps he too had had enough of them, for the time being at least.

In New York the brothers visited the Metropolitan Museum and the Frick Collection – Graham had just become art critic of Canada's one intellectual weekly – took a boat trip round Manhattan and went to Minsky's where they saw 'the immortal Gipsy Rose Lee do her bumps and grinds'.[51]

Back in Toronto, they decided to give a party of their own. They would invite their father and his friends; and Graham would invite his own new friends in the Toronto newspaper and art world. Only this time there would be booze.

It was Colin's last night, and the party was a roaring success. At eleven o'clock Graham and his father left to see Colin on to the boat-train to Montreal. After they had waved him goodbye Graham turned to ask his father whether he wanted to return to the party or go home. But his father had disappeared.

He was found, two days later, in a small hotel in the West End of Toronto, 'docile and drained'. Graham was now lodging with an old friend of his father's, an Englishwoman known as 'Lady Mary'.

'Campbell's not like other men,' she told him. 'He really just can't touch it. One glass – even a sherry – and he's off and away into some dark private world of his own . . .'

She warned Graham to let him be, not to disturb the balance he had achieved only with difficulty. She knew Graham didn't like his father's friends but said, 'He's better their prisoner.'

Graham protested that his father was a fine singer, a bard, a poet; 'and here he is surrounded by a lot of equivocation and humbug.' Better that way, 'Lady Mary' retorted, than that he should be unable to perform at all. At least he had been able to pursue a second musical career which, if less glorious than the first, had been of value to himself and others. She told Graham she had invited him to stay with her in order to get him away from his father: '. . . your continued presence, at close quarters, is too rich for his blood.'[52]

Graham accepted the rebuke. He agreed not to 'upset the apple cart'. But from then on his father was a lesser figure in his eyes – diminished by his alcoholism and his homosexuality. Colin never had to come to terms with his father as Graham did; he never saw him again after 1935. He could continue to cherish the illusion they had both initially shared.

Colin returned to Europe – and the gas company. But by now he was determined to leave. Graham's success as a budding journalist and art critic may have influenced him. If he couldn't go to university, he would go to art college. He would never make a businessman, he just wasn't interested enough.

By the time he resigned, Colin's salary had risen to £300 per annum, and in addition the company 'generously gave me a golden handshake of £100'.[53]

He left Brussels at the end of December 1936 and came to London. There he stayed for several weeks at the Thamesside home of the painter Julian Trevelyan, before finding himself a flat in Chelsea 'in a sinister old slum where the ground-floor tenant was a cordial prostitute.' This was in Finborough Road, S.W.10; it had the advantage of being close to the Chelsea Polytechnic, where he first went to study painting, 'imagining, quite incorrectly, that the artistic centre of the capital was Chelsea (as it had once been, in Whistler's and Rossetti's day . . .).'[54]

In September 1938 – a fateful month in Europe's history – Graham McInnes came to England to be married. His bride, Joan Burke, was Australian; they had met at Melbourne University but had not seen one another for five years. Graham and Joan were married in Kensington Registry Office with Colin in attendance.

This was the first time Joan had met Colin, in spite of their common Australian background. She was not disappointed; he was everything Graham had led her to expect. He was the charming younger brother and, though he was apt to dominate his elder brother, Graham accepted that: he said that Colin was the cleverer of the two of them. Colin was poor but he was kind and Joan thought he was altogether marvellous when she first met him. She also met Mayou, when she and Graham spent a week on the Continent before they sailed to Canada to begin their married life.[55] By this time the threat of war had receded; Chamberlain had returned from his meeting with Hitler at Bad Godesberg, and the general feeling in England was one of guilty relief.

In late 1938 Colin gravitated to the Euston Road School of Drawing and Painting – 'please notice the modest arrogance of this austere and factual title'[56] – founded by William Coldstream, Claude Rogers and Victor Pasmore.

He met by chance 'a man who influenced me profoundly, and one of the few of my own generation whom I loved and admired entirely'. This man was Graham Bell:

He was a South African, tall, broad, tough, proud, violent, kind, gentle, sensitive, cruel, generous, dangerous and patient, affectionate and demoniacal. He had a mop of hair like a broom, tiger's or hawk's eyes, a jutting dilated nose, a bitter and sensual mouth, and chin like a knob-

kerry. His voice rang every change from cooing solicitude to vituper-
ation. He could be blindly ruthless and exquisitely tender, act decisively
or languidly, love you or hate you for no apparent reason. He was
formidably intelligent, deeply imaginative, and had great areas of blank
prejudice and stupidity. In appearance and temperament he belonged to
the pages of Dostoievsky.[57]

Graham Bell was himself a painter, but it was less as a painter
than as the intellectual spokesman of the Euston Road group that
he influenced Colin. Colin was impressed by his combative articu-
lateness, his Thirtiesish combination of political and poetic
sensibility. Bell's pamphlet, *The Artist and His Public* (1939), which
could be seen as a kind of manifesto for the Euston Road school,
remains, despite its fashionable Marxism, a work of considerable
power and originality. In addition, Colin may have been drawn to
Bell because he sensed that, like himself (though he was not yet
aware of it), Bell was essentially more of a writer than painter.

It was as a direct result of meeting Bell that Colin joined the
Euston Road school and moved, as he puts it, 'from a slum in
Fulham to a slum in Camden Town'.[58]

In this school of about thirty regular students, situated in a
studio with a stove and two enormous windows above a pin-table
saloon where a juke-box played over and over again such hits of
the late Thirties as *I'm Sorry I Said I Loved You*, Colin strove to
become a painter. Lance Thirkell thinks this was a time of deep
depression for Colin, the time when he felt most inadequate.
While he was in Belgium, Lance remembers, Colin still had an
enormous sense of fun; even the job he could tolerate by mocking
it. Now he was doing what he had always wanted to do, but the
paintings he produced were dull and dreary. No doubt this was
partly the climate of the time and the influence of Euston Road,
with its social realist approach, but – according to Lance – 'he
had lost his original charm and gaiety and gone all brown and
dreary.'[59]

Poverty may have had something to do with it, too. Colin no
longer had a salary and he was reduced to such passes as design-
ing an '*ex libris*' plate for his old boss, Eric Dadson (who, in his
desire to help Colin without patronising him, paid him generously for it).

What he found attractive about the Euston Road school was
that it was, perhaps, the last authentic master-and-pupil academy which

has existed in our country . . . We saw our teachers paint, we visited them at their studios, we ate and drank and disputed with them. They got our paintings into shows with theirs [at the Leicester Galleries], introduced us to their patrons, and brought to the school older artists – Walter Sickert among them – and critics such as Adrian Stokes – in such a way that, although students, we could feel we were already fully involved in the artistic adventure.[60]

Yet Colin writes of his 'incapacity as a painter'[61] and, again, of his 'forlorn hope – since I had only inclination, and no natural talent – of becoming a painter.'[62] He may, of course, be doing himself an injustice, rationalising his later defection from painting; Sir William Coldstream remembers that he 'painted rather well'.[63] But he is probably right: the fact that he shared the Burne-Jones facility for comic drawing did not necessarily mean he would evince a talent for painting.

The experience of Euston Road, however, was not wasted: his familiarity with European galleries had given Colin a considerable academic knowledge of art, but by learning to look at people and things with a painter's eye he gained a practical insight into the painterly process which would be invaluable to him when he became an art critic. In addition to that, the endless gatherings in Charlotte Street cafés and pubs, the bohemian life of Fitzrovia – 'the nearest thing to Paris' is how Thelma Hulbert, who combined being 'secretary' of the school with learning to paint, remembers it[64] – gave a sense of community to one who was temperamentally a 'loner'.

The painters Rodrigo Moynihan and Thelma Hulbert both speak of Colin's pallor at this time – he was pale but healthy looking. And Thelma Hulbert adds, 'There were none of the eccentricities of his later appearance – no fancy caps or dyed hair! He had short-cut hair and was more *un*conscious of his appearance.' What he was really like, she hardly knew; it was a case of 'in for the painting and out with the chaps'. He was always very charming when he spoke to her, but there was no personal contact. To Coldstream, he was 'extremely civil, but wasn't very obviously approachable'. Rodrigo Moynihan found him 'an incredibly shy, withdrawn person'; and another painter, Elinor Bellingham Smith, who was then married to Moynihan, remembers him as 'quiet and sweet and frightfully good-looking – he looked like a Burne-Jones.' Nor will she ever forget how, one

Christmas – it must have been 1938 – when all the Euston Road crowd came to stay at Monksbury, the Moynihans' farmhouse in Essex, Colin noticed her fatigue and came and helped her with the washing up, while the others carried on playing darts.[65]

Even with Graham Bell, whom he so admired, Colin kept his distance, so that Bell could describe him in a letter to a third party as being 'so self-sufficient'.[66] Perhaps this was an understandable wariness on Colin's part, as Bell was so dominant a personality. Lawrence Gowing, for instance, who was then a student at Euston Road (and succeeded Coldstream as head of the Slade School of Art in 1975), recalls an evening in The Yorkshire Grey in Fitzroy Street when Rodrigo Moynihan, who did not share the aesthetic outlook of Euston Road though he was on friendly terms with the founders, drew him aside 'from one of the crowing choruses of scorn for any painting that affected a quality of the artistic, over which Graham Bell presided, to register a modest, mock-political dissent from the art-politics of the realistic wing.'[67]

It was Graham Bell who had them stay up half the night to paint poster adaptations of Goya's *Disasters of War* etchings and parade with them the following day to Trafalgar Square to arouse English support for Republican Spain – already a lost cause. Political debate was the stuff of Euston Road life: they all marched up and down Whitehall demanding Chamberlain's resignation and calling for 'an improbable popular front of Churchill, Cripps and the Communist Party'.[68]

'It is the fashion now,' MacInnes writes a quarter of a century later, 'to sneer at the leftward inclination of artists and intellectuals in the Thirties. I can only reply that for anyone of human feeling, it was impossible, in the Chamberlain era, to be an artist without being also some sort of radical . . .'[69] Colin's own radicalism was a recent growth; he was far more radical at the age of twenty-four than he had been at nineteen. This may be partly attributable to the deteriorating political situation, in which England – and Colin was constant in his patriotism – played so ignominious a role; but it was also the result of his Euston Road education and the influence of Graham Bell.

To follow the short trajectory of Bell's life to its sad conclusion: during the 'phoney war' he trained to be an RAF navigator and then, on 9 August 1943, he was killed in a plane crash at Newark in Nottinghamshire. He was thirty-three years old. From Gibraltar,

Corporal MacInnes wrote to a mutual friend: '. . . I was not a close friend of Graham's, perhaps because a weft of insincerity in my nature prevented this. But when I was with him I felt myself on the border of something enormous . . .'[70]

The Euston Road school did not long survive the outbreak of war; its people were dispersed, its activity doomed. Even before the death of Graham Bell it had already passed into art history.

5

In War and Peace

Despite the fact that he 'grew to love the army emotionally, while totally rejecting its ethos both intellectually and spiritually',[1] Colin suffered initially from the lack of privacy, the childish do's and dont's, rewards and punishments inseparable from army routine and discipline. He rejected the option of becoming an officer – a decision which Graham Bell described as 'a product of protestant pride'; adding, in a memorable sentence, 'He punishes himself for the weak charm of his ancestors.'[2] But by the end of 1940 he was one of a demonstration platoon of NCOs at Bulford, that archetypal military camp on Salisbury Plain, whose task it was 'to act as guinea-pigs for the Officer Cadet Training Unit there: that is, to perform the manoeuvres these privileged wretches were being slave-driven to perfect, with even greater panache and efficiency.'[3]

It was a grim time for Colin personally as well as, of course, for the nation as a whole, a time when ' "austerity" . . . the negation of all joy, was already settling like a sterile blight on England.'[4] In the midst of this encompassing gloom Colin received an invitation from the painter, Stephen Tennant, to visit nearby Wilsford Manor. Stephen Tennant's mother was Lady Glenconner, the beloved friend of Margaret Mackail; and it was at Wilsford, before and during the earlier war, that Angela Mackail had first met both her husbands-to-be. Since that time Stephen Tennant had transformed the Edwardian manor into 'a southern-oriental-English dream', where he himself 'crouched on the cushions looking like an exquisite, sad faun'.[5] The contrast between Bulford and Wilsford could scarcely be greater, but the image of MacInnes clumping along the road to Amesbury in his ammunition boots like some northern barbarian about to invade a Moorish palace is a consciously butch effect contrived, perhaps, to conceal the exquisite in himself.

By early 1941 Colin had had enough of playing soldiers on Salisbury Plain and was looking for alternative employment. He succeeded in having himself transferred to the Field Security

Service of the Intelligence Corps and was eventually posted to No. 1 Field Security Section of the 2nd Infantry Division stationed in the East Riding of Yorkshire. He was allotted the Bridlington area, by the sea, and his duties included writing weekly reports on security matters, lecturing and advising home guard and local army units on security, and carrying out any special instructions from divisional headquarters. In his spare time, to improve his knowledge of German, Colin took lessons in the language from a young woman in Bridlington. Her mother, however, infected with the spy-mania which gripped the country just then, grew suspicious of her daughter's pupil, who seemed to have no military duties, never went on parade and wore no identification marks on his uniform. So she went along to the local police station and denounced him as a spy. The police reported the matter to their headquarters; the Chief Constable handed over the information to the Field Security Officer in charge of No. 1 Section, who in turn passed it on to his NCO on the spot – namely, Colin MacInnes. Thus Colin received orders to investigate his own activities.[6]

In October the 2nd Division was ordered out to the Far East; but Colin MacInnes and two other NCOs were retained to form the nucleus of a new Field Security Section for the East Riding. First, however, they were sent back to the Intelligence Corps depot at King Alfred's College, Winchester, for further training.

Life at the depot was made up of all that Colin hated most about the army: drill, motorcycle instruction and guard duties. In the end he could stand it no longer and, much to the surprise of the other section NCOs, applied for a posting to Gibraltar.

Before he went abroad he made his peace with his mother. She was living – as she did throughout the war – in Beaconsfield. He wrote her a poem which he called simply, 'Now that I find I love my Mother':

> I
> It seems that a beloved flower,
> Though tillage none, has sprung.
> As if our Nature would forbid
> An arid earth should keep it hid,
> And from untended ground has wrung
> Our blessing in this latter hour.

II
Did I, a babe, lean to your breast?
Did we in later years
Depart each other, led this wise
By temperament and family ties
Which discord brought, or by our fears
And wants opposed, and all the rest?

III
These longings rule us yet;
You yours, and I still mine.
Yet, though the night consume the day
And day blind night, night after day,
This strife gives birth to passing Time.
So too, strife past, our hearts have met.[7]

Such hopes were premature. Though the differences between mother and son might be resolved in a poem, they were far too deep-seated to be resolved *by* one.

Colin went out to Gibraltar at the end of November 1941 on the troopship *Rangitata*. The journey was a dangerous one through U-boat-infested seas. Indeed the *Rangitata* was torpedoed and sunk shortly after this voyage. But Colin and his section arrived safely at their destination. MacInnes looked back on his time on the Rock of Gibraltar as a kind of imprisonment: 'an experience by which none who endured it have been left unmarked; for the paradox of sunlight, no black-out at night' – that would have distinguished the Rock too sharply from the 'neutral' neighbouring Spanish coastal town of La Linea – 'and shops groaning with propaganda goods in the only remaining allied foothold on the European mainland, accompanied an exclusively male society (except for eighteen, I think, Wrens), the tantalising daily spectacle of forbidden Spain, and for most of us locked up there, a two-year stint to do.'[8]

Yet at the time Gibraltar was a lively enough spot. It was the focal point for all escapees from Occupied Europe. There was a steady stream of Poles, French, Dutch and Belgians, who stayed briefly in the various hotels before they were shipped off to Britain to join the Free Forces. These birds of passage relieved the monotony of military life and gave it a cosmopolitan flavour.

Colin shared with two other NCOs a hotel room which became known as the 'three corporals' room'. They set out to make it as unmilitary as possible: Colin left copies of Cyril Connolly's literary magazine, *Horizon*, to which he subscribed, strewn around the place; and one of the other corporals, Hudson Smith, who was a jazz fan (and introduced Colin to the singing of one of his later idols, Billie Holiday), contributed a wind-up gramophone and a pile of 78 records. Both Colin and Hudson Smith took advantage of the regulation whereby security personnel did not have to wear uniforms but could dress in civilian clothes.

The third corporal, Roland Atkinson, a former reporter on the Continental *Daily Mail*, wrote of Colin in the section diary: 'He writes more, reads more, works harder, cleans more articles, argues more, learns more Spanish, fools more people, gets around more, drinks more, coughs more, and sleeps less than any other member of the section.'[9]

Hudson Smith explains that Atkinson was easily provoked into argument by Colin and invariably came off worse. Atkinson later came to think of Colin as 'something of an intellectual bully' and found him generally secretive. Hudson Smith, who was closer to Colin, also found him somewhat secretive. Though he shared a room with him for two years he never suspected Colin of homosexual proclivities; even in retrospect he says that Colin 'betrayed few signs of sexual ambivalence'. On visits to the border town of La Linea Colin was not to be tempted into any of the numerous brothels there; but he did, on the other hand, manage 'to lay one of the prettiest Wrens on the Rock'. Considering that 'their virginity was guarded by a formidable Chief Wren like the gold in Fort Knox' and that they were so vastly outnumbered by males that they would scarcely look at anyone below the rank of major, this was no mean achievement. Yet Colin, 'with typical secrecy', said nothing of this conquest to Hudson Smith till years after the war.[10]

Colin was cynical about routine security work and, because of his excellent French, he was soon seconded to the Interrogation Board whose task it was to screen refugees. He found this far more congenial and made several friends among the French and Belgians who succeeded in making their way to Gibraltar.

As a result of this, perhaps, when he returned to England he was offered a 'special job' – in other words, a chance to join the Secret Service. But he did not take to the cloak-and-dagger ambiance and was soon back in his army unit. There he was promoted to sergeant.[11]

MacInnes finally entered the war with the Normandy landings in June 1944. He was nearly thirty. His experiences over the next year or two are described in great detail, and with a minimum of fictionalisation, in his novel, *To the Victors the Spoils*. After the invasion got under way he found himself, as he puts it in a later article, 'senior sergeant in a unit comprising an officer plus batman-driver, a fellow sergeant, and 14 junior NCOs. The duty the army had assigned to us was to flit over liberated and occupied Europe hunting for spies, saboteurs, national socialists and suchlike.'[12]

While he was thus engaged he received news of his father's death in Canada; James Campbell McInnes did not survive the last winter of the war. His male friend and companion sent Colin a telegram but, not knowing where he might be found, sent it c/o Angela Thirkell. Instead of redirecting the telegram she merely enclosed it with her next letter. Colin did not forgive her for that.[13] But for the moment he had other things on his mind.

In *To the Victors* Sergeant 'Mac' is recognisably MacInnes himself. For him, as for the other NCOs, tackling Gestapo agents and sympathisers is a test he is not at all confident of passing. He is excited by the 'amorality with which the mental climate of Intelligence work is saturated'; he is both fascinated and disgusted by the human weaknesses it reveals. Yet to begin with he is so anxious for his 'spiritual virginity' that he holds back. Indeed, he is accused by another NCO of being 'pro-German'.

'What does that mean, "pro-German"?' he retorts. 'Once we get there, you'll be calling me "anti-German". All I'm telling you is that a great many, of which you're one, will miss what's remarkable in them, admire what's inferior and won't see how their qualities are related to their defects. And that very soon, your sentimental hatred will turn to sentimental adoration.'[14]

MacInnes himself changed in the opposite direction – from sentimental adoration to sentimental hatred. In life as in his novel he extolled the Germans for their virtues, or the virtues he associated with them – their 'innocence and purity of instinct', their single-mindedness and their extremes of despair and ecstasy: 'They're great givers. That's why, when they gave themselves to Hitler, they gave themselves completely'[15] – but when the time came he was ready to turn on them like a disappointed lover or avenging angel.

It so happened that a young poet called Robert Waller, whom Colin had originally met in Euston Road days through their mutual friend, Graham Bell, was also in Germany. He was an instrument mechanic in the Royal Tank Regiment. He drifted through the war as a private soldier, living in a world of dreams, scarcely even conscious of which country he was in. One day Colin descended on his unit in a Mercedes he had somehow acquired and asked his commanding officer if he might take Private Waller with him on a mission. The officer agreed. Waller had no idea why Colin wanted him; all he knew was that he was chasing Nazis. Colin's way with them, he soon discovered, was to treat them with the same brutal arrogance as they had exercised on others.[16]

Once, when they were driving through the countryside, they came upon a large country house, set in its own grounds, with wrought-iron gates and an imposing sweep of drive. It seemed to be a hotel; it was full of wealthy, bourgeois Germans having lunch. Such a sight roused Colin's ire. He drove straight up to the house and demanded to see the manager. This individual was visibly startled at the appearance of two British soldiers; he was only too ready to comply when Colin ordered him to clear the restaurant and set a table for two in the middle of the room. MacInnes and Waller ate their meal in solitary (and for Waller, uncomfortable) splendour while the displaced guests peered in at them through the windows. When they drove off they found the gate at the bottom of the drive was shut. Waller was about to go and open it when Colin restrained him. He drove back up the drive, summoned the manager again and told him to open the gate. But the manager did more than that: in addition to opening the gate he lined the drive with members of his staff. 'Did you see the look in his eyes?' Colin asked as they drove away. 'Yes,' Waller replied, 'it was admiration.'[17]

The single most appalling discovery the Allies made as they advanced into Germany was of the concentration camps. Robert Waller was with MacInnes when the first rumours of Belsen were circulating among the troops; MacInnes was anxious to go and see for himself, but Waller preferred to stay away.

'I went out yesterday,' Mac says, in *To the Victors*, 'but they wouldn't let me in. It's closed to sightseers now, they said . . .'[18]

Nevertheless, MacInnes managed to get hold of some photographs of Belsen which he took to a shop to be printed and, when the wretched shopkeeper prevaricated, got tough with him and ordered him down on his hands and knees. Waller, who was with Colin, thought he was being unnecessarily sadistic and remonstrated with him afterwards; but Colin merely shrugged and said it was better to be humiliated than shot.[19]

MacInnes suppresses the sexual aspect of his experience in *To the Victors*: all he offers is the occasional mutual affair with some sad girl. But the women in the novel are peripheral; it is the relationships between the men which count.

Waller suggests that the war did not so much change Colin as 'liberate' his homosexual and powerful sexual dream tendencies. The army offered maximum opportunity for homosexual indulgence and Waller remembers that, while they were together in north Germany, Colin boasted of having slept with the entire police force in one place. Before the war, Waller recalls, 'he was shy, sensitive, never pushed himself forward; when we went to the pub he always sat at the back listening . . . But then he became this sardonic, ferocious character. He once said that, as far as he was concerned, the Germans won the war.'[20]

The war undoubtedly had a coarsening effect on him. 'That's one thing to be said for soldiering,' Mac says at the end of *To the Victors the Spoils*:

you certainly get to find out what you really are. And you certainly get to know how parts of your nature were held in check before by fear of the consequences. You soon discover that there's no such thing as a small evil, one dirty little act. They're all the same, they all carry you the same way. Once you're caught up in it, you really are caught up in it. And if you know what you're doing, you begin to fear your own enjoyment.[21]

After six months of arresting, interrogating and imprisoning people, Colin had had enough. 'These people were odious,' he writes, 'I had no sympathy for them, but this tearing away of frightened monsters from their screaming wives and children did begin to prey on my nerves.'[22] By the time the German army surrendered, the invading forces had reached the Baltic, and Colin's unit somehow found itself on the wrong side of the armistice line. They were the only British troops in a town full of German soldiers, deported Allied workers and German refugees. A 'ridiculous old German General' and an 'extremely shaky Nazi

Burgomaster' attempted to keep some sort of control; but they were only too eager to hand over responsibility for order to the first Allied soldiers who came along.

The first day he was in the town, Colin heard there was a prison full of Allied political prisoners, many of whom were dying. The Allied civilians who told him about the prison urged him to get the prisoners released. He went there and saw how volatile the situation was: there were 1,400 or 1,500 men in a prison built to house half that number; they were a mixture of Allied and German, political and 'criminal' prisoners; they all knew the war was over and were therefore impatient to be released; the German warders were no longer sure of themselves and had become trigger-happy.

Colin reported back to his officer, who said: 'Prisons aren't our pigeon, Sergeant. They're a Mil. Gov. matter. Besides, our job's arresting people, not releasing them.'[23] This was precisely what appealed to Colin: it would make a pleasant change to release a few people. He stressed the danger of a riot and the captain finally agreed to refer the matter to higher authority. Military Government gave its blessing, and Colin and another NCO took over the prison.

MacInnes and his fellow sergeant went through all the documents relating to the hundreds of Allied prisoners – political and criminal. It was often impossible to distinguish between the two: what was a criminal offence in German eyes was likely to be an act of heroic resistance from an Allied point of view. So they decided to free all Allied prisoners and let the individual nations' missions sort out their own people.

Colin's spell as prison governor ended with the evacuation of the Allies. Nation by nation, they left the prison in lorry loads, waving home-made flags and singing their national anthems. Even the German warders, watching surreptitiously from windows and doorways, were impressed. After that, the proper authorities took over. 'Heartily sick of the prison,' Colin was glad to leave. His one regret was that he 'hadn't simply, in the first few hectic days, opened all the cells and let everybody out.'[24]

His days in the army, too, were nearly over. At first he had been a reluctant soldier, but he was soon won over. In an article written twenty years later he listed the virtues of military life as he saw it – the unexpected egalitarianism, the unlikely friendships and the blissful irresponsibility: 'If you do what you're told you don't have to do anything else, and your whole inner life becomes free, contemplative and protected. No one can relax as soldiers can: no one – except, perhaps, in a monastery or prison – can dream as richly.'[25]

MacInnes was demobilised on 25 April 1946. He had already made his first broadcast – for the French Service of the BBC – on 4 April. As an aspiring writer who had studied to be a painter, he naturally gravitated towards art criticism, though he eked out a living by giving lectures on art as well.

He moved into a flat at 4 Regent's Park Terrace, within earshot of London Zoo. The house was rented by Robert Waller, who had recently married and lived on the ground floor with his wife and his mother-in-law; MacInnes had the top floor and a room on the floor below which he sublet.

There were parties in the house and sometimes Angela Thirkell came. Waller remembers that she was quite a draw. She would stand there, stiff and upright, making Edwardian remarks: 'Playing the arch-reactionary had become her life-style, which she was in a way commercialising.' But she was true to herself and Waller liked her. Colin would come in with her, smiling and polite. But he made faces behind her back to dissociate himself from the remarks of this embarrassing, if now eminent parent.[26]

Throughout the war Angela Thirkell's reputation as a novelist had been growing on both sides of the Atlantic. By the end of the Forties her American fans were forming themselves into 'Thirkell Circles'. In England, too, though she might be a hate figure to the *New Statesman* and 'the safest bet for oblivion' according to its reviewer, Philip Toynbee, her fame brought her a considerable fan mail, including many letters from servicemen and prisoners of war.[27] 'To the wit and literate high-jinks of the Barsetshire novels,' Graham McInnes writes, 'she added . . . a spice of well-bred courage and county phlegm which went well with the mood of the Blitz and the V-bombs and ultimately the Victory. But alas, peace brought in her eyes, not a return to any arcady, but Mr Attlee whose government she feared and detested.'[28]

The post-war world was not at all to Angela's liking. Her

adored father had died at the end of 1945 and Margaret Mackail, though she lived on into the Fifties, was more or less an invalid; her daughter made no bones about saying what a sore trial it was to look after her. Personally and politically the outlook for Angela Thirkell was dispiriting. She provocatively entitled her novel of 1946, *Peace Breaks Out*. 'If Churchill had been in,' someone in the novel says, 'we'd never have had this peace.' When Churchill lost the post-war election, the author comments, 'millions of people felt a sudden sense of desolation, of being children deserted in a dark lonely wood; much as they had felt it in that black winter when their ruler deserted them. Other millions saw the dawn of an even Braver and Newer World, as if the present brave new one were not unpleasant enough.'[29]

Angela Thirkell had become the mouthpiece of the embittered and embattled upper middle class who saw in Churchill's electoral defeat a betrayal, an act of monstrous ingratitude, of political vandalism. 'They' were now in power, and look what a mess 'They' were making of it. 'And when,' says Mrs Morland/Thirkell,

I saw the way They managed it [VJ Day]; when Anne Knox started for London and got as far as Barchester and had to come back because the papers hadn't come and they very rightly don't listen to the wireless, though I daresay we shall all be compelled by law to listen to it soon, in which case I shall go and live with Lord Stoke because he is deaf; then I lost Faith. Not that I ever had any . . .[30]

MacInnes, by contrast, found post-war life in London, with its black market and spivs, attractively familiar; it was all of a piece with his wartime experience. 'I recall, for example,' he writes,

a restaurant in Camden Town to which people came by night from all over the metropolis, where heavily rationed foods were constantly available, and which somehow avoided prosecution. I remember a pub (run by a former army comrade) where whisky in bottles, intended for export, was obtainable. I knew a man who had Service contacts and could arrange for petrol, though this was dicey because army petrol was coloured puce. As for the spiv, he was a rogue, but for women who wanted impossible nylons, or that legendary object of desire, the new LP record, or the fabulous ball-point pen that cost 34*s*. 10*d*. in the shops (now 6*d*.), the spiv seemed a kind of Robin Hood . . .[31]

In November 1947 Colin became art critic for the *Observer*. He sent in his first review, on academic painting, on Guy Fawkes Day; and though it did not amount to much in the way of fireworks, it was subjected to a number of editorial emendations – as Colin

discovered when he received the proof. These alterations seemed
to have no other purpose than to weaken the piece – for example,
'which the Impressionists ignored completely' was watered down
to 'which the Impressionists tended to neglect'; and what he wrote
of Sir Alfred Munnings's artistic gifts, that 'they make no appeal
to me personally', was rendered thus: they 'appeal to me personally far less than to many others.'[32] MacInnes protested against
such a mealy-mouthed approach. In the event, he won his first
skirmish with an editor and the newspaper printed his original
text. After that they let his words stand, though for as long as he
was writing regularly for the *Observer* he kept a scrapbook in
which he religiously pasted the proofs of his reviews alongside the
published versions.

A more serious row took place over the 180th Royal Academy
Exhibition at Burlington House. On 2 May 1948 the *Observer*'s
editor, Ivor Brown, used the occasion for a philistine attack on
modern art. 'Wiser men than I,' he wrote, perhaps in deference to
his art critic, 'will tell you whether what you see is Good Art. But I
can guarantee the presence of Good England . . .' He took the line
that what was good enough for the Old Masters should be good
enough for us: 'It appears, for some reason which I can never
understand, that the art which represents is perfectly respectable,
even admirable, in Old Masters. But what with them was virtue,
with us is vice. To be a new master you must vomit up your
sub-conscious or mass the hallowed cube . . .'[33]

MacInnes, whose review of the exhibition was to appear in the
following week's *Observer*, took offence. He felt that Brown had
not only upstaged him, but also discredited what he would have to
say in advance: it was as if he were inviting his readers to ignore
what his critic said. It was an intolerable position and MacInnes
resigned forthwith, after just six months at the job.

As a critic Colin was loyal and generous to his friends. This was
not so much a form of nepotism as a desire to have others share a
genuine admiration which allowed no distinction between the
personal and the professional. In a broadcast, for instance, he
described modern French art, deriving from Picasso and Matisse,
as 'mannerist' and singled out, as an exception to the prevailing
trend, Mayou Iserentant. 'Her extraordinarily personal and
poetic art,' he told his listeners, 'lies outside the mannerist
currents.'[34]

Because of his connections with the Continent, MacInnes was a frequent visitor to the Anglo-French Arts Centre in St John's Wood. It was there he met another aspiring art critic, David Sylvester, who, for twenty-five shillings a week, rented his spare room in Regent's Park Terrace.

MacInnes loved to typecast his friends; and woe betide them if there was any deviation from the image he had of them. In David Sylvester's case Colin took a romantic attitude to his Jewishness which Sylvester found positively claustrophobic. MacInnes would later do the same sort of thing with blacks – to such an extent that one black man was heard to complain, 'Man, that Collins [as they often called him], he make you feel *so black*.'[25]

At one time he even kept an album with people in categories. Herbert Read, for instance, featured in it not as a writer, but as a soldier – because of his First World War DSO and MC.[36] David Sylvester recalls that MacInnes invented a game (though Mac-Innes attributes it to Sylvester) in which friends – or famous people – are classified according to whether they are temperamentally 'Greeks', 'Romans' or 'Jews'. Thus, Jew = 'moralising, prophetic, radical-traditional'; 'Greek = 'life-loving, crafty, hedonistic-spiritual'; and Roman = 'authoritarian, organisational, grandiose, rhetorical'. Colin himself claimed to be 'a Jew, in love with the Greeks, who detests the Romans.'[37] Perhaps, though, there was more of the Roman in him than he cared to admit.

He certainly carried over something of the wartime interrogator into civilian life. 'A writer,' he wrote in the notebook in which he inscribed maxims and pensées, and which he labelled 'Thoughts', 'when he meets a person, tries to stir up the mud in his soul.'[38]

He also wrote, 'It is impossible to be generous unless you have nothing'[39] and, suiting the action to the word, promptly gave away most of his possessions. All at once great gaps appeared in his packed bookshelves; and they were quickly reduced almost to nothing. *'Je suis dans une période de dématérialisation,'* he told a friend.[40] He also removed from the walls of his flat a number of paintings (mostly by Mayou Iserentant) and left them in the care of an old friend.

It was as though he were clearing the decks in order to get down to the serious business of becoming a novelist. To Robert Waller, who was now a BBC radio talks producer in Bristol (though Waller's mother-in-law, Mrs Truman, still resided on the ground floor of 4 Regent's Park Terrace), he wrote:

. . . Here I sit and write pages of fiction. It is late to begin, for so much is terrible, and has to be dropped into Mrs Truman's dustbin again and again. I have really finished only one book, after writing it three times, and even it is not finished as I should wish.

When one writes, all one's defects emerge from hidden corners! The virtues will not appear without bringing along, uninvited, their brothers and sisters, the defects. Vulgarity, pretension, facetiousness and self-adulation are some of their many names. I spend my time picking them up like cockroaches off my pages, and cracking their heads.

The notion that one can do journalism (however elevated) or critical work, and also write fiction, is a complete error. I have abandoned everything of that sort. That leaves the material problem, but to one enjoying good health and having no dependents, there is no material problem, I have discovered. But rather than write for the *Observer*, e.g., again, I would prefer to drive a truck.[41]

The years 1949, 1950 and 1951 seem to have been rather indeterminate ones in Colin's personal life. He was in his mid-thirties and had not yet, in current homosexual parlance, 'come out'. If he had been active homosexually at the end of the war in Germany, that was because wartime conditions licensed special behaviour. Since the war, it appears, he had been living a largely chaste and self-sufficient existence.

His 'Thoughts' book strengthens this impression of personal indecision. 'With one woman to love, and one friend to tell the truth to, you can travel through the jungle of society in the necessary second gear,' he writes at one point. At another: 'Let us be less illusioned about friendships and friends; it never goes deep. The only human bonds that lift us out of loneliness are those of the flesh – even when indifference or hatred are also present in them.' 'The dangerous Puritan,' he warns himself, 'is the Puritan who boozes'; at the same time noting that 'homosexuals sip half-pints.' Another reference to homosexuality comes in his critique of Benjamin Britten's opera, *Peter Grimes*:

'The theme and tragedy of P. Grimes is homosexuality and, as such, the treatment is quite moving, if a bit watery.

'Grimes is the homosexual hero. The melancholy of the opera is the melancholy of homosexuality.'[42]

In the midst of these more or less random thoughts comes a sudden, startling *cri de coeur*:

I sat up in the night writing letters. I worked on through the night because I wanted to catch up with my work, because I was behindhand and wanted a new start.

I went to bed after breakfast.

I slept all through the morning and was woken in the afternoon by the phone bell, with a call from the woman I had been writing to.

She said, 'The chairs and sofa look idiotic without you.' I said, 'I shall come back soon.' She said, 'They look idiotic.' I said, 'Don't move them till I come back.'

She said, 'Do you love me always, always, always?'

I said, 'Always, always, always. Always, always, always. Always, always; always, always, always.'[43]

One can only speculate as to the woman's identity: possibly it was Mayou Iserentant. But the last word reverberates with poignant longing.

Small wonder then, that, caught between the 'melancholy' of homosexuality and the impossibility, as he saw it, of a 'fulfilled' life, MacInnes should complain: 'I am the donkey who hesitated between two thistles and died of starvation.' He writes, 'If chastity were not considered a virtue, it would be quite attractive.' Virtue repelled him – 'I cannot bear, cannot support, the sight of the consciously good' – and evil exercised a fatal attraction, even against his better judgment: 'This idiotic preoccupation with evil . . . fly and spider attitude to it . . .' His ambition was 'to be a sinner who doesn't sin.'[44]

He was inclined to blame his problems on heredity – 'generations of alcoholics' on his father's side and of 'morbid, gloomy introspects' on his mother's. 'I have always felt,' he wrote, 'that I am like a man driving a car he isn't sure of . . .' At the same time he took comfort in the belief that 'those who *support* and "cure" an inherited ill-health are specially worthy . . .'[45]

MacInnes's career as a novelist got off to a flying start when the *Daily Graphic* nominated *To the Victors the Spoils* as its first 'Book of the Month'. But it was not an unqualified success. The *Sunday Pictorial*, for instance, described it as a book that 'leaves a nasty taste',[46] objecting to the portrayal of British soldiers as looters rather than heroes. And even as sympathetic a reader as Robert Waller feels that MacInnes exaggerates the amount of looting that went on in the wake of the invasion of Germany. 'There was looting, of course,' Waller says, 'but Colin enjoyed indicting his own countrymen.'[47]

Despite his resolution to become a truck-driver rather than return to art criticism, MacInnes really had no option if he was to earn his living by his pen. So in January 1951 he accepted the first of many invitations to take part in the BBC radio programme, *The Critics*.

The Critics was broadcast on the Home Service (which was later to become Radio 4). Though it was a less highbrow affair than its successor, *Critics' Forum* (on Radio 3) is today, the format of the programme was much the same: a film, a book, a play, an art exhibition and sometimes a radio programme were discussed by a team of critics, each of whom was responsible for starting up the discussion of his particular topic. Colin was generally the art critic, though he was occasionally radio critic. David Sylvester, who was himself one of *The Critics* in the later Fifties, remarks of Colin that he 'had the knack of performing in a middlebrow context'.[48] Another critic went so far as to dub him 'the Commander Campbell of *The Critics*', after a famous contributor to another popular radio programme, *The Brains Trust*.

Colin was by no means always reverential towards artists. About Henry Moore, for instance, he composed in an idle moment this parody of the Music Hall song, 'Don't Have Any More, Mrs Moore':

> Don't make any more, Mister Moore,
> Mister Moore, please don't make any more.
> The more you make, the more you make, they say,
> But enough is as good as a feast any day.
> If the Tate buys any more, Mister Moore,
> They'll have to take the house next door,
> 'Cos each reclining figure
> Gets heavier and bigger –
> So don't make any more, Mister Moore.[49]

In addition to his regular stints on *The Critics*, MacInnes succeeded in establishing himself generally as a thoroughly professional broadcaster. He also completed his second novel, *June in Her Spring*, which he dedicated to Mayou Iserentant.

'It is my idea of a hymn to pure animal love in youth,' he wrote. 'I don't know what anyone else will think of it – I wrote it straight off, exact opposite to laborious "planning" of *The Victors*.'[50]

The theme of the book (which remained Colin's favourite among his novels) is young love thwarted by hereditary forces –

on the girl, June's side, by madness in the family; on the boy, Benny's, by 'sexual perversion'.[51] Benny only learns about his (dead) father's homosexuality from his guardian, Henry Bond, towards the end of the novel. One reader, at least, must have read the following passage from its climax with mounting horror and distaste:

'But my mother . . .'

Sadness and pity appeared in Henry's eyes. 'Benny, dear boy, your mother – oh, forgive me this truth! – was no more to him than an episode . . . one of many, disastrous all of them to his happiness and career, flights from his duty in those awful alcoholic fits that made him a savage monster . . . I see him standing now (and Henry rose) with the first choir and orchestra of Europe massed behind him, swaying with dark eyes like a falling angel, missing the beat from the conductor and coming in blindly, late behind the music – a catastrophe! And I (Henry wrung his hands), estranged from him just then in one of our many awful quarrels, watching this horror from the balcony! And he! a man who sang before prime ministers and kings, the object of this public mockery, all the while standing there singing with his voice as noble as it ever was but bars behind the music! And why was this? It was because he'd drunk like a beast and all his thoughts were centred for a while on some worthless woman whose very name I cannot even now remember!' Henry clenched his fists then beat his breast once, and loosely dropped his hands. 'Some men are born,' he said, 'who are not fit for women . . . You are so like your father, Benny . . . Be true to your own nature . . .'[52]

In the circumstances it is hardly surprising that Angela Thirkell preserved 'a stony silence' on the subject of her second son's literary productions.[53] Like some of her own – in this respect, at least – they were a little too close to life.

Colin ascribed her silence to smug superiority: 'I felt she was being tactful about my incompetent obscurity and her own illustrious achievement, which was of course doubly maddening.'[54] But in this he seems to have been repeating his father's error of imagining her to be invulnerable when it was only in self-defence that she sought to appear so.

Like naughty children, both father and son tried her to the limit with erratic and sometimes abominable behaviour. Then, when they discovered there was a limit, that her love was not boundless, they reacted as though it was they who had been wronged, not she. Colin had more excuse in that he was, to some extent, made to bear the sins of his father and rejected, not so much for what he was, as for what he might become. There was an element of self-fulfilling prophecy in this. In his attempts to break through to his mother, Colin came more and more to resemble his father in his outrageous behaviour; and in her attempts to defend herself from this living replica of the now despised, but once loved and then feared James Campbell McInnes, Angela Thirkell withdrew ever further from him.

Something of this mutual suspicion and deepening hostility must lie behind an observation of Colin's in his 'Thoughts' book, dated 1952:

Evidently age does bring some 'automatic' wisdom, since A.T., who has behaved with passion more than wisdom, now has a sly, hard, sardonic look in her eye, which she darts out at you in a penetrating, disturbing way.

Her unspoken thought is, your achievements do not match your pretensions.[55]

For the most part Colin tried to suppress his relationship to Angela Thirkell. He was intent on 'a kind of literary matricide',[56] and the author's note on the dust-jacket of both *To the Victors the Spoils* and *June in Her Spring* acknowledges only one parent — James Campbell McInnes. Yet mother and son did make one public appearance together and that was a couple of years later, in 1954, when Colin, desperately short of cash, had the brilliant idea of interviewing his mother on radio.

The broadcast itself, however, was fairly innocuous. Angela Thirkell reminisced about her childhood and forbears and gave vent to some of her dottier prejudices; but Colin refused to rise to the bait. He ostentatiously addressed his mother throughout as 'darling' — an endearment which she conspicuously failed to return until the very end of the programme when she offered a single, valedictory 'dear' like a peck on the cheek.[57]

Part two

MacInnes in Babylon

6
City of Spades

Sometime during the Fifties Colin wrote a novel which he called *Fancy Free*. It is his attempt at a sex novel – more didactic, though, than pornographic. Despite the range of sexual possibilities on offer, and the explicit descriptions of the various conjunctions, the novel is only intermittently arousing. Though MacInnes himself, in his later years at least, was keen to have the book published, its publication would scarcely enhance his reputation. It is not a good book; but it is an extraordinary psychological document.

The novel is set in turn-of-the-century Australia and opens in Tasmania, where – so it begins – 'On his fourteenth birthday Dugald was seduced, not unwillingly, by the aboriginal dustman . . .' This (unnamed) aboriginal buggers him with his huge cock, then jerks him off while Dugald, in ecstasy, licks the aboriginal's arse (in what is probably the most erotically felt scene in the book). But this being MacInnes, the aboriginal has a lesson to impart:

'I don't want you to become a little fairy [he tells Dugald]. It's no sort of life and, besides, it wouldn't suit you, I don't think.'
   'So what must I do then, mister?'
   'What you must do, son, is become a fucker, and not become a fucked. It's simple as that. Boys or girls, up the pussy or the arse, whichever you prefer, but you've got to remember there's a cock between your legs and you're a *man*.'

Dugald, eager to prove himself a man, begins by buggering the school tennis champion, a bigger boy than himself; and then, in a somewhat bewildering sequence of events, ends up in bed with the boy's mother, 'the ginger woman'. The prospect of fucking *her* fills him with anxiety:

The woman started fondling and kissing him, and this made matters somehow worse. There was so *much* of her! That mouth a mile wide, that thick tongue, those tits all over his face and chest – she must have about eight of them! And when he put his hand round on her arse, it seemed enormous . . . 'You getting bashful?' the ginger woman asked him kindly. 'Never mind, just close your eyes and leave the rest to me.'
   He felt her loosening his pants and wriggled as she pulled them off.

Next he felt her hot wet lips on his prick and bollocks, and when his cock disappeared inside her mouth like an asparagus, he felt he'd never be able to give her everything she wanted. One of her fingers was trailing round his arsehole, too, and this made him feel insecure because he felt it was *she* who was going to fuck him, not the other way round as it ought to be.

The woman, sensing his withdrawal ['reluctance' crossed out], took one of his hands and slipped it up inside the knickers onto her hot, sticky, hairy cunt. This was the test, she thought! If he liked that bit she'd got him – and womankind had got him too forever! . . .

But Dugald remains sluggish until he remembers the aboriginal dustman. Then he 'thought of how the abo must have felt as he bent over himself, Dugald. And as soon as he thought of the abo, Dugald felt his cock bound up as if it were going to shoot off his groin, and his bollocks tingle . . .'

Under this stimulus he performs satisfactorily and afterwards kisses the ginger woman 'affectionately rather like an incestuous son'. But the scene so fastidiously rendered is devoid of the eroticism of the earlier seduction by the aboriginal or the 'fierce but kindly ravishing' he next receives at the hands of a friendly party of itinerant 'rabbiters'.

Fancy Free is a picaresque novel: it moves from one sexual encounter to another as Dugald sets out on his journey from Tasmania to the mainland of Australia in search of his parents. He does not even know if he has a father; all he knows is that his mother lives in Queensland. Along the way he meets Beth, a typical homosexual's dream boy-girl: 'Dugald was delighted to see that Beth had a body very like his own – a girl's body, sure enough, but taut and tense and lithe and slender. Not a great *female* like the ginger woman was . . .' Beth disguises herself as a boy when they cross the Bass Strait as deckhands – though it's hard to see that any disguise is required since she already 'had her hair cut cockatoo-style like a boy's, and wore a boy's shirt and trousers.' And just so that Dugald's cup of joy should overflow, she 'really only cares for arsehole'. The one advantage this boy-girl has over the real thing, so to speak, is that she can (and does) get pregnant, making 'fulfilment' possible.

Once on the mainland the too-young lovers are forcibly separated and Dugald is sent to a convict camp where he must again prove himself a man. But there can be no question of his preferred role:

'The tow-haired kid, unfortunately for Dugald, had an eager

arse, and blackmailed our hero into fucking him more than he
really felt inclined to by threatening to tell the older men that he,
Dugald, really wanted to be screwed himself . . .'

Dugald and Beth (who now have a son) are eventually reunited
and reach Queensland. There Dugald is delighted to discover not
only that he has a father but also that his father is a 'Chink' – a
Chinaman – and 'abominably sexy' to boot: 'To see him was to feel
the cunt or arsehole tingle with amazed anticipation, not un-
mixed with fear . . .' This meeting of the young and not-so-young
generations is a prelude to a riot of incestuous and semi-incestuous
intercourse. Dugald is invited to watch his father and mother
screw – and it is his father's equipment which holds his spell-
bound attention. Then he and Beth perform – much to the
latter's chagrin – for his father's delectation; only this time the
virile 'Ling' joins in, forcing an entry in Beth's well-used rear. The
inevitable climax to all this interfamilial fucking is Ling's rogering
of his own son, after he has partially anaesthetised him with
opium:

'. . . And when at last his father hoisted Dugald's legs over
his shoulders, and impaled his willing arse on his monstrous
throbbing cock, the boy felt his dad's riding him was a delight he'd
always longed for . . . this was the finest fuck he'd ever had in his
existence.'

But then post-coital shame and opium-induced 'darker
thoughts' take hold of him. Dugald fights the father whose
dominance he desires even as he resists it. He throws a dagger
which by chance rebounds off a wall and kills his father. He
is immediately filled with remorse, though his dying father
exonerates him from blame.

The remainder of the tale concerns the lubricous desires of the
'planter's son' – 'a tall fairy in his thirties, lean and peroxided,
and sharp in the way queers are, yet not ill-natured' – who has
inherited the estate on which Dugald's late lamented Chinese dad
had been foreman. Dugald is approached by this effeminate to
see if he will arrange 'a collective rape'.

' "You mean for free?" said Dugald rather brutally.

'The planter sighed. "I'd prefer it for love, of course . . . One
does like to feel one's wanted . . ." '

The planter gets his wish, but not for love. Dugald persuades a
group of cane-cutters that it would be in their interest to oblige

him. There follows an orgy in which the masochistic planter is beaten and buggered to his heart's content.

Afterwards, 'like a phoenix soaring from the ashes, the planter arose exhausted with tears in his eyes, but bravely beaming with satisfied approval at his tormentors. "Well!" he said weakly, "that was an hour of my life to remember, if you like!" The cane-cutters grinned and toasted him with bottles, their faces filled with amiable contempt.'

The affair ends well, with the planter handing over his estate (voluntary abdication or forcible abduction?) to his workers to run communally; while Dugald's mother, the widow 'Rue', finds happiness in the arms of Ling's natural successor as leader, an ex-cattle drover whose egalitarian approach to land-ownership is in stark contrast to his *machismo* in sexual relationships. ' "Remember this prick," he said severely. "And if I find you playing with *any* other – that is, without my permission – I'll first ram it up your arse and give you a rupture, and then bite your pussy in a way you won't forget." ' But Rue, like Edith in Angela Thirkell's *Peace Breaks Out* – 'a true woman who adored the hand that held her in check'[2] – only 'whispered thickly' in reply. MacInnes endorses both the cattle drover's anti-authoritarianism in the workplace and his authoritarianism in the home without apparently being aware of any contradiction.

This novel is obviously Oedipal, but not conventionally so. In Sophocles's play, Oedipus kills his father and marries his mother in ignorance, though in Freud's interpretation he does it, so to speak, 'accidentally on purpose' so that he may assume his father's role and come of age. In MacInnes's tale, Dugald kills his father not in ignorance, it is true, but still by mistake; but there all similarity ends. It is not his father's, but his mother's role he aspires to. But that will never do, it is too humiliating; he does not want to end up like that 'fairy', the planter's son, who gets his kicks from being abused and is treated by other men with 'amiable contempt'. So by an effort of will, rather than through natural inclination, he seeks to emulate his father and be a 'fucker', not a 'fucked'. Phallocracy rules in *Fancy Free*.

MacInnes's patent dislike of women – his need to put them firmly in their place – is the mirror-image of his mother's rejection of the male sex after her two unhappy matrimonial experiences. In her novel, *Ankle Deep*, Angela Thirkell looks at her fictional self through the eyes of a lover *manqué*:

She was so entirely dominated by her mind that her senses would never be allowed to take their way. If she could once be carried off her feet, she would, he believed, have been capable of any self-abandonment, and shown him a side of herself which, even in dreams, he had hardly dared to suspect. But he was not capable – and without conceit he believed that no other man was capable – of penetrating her defences. Fear and unhappiness, of a kind which he could guess only too well, had forced her away into herself – in no other way was her horror of physical contact explainable.[3]

It was in reaction to his mother's withdrawal from all sexual contact – 'her writing years,' he maintained, 'were those when she had ceased to love the world'[4] – that Colin put such an emphasis on 'animal' life. Like her, he was dominated by his mind; like her, too, he was capable of any self-abandonment. The difference between them was that he was prepared to act out what she would scarcely even contemplate: *his* mind determined that his senses *should* be allowed to take their way.

The trouble was – as Robert Waller points out – that he had his father's sensuality and his mother's will-power.[5] Unable to strike a balance between the two, he oscillated wildly from one extreme to the other, from drinking heavily to not drinking at all, from sexual indulgence to total abstention. In spite of his commitment to the physical, there was something monkish about MacInnes. Many people noticed it; and he himself knew it, even cultivated it in the austerity of his surroundings – the succession of rooms he lived in, devoid of books and of any furniture that might be called luxurious.

The writer Monty Haltrecht, who, against his better judgment, allowed Colin to rent a room in his central London flat in the early Sixties, remembers the day he moved in: 'After some talk, he stood up, arms crossed over his chest, and said, "MacInnes retires to his cell" – all weight withdrawn, very saintly. Yes, there was something monkish about him.'[6]

If in his mid-thirties Colin grew to resemble his father in both his alcoholism and his homosexuality, then his mental cruelty, his ability to say cutting or wounding things, came from his mother; James Campbell McInnes was not clever enough to be cruel.

In terms of his sex novel, MacInnes was less like his hero, Dugald, perhaps, than the despised planter's son. He was a masochist. But he was ashamed of his masochism and therefore full of self-contempt. So he drank to forget; and so he trapped himself in a vicious circle of sexual and alcoholic indulgence, remorse, renunciation, and then indulgence again.

A pre-war acquaintance at Chelsea Polytechnic, Michael Law, who often saw Colin in Soho in the Fifties, compares him with another Soho figure of the time:

Both [were] almost totally homosexual; [they had] the same anger, temper, petulance, exasperated violence. While being socially destructive towards friends and acquaintances, both had a predilection for suffering at the end of the day, for being paid back, as it were – it was a very moral thing. They looked for the rough, so despised the bland and the smooth. Perhaps they were seeking a just retribution for being bitches in the first place.[7]

This tallies with what the art critic and erstwhile director of the Whitechapel Art Gallery, Bryan Robertson, who probably knew Colin as well as anyone in his later years, says of him:

He could not, it seemed, have a sex relationship with an equal. Psychologically, this no doubt related to his mother's rejection of him – it's a classic pattern . . . His attitude to his sexual partners was rather like the attitude of some artists towards their dealers: 'Wouldn't have them to dinner.' He was by nature a warm, tetchy queen; but he would have hated such a description, regarded the type with scorn, not been at ease with it . . .[8]

MacInnes's discovery of blacks, his drinking and his homosexuality developed simultaneously. From the end of the Forties, his social and sexual odyssey took him to the heart of African and Caribbean London – the Soho clubs, the Tottenham Court Road pubs and dance-halls and the Dickensian purlieus of Cable Street, with its dives and gambling-dens. He became 'what the Americans call a nigger-lover' and rejoiced at the arrival in Britain of people who brought 'an element of joy and fantasy and violence into our cautious, ordered lives'.[9]

But it was the early summer of 1952, when the Katherine Dunham Dance Company came over from the United States for its second London season, that was the honeymoon period of Colin's love affair with the 'Spades'.

Katherine Dunham's company consisted of black dancers, the majority of whom came from the northern cities of the United States, and musicians – drummers – who were Cuban. She herself was half black, half French-Canadian; she had studied ballet at high school, and gone on to do a degree at Chicago University. An anthropological lecture she attended sparked off her quest for an authentic Afro-American dance form. She spent the year 1937-8 in the Caribbean where, she felt, she might find 'the cultural heritage' of which black Americans had been deprived. Eventually she founded her own company and dance school in New York. She first toured London in 1948, when the contrast between her rich and vivacious dances and the post-war austerity which hung like a pall over the city ensured an instant and tremendous success.[10] By 1952 the atmosphere had changed and her second London season was not quite so rapturously received.

MacInnes had missed the first visit of the 'Dunhamites'. Ballet was not his favourite art-form; indeed, in the first of his 'London' novels, *City of Spades*, he refers to it as 'this sad, prancing art'. So his enthusiasm for the Dunham company was first and foremost an enthusiasm for its individual dancers. 'They are quite extraordinary: like innocent orchids,' he wrote to Robert Waller. 'If it wasn't, my dear Bob, that when mentioning this to you I imagine I feel chill winds of disapproval blowing up to me from Bristol, I'd tell you more . . .'[11] Though he had fallen in love with the entire company, Colin was particularly attached to one dancer, who suddenly had to return to the United States.

'Have just been seeing off, at Airways Terminal,' he wrote to Waller, 'the white-toothed Charles I brought round on Sunday. His father has died suddenly, and he's flying off to Cleveland Ohio. Very sad for me, as he is my favourite Dunhamite.'[12]

Worse was to follow. Colin had been making elaborate arrangements with Waller for entertaining, and being entertained by the 'dark angels', as he rather romantically (and patronisingly) called them, in Bristol when the Dunham company's tour of the provinces folded.

I am very dejected, because they were a great ray of sunshine in my life, and, as well as the sex attraction, I made a great many friends among them whom I won't easily forget. Well-a-day! Fucking Hell . . .

I'm sorry too that you won't see them. I know you're favourably disposed, yet I think the reality would have exceeded even your imaginings. You get all the usual physical and emotional beauty of Negroes *plus* a higher American sophistication and education, *plus* an understanding of Art: an irresistible combination.[13]

The Dunham idyll was an oasis in MacInnes's emotional life. 'Oh, intolerable sight of the Katherine Dunham dancers,' he raved in the privacy of his 'Thoughts' book. 'Such animal beauty makes the streets and the days unbearable! What is there to compare with animal beauty, grace and intelligence? Nothing [footnote: 'animal courage']. It is a terrible punishment to grow old and die.'[14]

The Dunhamites were not only black and beautiful; they were also westernised. They could be taken out to dinner, introduced to friends like Robert Waller; they read poetry; they were socially, as well as sexually, acceptable. While Colin was with them he could almost believe that a compromise between his social and sexual desires was possible. But even if the Dunham tour had not ended prematurely, it is unlikely his euphoria would have lasted. What had attracted him to blacks in the first place was their *un*acceptability, the fact that they were 'outsiders'. To put it crudely, what he wanted was to be raped by a big black, a 'primitive', or – better still – by several.

Hence his preference for Africans over either West Indians or black Americans – they were 'more authentic'; they were the real thing. Ricky Hawton, the original for 'Johnny Fortune' in *City of Spades*, was a Nigerian. He moved in with Colin in late 1952; for a few months they were 'inseparable'; and 'in terms of life and understanding it, he gave me more than I could give him.'[15] Yet Ricky, unlike some of the male dancers in the Dunham company, was essentially heterosexual. As a result Colin suffered 'the particular torture of a homosexual's love . . . that he most admires and covets a man who does not love men.'[16]

Just after Christmas 1952, Colin wrote to Robert Waller to explain why he had not been able to meet him in Bath: 'Richard Hawton Samuel Erizia's temperature shot up overnight to 101, and then, on the Thursday, to 103 and he began spitting blood. Dr Ernst Cohn arrived and diagnosed 'flu . . . So I didn't feel I should leave Richard, much as I wanted to come.'[17] A few days later he reported: 'Have just delivered Richard Hawton Samuel to Charing Cross Hospital with a temperature of 103½ and pneumonia: hope they don't avenge the Mau-Mau murders on him . . .'[18] On this occasion Ricky recovered and, in the spring, he went off to Manchester 'to seek his fortune'.[19]

His illness, though, was an additional anxiety for Colin at a time when he was anyway depressed. He admitted to Waller, 'It's only dawning on me gradually how terribly cast down I've been by the reception, or lack of reception, of *June* — I thought I was indifferent — vanity! One is discouraged by nothing more than by the obvious banal failures — the lack of *success* . . .'[20]

June in Her Spring was published in the autumn of 1952 and by late November its immediate fate was apparent.

'This has been the reception,' he wrote:

a *few* eulogistic reviews, and otherwise spontaneous boycott: we've checked up through spies, and critics just won't handle it: won't attack it even.

A number of Public Libraries . . . have banned it.

I'm irritated and disappointed: no attack — the 'British' method, ignore its existence.[21]

To another correspondent, MacInnes wrote that it was not at all the reception he had hoped for: 'It is an innocent work, in my opinion!'[22]

June is, for the most part, an innocent and quite unexceptionable boy-girl love story; but it touches on the taboo subject of homosexuality. That was the trouble.

The year 1952 had seen a record number of indictable homosexual offences in Britain. In his book on homosexuality, *The Other Love*, H. Montgomery Hyde writes:

In 1938 there were 134 cases of sodomy and bestiality known to the police in England and Wales. The number in 1952 was 670. During the same period the number of attempts to commit 'unnatural offences', including indecent assaults, increased from 822 to 3,087. Offences of gross indecency between males went up from 320 to 1,686. Importuning also increased substantially, 373 cases of proceedings in London alone being reported in 1952.[23]

Among the reasons offered for this extraordinary increase by witnesses who appeared before the Committee set up in 1954 under the chairmanship of Sir John Wolfenden to consider the law and practice of both homosexuality and prostitution (conveniently lumped together) were: a general post-war loosening of moral standards, a burgeoning of homosexual behaviour as a result of the war, during which men had lived in unaccustomed intimacy with one another and had gone for long periods without female companionship; and a weakening of family ties. But these explanations, if indeed they had the slightest validity, paled into insignificance beside the factor which the Wolfenden Committee recognised only with the utmost reluctance: 'Most of us think it improbable that the increase in the number of offences as known to the police can be explained entirely by greater police activity, though we all think it very unlikely that homosexual behaviour has increased proportionately to the dramatic rise in the number of offences recorded as known to the police.'[24]

In other words, the dramatic increase was not so much in homosexuality as in police activity. Before the war, uniformed policemen would occasionally raid public urinals in search of homosexual offenders, 'but these raids were quite open affairs, and the police were not then in the habit of employing good-looking young detectives in plain clothes to act as *agents provocateurs*, as they later did. This detestable practice, which began after the last war, reached its height in the anti-homosexual drive instigated by the authorities in the early 1950s.'[25]

H. Montgomery Hyde was himself an MP at the time (indeed, his support of homosexual law reform eventually cost him his seat, his constituency association being unwilling to re-adopt as their candidate in 1959 a man 'who condones unnatural vice'). Yet when he raised the question of *agents provocateurs* in the House of Commons, he was astonished to hear the Home Secretary 'completely reject the suggestion that it is the practice of members of the Metropolitan Police to act as *agents provocateurs* in carrying out duties which, though distasteful, are essential to the preservation of public order and decency.'[26]

The persecution of homosexuals was stepped up as a result of the defection to the Soviet Union of the homosexual British diplomats, Burgess and Maclean, in March 1951, and the McCarthy witchhunt of communists and homosexuals in the United States. It was not until 1953–54 that the police overreached themselves and prosecuted one or two individuals with the courage and the capacity – as well as the social confidence – to answer back.

Two books appeared in 1955: Peter Wildeblood's *Against the Law* described the experiences of Lord Montagu of Beaulieu, Michael Pitt-Rivers and himself in the celebrated 'Montagu' case; and Rupert Croft-Cooke's *The Verdict of You All* documented the frame-up which resulted in his spending some months in Wormwood Scrubs gaol. Both these books exposed the injustice of the homosexual witchhunt and were timely reminders to the Wolfenden Committee of the grievances of homosexuals.

MacInnes's attitude to homosexuality, on the face of it, was eminently sane and reasonable:

. . . I believe myself the whole subject is much simpler than it may seem, or 'we' have made it: it is an ancient, timeless, permanent human situation, rooted in nature with a million other natural phenomena. Distortion begins *either* when a cult is made of the practice, or a cult is made of the persecution of it: both attitudes are blind and neurotic, in my opinion. In some ages, apparently, and in some countries and individuals even now, a balance is reached and life goes on unharmed . . .[27]

But while he insists that homosexuality is perfectly natural, what he offers as an alternative to the 'fulfilled' heterosexual/family life is not homosexuality, but *bi*sexuality.

'Unless [the homosexual] escapes at least into bisexuality,' he writes, 'his creative life has the severe limitation that he is doomed to a half-ignorant, ill-proportioned vision of mankind: a closed-circuit vision like Michelangelo's, with its disturbing undue pre-occupation of a great spirit with the flesh.'[28]

According to this account, bisexuality is an 'escape' from homosexuality, which is itself 'a crippled state of being'. Whether or not this is generally the case with bisexuals, it certainly was with MacInnes: he did not take the escape route very often, though he did have occasional heterosexual involvements. But the possibility was there; that was what counted. On the positive side, it meant that he never succumbed to the ghettoised, 'homintern' view of life. But it also meant that to some extent he was living a lie, deceiving himself as to his own nature.

Colin's obsession with blacks was putting a strain on some of his older friendships. Mayou Iserentant wrote from France accusing him of 'sinking into an unhealthy "simplicity" '.[29] But he put that down to jealousy. Robert Waller was alarmed by the 'terrible stories' that filtered through to him in Bristol 'about unpaid bills and Negroes lying around drunk' at 4 Regent's Park Terrace;[30] and a quibble over an electricity bill escalated into a bitter feud in which each analysed the other's character and behaviour.

'The instinct you have to admonish me . . .' Colin wrote in one letter, 'springs, I think, from a belief you have that my conduct in general is not what you might wish it to be; and perhaps also from a certain envy at the liberty that accompanies it . . .'[31]

In another, he returned to the question of his 'sensual allegiances' and asked:

What, my dear fellow, do you *know* about them? . . . In my sex life, I have always (no, almost always) done what I'm sure *bloody few* in this world have done, always taken the burden of sin off the other person, always preserved their humanity intact. (It is this, not vestiges of morality, that has preserved me from spiritual damnation.) When I think back over my negro period, for instance, I am amazed at the load I have carried for them in every possible way. What do you even know about all this?[32]

Leaving aside the fact that he was already referring to 'my negro period' as a thing of the past, three years before the publication of *City of Spades*, what he meant, presumably, was that, even though money might change hands as, directly or indirectly, he paid for his sexual gratification, this did not absolve him from human responsibility. But like the Scottish preacher who noted in the margin of his sermon, 'Weak point here, shout like hell,' he protests too much, and the suspicion remains that he was guilty of treating his lovers as sexual objects.

In the final analysis, he was prepared to admit that his life was 'in most respects catastrophic and a disaster'.

'Why this should be,' he went on, 'I don't quite know, since what you would call vice bores me so painfully, and what you take for spiritual pride is as much . . . an ingrained loneliness of spirit that goes back, I should say, to circa 1917' – i.e. when he was three years old and his father disappeared from his life –

has shown few signs of altering, and probably never will. Yes, my dear chap, my life on the spiritual (and artistic) plain is crippled and thwarted. *But*: unregenerate to the last, I would not trade my angry solitude, my exasperated contempt, my anti-social arrogance, no, no, not at any price, for the *dreadful moment* at which a human being becomes a judge and tries to eat somebody else's soul.[33]

Waller, on his side, grew tired of Colin's 'exasperated arrogance':

I began to feel that unless you conformed entirely to what he thought you ought to be and did what he thought you ought to do, you were some kind of immature, naive child unworthy of his attention. This feeling of either having to submit to his will or be banished from his presence finally led me to refuse to do several things he thought I ought to do. This enraged him and he constantly tiraded against me (usually when drunk), so that finally I had no further wish to see him.[34]

The final break, though, was still some years off. As fellow professionals in the broadcasting world, MacInnes and Waller kept up at least the appearance of friendship. In the summer of 1954, Colin reported to Waller:

Am also appearing in July, to my disgrace, on the telly – chairman of a programme called Authors in Focus, or Focus on Authors, can't remember which. Horrid, horrid, horrid, but I should like to master that 'medium'. Do you realise that all we 'broadcasters' are really turning into actors – a new branch of the profession (of which clergymen, auctioneers, bookmakers, street vendors, sergeant majors, orchestra conductors etc. were earlier adjuncts) . . .[35]

Television was still something of a novelty in the mid-1950s, and radio had not yet been reduced to the status of a poor relation. Among radio performers, some – like Gilbert Harding – became television stars; others – like René Cutforth and Colin himself – never quite succeeded in making the transition to television, feeling more at home in a verbal, rather than a visual medium. Colin's attitude to the BBC itself remained ambivalent; his advice to the poet, Charles Causley, was: 'Never join the BBC. Always approach it as a buccaneer: plunder it and get out. They'll always come back to you.' He also said, 'To be a successful broadcaster, the BBC always likes you to be terribly good at something else.'[36] Writing novels was Colin's ticket to self-respect; broadcasting, being a radio personality, largely induced self-contempt. But it satisfied a craving for celebrity and paid at least some of his bills.

His financial situation was generally so precarious, however, that he had taken to writing begging letters to his old chief, Eric Dadson. Dadson never lent money on principle, but he did send Colin occasional hand-outs in response to these requests. In September 1954, in an extraordinarily tactless preamble to one such request, Colin wrote:

Dear Eric, May I tell you my troubles? For the last two years I have been earning over £1,500 a year by radio and journalism, working at about 50 per cent of my capacity. The other 50 per cent has been spent boozing and indulging in expensive sex like a lunatic – throwing money away in an idiotic fashion as if I was a millionaire, though I can't say I altogether regret it. Until more or less recently I have kept one jump ahead of my creditors, but now they have caught up with me, particularly the Income Tax. I am now 40, and see that if I don't settle down I'll make a mess of what's left of my life, and I'm making an effort to do so [sic]. I'm not sure that I'll succeed, but I think I shall principally because I am now so *sick* of the wild life and get little pleasure from it. I am working quite hard, drinking much less, giving up orgies, though I break out from time to time . . .[37]

A few months later he wrote and apologised to Dadson for having 'unloaded all that on you'; he claimed to be 'on an even keel once again'. But he still asked for a loan of £200.[38]

By this time he was a regular broadcaster on *The Critics*. Though he objected to its ineffable chattiness, he justified his continued participation on the grounds of professionalism:

I took this job on like any other. The real reason was financial. The annual stints of six programmes on *The Critics*, with 'repeats', earned me a great deal more than I had for either of my first two novels; and incomparably more than the 'serious' periodicals I really wanted to write for exclusively could afford to pay me.[39]

This did not prevent him from biting the hand that fed him when an opportunity presented itself. The producer of *The Critics* unwisely allowed there to be a discussion of the BBC's cherished Reith Lectures on the occasion of the first of the 1954 series, given by Britain's ex-ambassador at Washington, Sir Oliver Franks. The idea was to talk about the Reith Lectures as an institution and only refer in passing to Sir Oliver's initial lecture. Inevitably, though, the critics discussed what they had heard; and the result was an almost unanimous thumbs-down (Harold Hobson's was the one dissenting voice) to this particular lecturer as well as to Reith Lectures in general.[40]

This presented the BBC with a dilemma: should one radio talks department production be permitted to criticise another before the latter had even properly got under way? BBC officials reacted swiftly: with no explanation or apology either to the listening public or to the participants, they simply expunged the radio section of that edition of *The Critics*. This meant that Michael Ayrton, who was the radio critic (Colin was art critic) and had led the excised discussion, had a spectral presence in the broadcast programme, remaining only as an unidentified voice.

Walter Allen, who was chairman of *The Critics* on this occasion, began by supporting the BBC line of argument, then wrote an article for the *New Statesman* under the pseudonym 'William Salter', in which he criticised the BBC for 'behaving arbitrarily' and maintained that it had 'made a public fool of itself'.[41] But it was MacInnes whose fury sparked off the row. The BBC, he said, should apologise to its critics. A number of acrimonious letters passed between him and the Controller of Talks, Mary Somerville; and as a gesture of protest MacInnes refused to take part in the final programme of the series. (This did not prevent his being invited – and accepting invitations – to participate in a further series the following year and thereafter.)

Elspeth Huxley, who was another of the critics involved, remembers it twenty-five years later as 'a storm in a teacup . . . [with] the BBC as usual being pompous, and Colin I think a bit prickly and on his dignity.'[42] Colin himself did not so readily forgive or forget – particularly where the authority involved was a woman. A year later, after another series of *The Critics*, he wrote to Robert Waller:

At the final luncheon of the Critics, we were honoured by the attendance of Dame Mary Somerville – the first time I had had the displeasure of meeting her. She tried the *grande dame* treatment on me, and I replied with my Sergeants' Mess style, which cooled her. She belongs to a distant Girton- [Somerville, in fact] Manchester Guardian age of refined anti-vulgarity, she takes herself very seriously and believes the world can be improved. A capable horror, I thought . . .[43]

He made use of his sergeants' mess style on other occasions, too, such as the dinner party at which the woman sitting next to him asked if it were true that he was a queer. 'No,' Colin is alleged to have replied, 'but it won't do *you* any good.'[44]

Early in 1955 he was invited by the British Council to undertake a lecture tour of East and Central Africa. Needless to say, he embraced the opportunity of visiting the continent that for him was already swathed in romance. For seven weeks he travelled through Uganda, Kenya (where the Mau-Mau struggle for independence was still in progress and the black population subject to curfew), Tanganyika, Nyasaland and Northern Rhodesia (as they then were).

He went ostensibly to lecture on art; but by the time he reached Nyasaland and was addressing a mixed group of European, African and Asian teachers – or, more precisely, *un*mixed, since each race left a space between itself and the other two – art had become 'the pretext for a demonstration of the unity of human creation among all peoples'.[45]

In print, MacInnes was careful, if not to exonerate the European settlers, at least to plead extenuating circumstances for their attitudes. Certainly they welcomed any chance to put forward their favoured 'solution' to the racial problem, but 'in this the Europeans aren't alone to blame. Many of us, in England, have a nasty habit of automatically damning our own kind. I invite any such to spend even half an hour with an Asian or African who thinks, like the lunatic settler, that he has a "solution".'[46] Yet in his behaviour he was often offensive and left a trail of wounded sensibilities in his wake (though not quite so spectacularly as he would do on another African tour fifteen years later). On those occasions when he 'escaped from his hosts' and wandered in the African parts of whichever city he was visiting, the sense of relief must have been mutual.

MacInnes in a smoke-filled African hut, or wandering among Arabs 'turbaned and wrapt up in antiquity',[47] watching the Zanzibari *dhows* in the harbour at Dar-es-salaam, saw himself doing in Africa what his illustrious cousin, Rudyard Kipling, had done in India: they were both social explorers familiarising themselves with the bazaars and native quarters of exotic cities, while their more prosaic fellow-countrymen confined themselves to barracks in their identical European villas strung along roads named after generals . . .

Some months after his return to London Colin was arrested at 'a squalid gambling house in the East End' in the small hours of a Sunday morning – along with everyone else present – on what turned out to be a drugs charge.[48] This was 1955, not 1965 or 1975 when such a charge would scarcely have raised an eyebrow. In 1955 there was still an almost Dickensian aura of mystery and foreignness about drugs – the very words 'Indian hemp' conjured up an atmosphere of the opium den.

The officers who arrested Colin and his black companions were not local police, but CID. When they arrived at the nearest police station, Colin thought he detected some hostility between the ordinary cops on duty there and the men from the Yard, whose methods were far from gentle. It did nothing for his peace of mind when the man who had been questioned before him came out crying. 'Negroes do not often cry,' he writes.[49]

Then the detectives beckoned him in, calling out, 'You!' He answered, 'I've got a name, you know.' They waited until he came through the door, then one of them slugged him expertly on the back of the neck so that he slumped on to the floor. When he refused to be fingerprinted, they started to set about him in earnest. With a courage born of desperation he told them they had been seeing too many American films. This seemed to give them pause. Abruptly they changed tack and handed him over to a nice, fatherly copper who gave him a cigarette and reasoned with him where the others had used force. Still he refused to let them take his fingerprints; nor, since they would not let him see the list, would he sign for the articles they claimed to have removed from him.[50]

It was not until the Monday, when all the accused had to appear before the magistrate, that he learned he was charged with being in possession of drugs. He was allowed bail, but not before he had agreed to be fingerprinted. In this, the magistrate succeeded where the police had failed.

Although his arrest gave him a certain kudos, and established a kinship with the outcasts and villains he admired, Colin's gut reaction was a middle class one of the kind he affected to despise. How dare they? was his unspoken thought. He complains, in a later article, that the police 'made no attempt whatever to find out who I was – or indeed ask me anything but my name and address and to be fingerprinted. I don't of course mean that because I am "educated" I was entitled to favoured treatment, but I do think if they had asked me a question or two they might have had second thoughts.'[51]

In the end, of course, he did get favoured treatment. All but one of the dozen or so black men who were arrested with him were convicted, though they too proclaimed their innocence (Colin's view was that some – those who were merely 'dossing down on the floor' – were indeed innocent, while others may well have been guilty: 'It was that kind of a place.')[52] Only Colin and one of the other defendants could afford a lawyer.

Angela Thirkell overcame her reluctance and distaste to the extent of offering Colin the services of the Queen's lawyers, but Colin rejected her offer. He took instead the advice of a friend who ran an East End tailoring business, was an actor and would later be his landlord, Alfred Maron (to whom he dedicated *Absolute Beginners*), and went to Barney Greenman, of the firm, Wiseman and Greenman.[53]

Colin's relations with his mother had now reached their nadir.

When she heard he was in trouble with the police she wrote, 'He is 41 – too old to make a fool of himself.'[54] Though she felt obliged to offer him legal help, she was appalled by his behaviour and anxious that it should have no repercussions on her other sons' careers. Lance worked for the BBC; Graham was a Canadian diplomat and had spent the previous three years in India. When he and his wife, Joan, returned to London in 1955 they found a very different Colin from the one they had known and loved: he was drinking heavily and he was aggressive and unpleasant – to Joan in particular.[55] But his behaviour towards his mother was even worse.

One night he had gone round drunk to Shawfield Street in Chelsea, where she lived, and created a violent scene. Angela reacted as she had done in the past to similar outbursts from James Campbell McInnes – with an icy calm. 'Probably I ought to have had hysterics on the spot – but one just doesn't,' she told the friend who typed and vetted her novels for her, Margaret Bird. 'I don't think I shall ever recover; one's mind can reason, but one's body reacts automatically.'[56] Her rejection of Colin was now absolute and she ratified it, as it were, by cutting him out of her will. 'A woman's tender care,' she wrote to Gordon Haight, an American friend and the biographer of George Eliot, '*can* cease toward the child she bears . . . and mine has ceased. In the middle forties one does *not* behave like a drink-sodden fiend – even to a mother.'[57]

The solicitor, Barney Greenman, advised Colin that he would stand a better chance of acquittal on the drugs charge if he took his case before a judge and jury. It would cost more than going before a magistrate but, whereas magistrates tended to go along with what the police told them, a judge and jury could be more sceptical. Colin agreed and Greenman picked the barrister, James Burge (who later defended Stephen Ward in the Profumo case), to undertake his defence.

Colin insisted that he had been framed, that the drugs were a plant; and Greenman and Burge had the greatest difficulty in persuading him that 'you don't win medals fighting the police head on.'[58] The jury, they told him, would be anxious to let everyone off the hook. By insisting that he had been framed he would only increase his chances of a conviction, and in those days a drugs conviction was a serious matter – it precluded travel to the United States, for example. The lawyers put it to him that his best line of defence would be 'honest error': after all, the police could have made a mistake. Reluctantly, and only after a great deal of persuasion, did Colin accept this professional advice; he would much rather have been a martyr in the cause of truth. Ten years later he wrote, 'I am ashamed to this day I did not have the guts to say what really happened.'[59]

His case came up at the London Sessions, Marylebone High Street, in November 1955, three months after his arrest. He warned the various producers and editors he worked for – at the BBC, on *The Times* (for which he wrote occasional art features) – that he was appearing in court, in case they wanted to cancel or suspend programmes or articles he was doing for them. He had some trouble finding character witnesses, though eventually his publisher, James MacGibbon, and the BBC producer Douglas Cleverdon ('both Celts, incidentally') agreed to speak up for him. In the event they were not called upon to do so.[60]

James Burge had no difficulty in eliciting inconsistencies in the police officers' evidence. In addition, it was the defence case that MacInnes was a writer in search of material. When cross-examined by the prosecution lawyer, Colin was asked: 'If you consort with people of this description, would it not be natural for you to pick up their habits?' He replied that a journalist who consorts with people who smoke weed no more has to be a weed-smoker than a lawyer who defends a murderer has to have committed murder.[61] His educated accent, his intelligence, his sober dress and appearance, all created a favourable impression on the judge and jury and he was duly acquitted.

The case cost MacInnes over £200 in legal fees (a large sum of money in those days), not to mention the loss of earnings involved. In gratitude to his lawyers he sent them each a box of Havana cigars. James Burge – with whom he discovered a bond: both had been habitués of 'a coloured club (now closed) called "The Nest" '[62] – wrote in reply: 'Thank you very much for the delicious cigars. I have smoked one already and appear to have no ill effects . . .' Quite witty of him, Colin thought.[63]

Yet Colin's arrest and trial had a profound effect on him. 'In a way,' he said much later, 'I'm glad of the experience – I learned that the law is a game of chess, nothing to do with right and wrong. But it's impossible to come out of it unmuddied.'[64]

Colin's problem, as ever, was one of facing two ways simultaneously. Ultimately he was unable to let go of conventional thoughts and feelings long enough to discover the new purity which he believed might be reached through excess. He was no Genet; he did not submerge himself in the underworld, as the Frenchman did, and construct a universe which, in the activities of whores, ponces and criminals – as in a distorting mirror, or apt caricature – reflects our own features all too clearly. Like Orwell rather, he 'went slumming', making forays into the nether regions while retaining a base above ground. Thus he would always remain an observer, a voyeur, a journalist, an outsider even – though he was, as he characteristically put it, very much an 'inside outsider'.

In the summer of 1955 Colin had been reading *The Horse's Mouth* and other novels by Joyce Cary, who was then in vogue, for a BBC arts programme; and the conclusions he reached about the creator of Gully Jimson *et al* could largely – *mutatis mutandis* – be applied to himself:

I think his mind is *conventional* (though a 'conventional' person would not think it so) – i.e., his notion of the 'liberal imperative', his orthodox (though not in the sense of any particular faith) religious ideas, and his 'romantic' (really Somerset Maugham) conception of the artist: what I *don't* understand is why it took him as long as it did to become a success . . . Only in the African stories is there any mystery and passion – but this is pinched from the Africans.

Living off the emotions of the Africans, at second hand (as I do), is simply not good enough, though. If our world is not interesting enough, one must try and invent one that is . . .[65]

As with Cary's *Mister Johnson*, the liveliness of *City of Spades* (my own favourite among MacInnes's novels) may be partly attributable to the borrowed plumage of the Africans – and, to a lesser extent, of the Caribbean and American blacks – who people its pages. But its fascination is also due to the tangle of emotions – affection and exasperation, desire and despair – which these people aroused in the author's breast.

At the risk of over-simplification one might say that at the time of writing *City of Spades* MacInnes was politically optimistic – '. . . That race crap's changing fast, believe me,' says the homosexual Alfy Bongo, echoing his creator's more sanguine thoughts. 'In ten years' time or so, they'll wonder what it was all about'[66] – but personally pessimistic. Theodora Pace, who loves and loses Johnny Fortune in the novel, and was – as Colin admitted – an aspect of himself, writes to her friend, Montgomery Pew:

What's clear to me now, Montgomery – although I know you won't agree – is that love, or even friendship, for those people is *impossible* – I mean as we understand it. It's not either party's fault; it's just that in the nature of things we can never really understand each other because we see the whole world utterly differently. In a crisis each race will act according to its nature, each one quite separately, and each one will be right, and hurt the other.

It's when you see that *distant* look that sometimes comes into their opaque brown eyes that you realise it – that moment when they suddenly depart irrevocably within themselves far off towards some hidden, alien, secretive, quite untouchable horizon . . .[67]

The essay, 'A Short Guide for Jumbles', which MacInnes describes as a distillation of *City of Spades*, ends with an almost verbatim answer to the question of whether it is possible for black and white to be friends. But when the essay was reprinted in *England, Half English* in 1961, MacInnes took the opportunity to revise this bleak judgment. In a postscript he adds that

the years which have passed proved to me . . . that an African or a West Indian, and an Englishman, can be friends. A great deal, of course, is against this happening . . . the colonial relationship . . . the world-wide 'colour' situation . . . the truly formidable differences of social and physical background . . . but given goodwill and fortune, [even this] is surmountable.[68]

Although Colin became less pessimistic about the possibility of interracial friendship, he no longer spoke of love. He continued to form more or less enduring relationships with black people, as he did with whites, but he never recaptured the intensity of emotional attachment he experienced with both Ricky and Charles in the early Fifties.

7
Soho Bohemia

Just as MacInnes had been attracted to Fitzrovia in the late Thirties, so he inevitably gravitated towards Soho in the Fifties. Each was the bohemian centre of its time. Now Soho is largely sex shops and Chinese supermarkets; but in the Fifties London's 'square mile of vice' had a charm, a quaintness even, that had not yet entirely been obliterated by commercial exploitation. In those days there were live prostitutes on the streets rather than blue movies behind closed doors; even the vice was on a human scale. The criminal element gave it glamour, while the 'dear old Italians and sweet old Viennese who [ran] their honest, unbent little businesses'[1] made it surprisingly homely. But its most attractive feature for Colin was that 'there, as is rare elsewhere in London, the denizens live in the streets, and do not merely use them – as is the custom elsewhere in English cities – as places to get from here to there.'[2] In addition there was a 'great variety of private clubs in which persons of racial, sexual and professional peculiarities can foregather,'[3] so that Soho was the perfect place for the misfit. There *nobody* fitted – that was the point.

Sometime early in 1956 – it is difficult to be precise with dates in a life as erratic as MacInnes's had become – Colin took a room above an art gallery at 20 D'Arblay Street in northern Soho, though for a time he kept on his flat in Regent's Park Terrace as well.

Gallery One had originally been housed in a condemned building in Litchfield Street, off St Martin's Lane, and Colin first went there in his capacity as occasional writer on art for *The Times*. He had often noticed the framed photographs at the gallery entrance and the sign: 'Ida Kar: enquire within'. The first time he climbed upstairs to the gallery itself,

there entered a man whom I took to be not the proprietor, but a kindly guest sent down to hold the fort and do the honours. He was wearing what I was to learn was his invariable uniform – a black corduroy suit, blue jersey (white for ceremonial evening wear), and, encasing his feet, a pair of blue Boris Karloff shoes. Surmounting the tall frame all this covered, I saw a mild, quizzical, amiably insinuating face with two candid, limpid and dispassionate brown eyes – in which one could sometimes detect, however, a penetrating, steely glint.[4]

This man was Victor Musgrave; and his wife was the photographer, Ida Kar.

Musgrave was unusual among art dealers in that he had no capital, only enthusiasm and an eye for talent. What Colin did not discover on his first visit was that it was through the offices of a prostitute (who was being evicted by the landlord) that Musgrave had acquired the premises in Litchfield Street:

. . . this girl was but one of many with whom he was on familiar terms. Now, we have all met persons who, for various official reasons, have known prostitutes, and others who, being regular clients, have found out quite a lot about them. But what was unusual was to find someone, like Victor, who, although not actually of their world in any strictly professional sense, was on terms of unaffected ease with them. As I soon discovered, Victor was, like myself, a noctambule, and we would often walk at night round Soho or Mayfair. When, armed against the chill, if it was winter, by the expedient of stuffing the morning's newspaper under his blue jersey, Victor would lope and pad along the thoroughfares of these two 'square miles of vice', it was something of a royal progress. For, from doorways and turnings, there would emerge, with cries of 'Hullo, Vic', a sequence of girls who would interrupt their vigils to chat with him – while I waited, somewhat impatiently, to resume an interrupted dialogue on higher things.[5]

Colin worried away at the 'secret' of Victor's friendship with 'the girls'. Once, when they were walking along together, Colin stopped and said in amazed admiration, 'And they *like* you'; adding, after a pause, 'They do like you, don't they?' And, after yet further consideration, 'You must actually *like* women.'[6]

'Victor Musgrave has, for prostitutes,' he writes, 'rather the same sort of feeling as some people have (if the comparison will be permitted) for actors, or boxers, or criminals, or soldiers – a sort of cult, of extreme interest and admiration.'[7] Precisely the feeling that Colin himself had for blacks. Indeed, as Victor Musgrave recalls, it was Colin who was guilty of interrupting their nighttime strolls every few yards to strike up conversations with passing black men – 'like an unofficial MP in his constituency'.[8] Despite the fact that the two of them shared a penchant for sub-worlds of one sort of another, Colin was by no means uncritical of Musgrave's easygoing attitude towards whores. While he found the 'complete absence of the instinct to judge them in any way' wholly admirable, he condemned the lack of 'anything like a moral evaluation of their lives' in Musgrave's unpublished book on prostitutes.[9]

David Sylvester remembers that when Colin was writing *June in Her Spring* he used to tell anyone who asked him what he was doing that he was engaged on a life of John Knox.[10] It was in some ways an appropriate answer. To the jazz musician, Kenny Graham, Colin was a moralist with a Calvinist streak which reminded Graham of his mother – and of a scene from a film in which a teacher is whacking a boy and saying, between strokes, 'GOD – IS – LOVE.'[11] Bryan Robertson is perhaps nearest the mark when he says that Colin was a moralist who endorsed Gide's dictum: 'Judge, but nods and winks to the accused.'[12]

Among the people Colin met as a result of his move into Soho was a young painter called Alexander Weatherson, who was still an art student at the time. Colin wrote enthusiastically, 'I have met a youth who is the great-nephew of the Comte de Montesquieu who was the model for Proust's Baron de Charlus.'[13]

Weatherson was under no illusions about his role in their relationship: he was, to begin with at least, 'a sprat to catch mackerel'[14] – meaning blacks. Colin could be crafty, he found, in his efforts to seduce. There was a Ghanaian youth to whom he had taken a fancy and promised to have his picture done. So Weatherson had to draw his portrait. The trouble was, once it was done it was Weatherson the Ghanaian wanted to take home on his motorcycle, not Colin. 'Colin sat there grinding his teeth,' Weatherson recalls, 'and in the end he yanked the boy off his motorbike and tore up the drawing. This was the subject of an apologetic letter . . .' Weatherson received many such letters, all apologising for the night before. Every evening then seemed to end in disaster, or 'he simply abandoned you somewhere, like the middle of Cable Street.'[15]

If Weatherson wanted to rile Colin he had only to mention psychoanalysis. Freudian explanations enraged Colin and any attempt at analysis on Weatherson's part met with the retort: 'Physician, heal thyself.'[16]

'Colin used to give Sandy Weatherson a terrible time,' says Terry Taylor, another young friend Colin made at this time. 'He really took it out on him.'[17]

Taylor lived in Soho and worked in a Wardour Street amuse-ment arcade, taking passport photos. His interests were 'jazz, soft drugs and hustling'.[18]

'I met Colin,' he writes,

in the Myrtle Bank Club, a Spade drinker in Soho. Two white spots on a coloured cloth. At first glance I thought he was Law. Within two minutes of talking to him I dismissed the notion. No policeman could be *that* good an actor – or so open. Or that human. Within an hour he'd given me his credentials: writer, gay, liberal, happily housing the colour-bug. His charm and intelligence impressed me deeply. One didn't ask personal questions (especially of strangers) on that scene but he broke the rule so naturally that I found myself with my guard down and willing to tell him anything and everything . . .[19]

The Myrtle Bank Club was in Berwick Street; you could not drink alcohol on the premises, but you could get chicken and rice, coffee and Coca Cola till four in the morning. The doorman was Caribbean, the cook African. MacInnes wrote at the time:

. . . There is a marked *esprit de corps* among Myrtle Bank habitués. The music here is only a juke-box – but with highbrow jazz discs rather than the more usual 'pops': currently, Dave Brubeck, Chico Hamilton, and old stalwarts like Fitzgerald, Armstrong and Sarah Vaughan. You can dance – though cats should remain cool if the tables are all occupied by diners. Perhaps not advisable, for girls, to come unescorted here – or anywhere, at night – unless they are fairly solid eggs.[20]

Colin's musical taste baffled Terry Taylor: he was always singing Gilbert and Sullivan or old Music Hall numbers, but he admired Billie Holiday; he didn't care for West Indian calypso, but liked African Highlife sounds. Colin's favourite African musican was Ambrose Campbell, a Nigerian who 'presided over his superb team of drummers' at the Abalabi Club in Maidenhead Passage – 'the most authentic *African* club in London', where, according to MacInnes, the foo-foo 'peels the skin off your larynx and burns your belly with exhilarating fires'.[21] Colin once took Terry Taylor to the BBC Gramophone Library – in the days before the demand for security passes made it impossible to wander in and out of Broadcasting House without being questioned about your business – and invited him to choose a record to play. Confronted with such riches, Taylor decided to go for something Colin might like. He selected Kenny Graham's Afro-Cuban music, which Colin did not then know. Colin was instantly converted; later he collaborated with Graham on a couple of articles about jazz and a stage musical which was never performed.[22]

Terry Taylor was in his early twenties when he met Colin. Though he had no ambitions as a photographer – taking pictures was merely an easy way of making money – Colin introduced him to Victor Musgrave's wife, Ida Kar, at Gallery One. Within a week Taylor had moved in with Ida Kar; he became her photographic assistant and she became his mistress – an arrangement which lasted for a year or two and apparently suited all parties involved. 'It was an entirely new world to me,' Terry Taylor says. 'Painters, writers, collectors. It was all very strange – but wonderful – and I felt completely at home in it. Sort of Frank Normanish. My new education wasn't all down to Colin: there was Ida, Victor, and Kasmin was Victor's assistant at the time.'[23]

Ida Kar encouraged Taylor to paint, but it was Colin who suggested he should write. In his self-appointed role as mentor, Colin fed him with books, mostly written in a colloquial style, and impressed on him that good writing was not necessarily grand or scholastic. The authors he particularly recommended were Swift – in particular, *Gulliver's Travels* – Colette, Firbank and Hemingway: a mixture, in the twentieth-century choices, at least, of the brutal and the baroque.[24]

For Taylor it was 'potent magic', and with Colin's encouragement he went on to write his novel, *Baron's Court, All Change*. But the benefits of the relationship were by no means all on one side: MacInnes made the teenage hero of *Absolute Beginners* a photographer; and when he came to write *Mr Love and Justice* and had as his protagonist a merchant seaman who drifts into poncing more or less by accident he was once again drawing on his young friend's experience – though Terry Taylor was never a merchant seaman. Taylor personified the paradox which is central to MacInnes's vision, that of an innocent corruption, of semi-criminality as the creative and daring alternative to a life of mindless drudgery. The Fifties may have been the decade of conformity, of *The Organisation Man*, but it was also the time when the seeds of Sixties' rebellion were sown and nurtured in the new and unaccustomed affluence. As Taylor himself says of Colin in his later years, 'When the Hippies emerged, he wasn't impressed. Perhaps it was all too middle class, mystical, and shone [with] what he may have considered was too much artificial light. The tougher, darker, working class white/black hipster of the 50s/ early 60s had already claimed his empathy.'[25]

MacInnes did not like pubs. He told a friend they were like banks – never open when you needed them most. The service was invariably slow and slovenly; the counters were never wiped; the food was a disgrace, and why didn't they serve coffee? Yet he did allow that there were exceptions; and among his Soho haunts was the 'French pub', as The York Minster (now the French House) was generally known. There he might expect to run into friends, or friendly adversaries like the Soho-based writer, Paul Potts. But he preferred drinking clubs which, being private – members only – fell outside the licensing laws and could be open all hours. In particular, he favoured the Colony Room in Dean Street, better known as Muriel's after its founder and proprietor, the late Muriel Belcher, a descendant of the famous pugilist of that surname.

In Colin's view, drinking clubs were what pubs were often supposed to be, but mostly weren't. Pub landlords were seldom either welcoming or particularly friendly, whereas club owners were obliged to be hostly: 'In the words of one of them (now retired), "It's a perpetual party where your friends pay for the liquor." '[26] At Muriel's, apart from MacInnes, regulars included the painters, Francis Bacon and Lucian Freud, the jazz singer George Melly and the writers, Dan Farson and – from the late Fifties – Frank Norman. Of Muriel herself, Colin wrote that she was 'a character often met with in films and fiction, but oh! so rarely in reality: the platinum-tough girl with the heart of gold.'[27]

The attraction of the drinking club, he admitted, was 'partly morbid'. To sit in Muriel's 'with the curtains drawn at 4 pm on a sunny afternoon, sipping expensive poison and gossiping one's life away, has the futile fascination of forbidden fruit: the heady intoxication of a bogus Baudelairian romantic evil . . . The pub, drear though it may be, is certainly more bracing – it offers none of the spurious comforts of this hankering for the womb . . .'[28]

An occasional visitor to the Colony Room in the Fifties was Francis Wyndham, though it wasn't at Muriel's, but at Billie Holiday's London concert in 1954 that he first met Colin. The Wyndhams, of course, had been family friends for generations;

and Ada Leverson, who was Francis's grandmother, was admired by Colin both as a writer and as the loyal and beautiful friend of Oscar Wilde. 'You have brought off a most diabolical coup,' he wrote to Wyndham in February 1956, '. . . in contriving to be both a Leverson and a Wyndham. No wonder you stalk through Soho like a crown prince who has forgotten where he put his kingdom. No wonder the Kabaka called!'[29] (This last was a reference to the exiled ruler of Buganda, whom both Wyndham and MacInnes befriended.)

Colin's friendship with Francis Wyndham may have stemmed from his interest in his family. 'He believed in heredity,' Wyndham says, 'not in a snobbish way, though. He hated that. But as with Africans and West Indians, he had a sort of anthropological interest in origins. It was part of the way he looked at people, not individualistically, but as representative of this or that.'[30]

At that time Wyndham was living with his mother in Trevor Square – 'lovely name . . . and lovely square: *very* much of the 1950s, may I say,' Colin wrote enthusiastically. But he wrote mainly to apologise for his customary party (mis)behaviour:

. . . there was I behaving like an *homme fatal* without fatality, in other words, unsociably drunk. Quite, quite dreadful. Oh dear. At the party, somebody said to me, and casually, which made it deadlier (even to a moribund), 'I think you're rather stupid': which is how true. Alas! I shall ask you, in a year's time, or ten, or eighty, if I may call again, and meanwhile beg to be kept on probation.[31]

The only predictable thing about Colin was his unpredictability: he would arrange to meet Wyndham somewhere – generally somewhere odd – then turn up hours late, if at all. When he did appear, they would go on marathon walks through the streets of London. Colin had a provincial's – not to say, colonial's – curiosity about the metropolis. Wyndham found him a stimulating companion: in company he might try to dominate, but get him on his own and 'one was willing to put up with quite a lot, he was so interesting. But then, one might be on a walk with him and quite suddenly he'd want to be rid of one, he'd get bored and irritable . . .'[32]

The BBC radio producer, Patrick Harvey, also recalls how 'you'd be walking along Mortimer Street in apparent amity when he would suddenly turn. It was very disconcerting, but the next time you met there was no reference back to it.'[33] Although Harvey found Colin 'quarrelsome and prickly' in his social behaviour, when it came to work he behaved quite differently – 'he got on very well with the rest of the team, took ideas from them, even from me myself . . .'[34]

MacInnes and Harvey worked together on a series of radio programmes on Music Hall themes – Love, London life, Soldiers and Sailors, Work, Holidays, and Friendship (a decade later Colin reworked these into his book on Music Hall, *Sweet Saturday Night*). These programmes, which were broadcast in the summer of 1956 under the general title, *The Boy in the Gallery*, amply fulfilled 'the gloomy prediction of the BBC executive who (so a kindly spy told me), when the series was mooted, said, "I'm afraid these programmes are going to be very popular." '[35] The first broadcast had an RI (Reaction Index, reflecting audience response) of 81 out of a possible 100, which is very high indeed.

MacInnes was aware that not everyone shared his enthusiasm for Music Hall. In an article in which he described the various sorts of Music Hall bore he classified himself as a 'Junior Romantic Anthropologist bore': 'those who are too young to have heard the real artists, for whom they have nevertheless conceived a sentimental attachment (as one might, say, for Mrs Siddons), and who have then invented neo-Orwellian theories about their art . . .'[36]

One of his own theories was about clowns. 'The real clown,' he opined, 'is essentially subversive: he is not just comic-pathetic like, for instance, Chaplin, but a person who thoroughly disturbs his audience by really making them wonder whether his world of upended logic is not in fact more real than their own sensible, ordered lives.'[37] Yet the story he tells of the great Swiss clown, Grock (strange, he thought, that a great clown should be Swiss), is more comic-pathetic than subversive, though it is not hard to see why it appealed to Colin.

'He always appeared,' he writes of Grock (whom he had seen perform in the Thirties),

with an immaculate stooge whom he insulted throughout his act. Driven to exasperation, the stooge would at last refuse to talk to Grock any longer. Grock continued to mock him, but the stooge remained obstinately silent. One then became aware that Grock himself was suddenly agonised by the thought that he was going to be isolated in his own mad world – abandoned by his sole human companion, and now utterly alone.

So he began to appeal to the stooge, who still said nothing. The appeal at last became so painful that I have seen whole audiences riveted by this demonstration of our essential human isolation.[38]

Grock's behaviour on stage was a paradigm of Colin's in life. Even Colin's face, as Patrick Harvey remembers it, was 'like a circus clown's – very white, oval face, dark eyes, wasn't it?'[39] Others were struck by his death-like pallor: Alfred Maron, for instance, describes him as 'faceless. Always had a face like death, pale face, pale eyes. It was his stature which was impressive, his voice and energy. He had a pale face, pale hair, pale eyes, pale lips. You had to listen to him. He had to exert himself in conversation to impress. He had no face, no nose, no eyes – it was a *dead* face, a bloodless, anaemic face. That's why you remember his clothes . . .'[40] The playwright Bernard Kops feels that he was 'borrowed from death . . . he couldn't get back into the human family . . . He was the most alone and lonely man we ever met.' The 'we' includes Bernard's wife, Erica, who has 'this image of him looking in through the window, wanting to join in the life inside, but unable to.'[41] Colin shared with Grock a first-hand knowledge of 'our essential human isolation'.

MacInnes's attitude to the BBC was becoming increasingly tetchy. He disputed the fee he was offered for a Music Hall programme in which he felt his expertise was being taken for granted rather than paid for, and managed to get it nearly trebled. His exasperation with a fellow contributor to *The Critics*, the *Observer*'s film critic, Caroline Lejeune (who was a friend of his mother's and, when Angela Thirkell died, completed the novel she left unfinished), came over on the air to such an extent that one listener wrote in to suggest they be put in different teams: '. . . one ends up feeling like an incompetent hostess who has asked the wrong mixture to a party.'[42] And after he received half the fee in advance for a documentary programme on art dealers, he put off doing any work on it for so long that the producer was obliged to raise the matter with his superiors, one of whom noted sourly that 'contributors of uncertain temper are apt to behave in this way as soon as some of the money is in their pockets.'[43] In truth, Colin was fed up with radio work, but could not afford to give it up.

He preferred to write for magazines like *Encounter* and *Twentieth Century*. The essay, 'A Short Guide for Jumbles', which came out in *Twentieth Century* in March 1956, for instance, established MacInnes as something of an expert on 'the colour question', even before the publication of *City of Spades*. Indeed, one of the reasons for his disenchantment with the BBC was that when he had put up proposals for programmes on the life of blacks in London, they had all been turned down; it was only now that he had succeeded in publishing what he wanted to write elsewhere that the BBC began to show any interest in the subject. As a result, early in 1957 he was invited to take part in a radio discussion about immigration (which then meant West Indian immigration).

'It's always seemed to me,' he said on that occasion, 'that there's something heroic about the quality of West Indian immigration here: I say heroic in the same sense as that of our own forefathers was when they left this country up to 50 or so years ago. Nowadays, of course, we in the UK still emigrate as well, but one might say that we emigrate to safety: often to an assured job, and with an assisted passage. But the West Indian sets out for the unknown with only his strength and brains and courage . . .'[44]

In a later essay MacInnes distinguishes between African and West Indian reasons for coming to Britain. The African

male visitors were either seamen, or students, or traders or, in a very great many cases, a category that has no Caribbean counterpart – young men who were propelled here by a *wanderlust* that possessed so many Africans when, as a consequence chiefly of the war, the world burst suddenly into Africa, and Africans wanted to burst out into the world . . . The case of the West Indians is much simpler: they have always been an emigrating people . . . a young West Indian (like an Irishman half a century or more ago) must seek his fortune elsewhere to prosper, even to survive.[45]

Africans and West Indians alike, however, got a chilly reception when they arrived in Britain; only their responses differed:

The Africans, though at first surprised and wounded when they discovered everyone was not delighted to see and greet them, soon shrugged their massive shoulders with resigned indifference: for I have yet to meet an African who does not think that to be one is an enviable thing, and that anyone who does not realise this is an imbecile greatly to be pitied. In addition, independence was already in the air, and colonial occupation had been relatively brief: so that there was no real conflict of loyalties, and the oblong blue passport was regarded merely as a matter of provisional convenience. But with the West Indians, it was very different. For generations, they had been nurtured on the idea of England, the distant mother, whose destinies they had shared for more than 300 years: whose history they knew far more intimately than most of us ever learned theirs: and whose language they spoke (with embellishments and, to my ears, in many ways, enrichment) with the intimacy (unknown to Africans) of a cherished mother tongue. England had sent their ancestors to the Caribbean, and had kept them there, in circumstances about which they were ready to be indulgent. In spite of everything, they felt themselves to be British: for centuries, they had helped make their mother rich and strong. Now, nationality laws which this motherland – not they, who had no power to – had just enacted, threw open welcoming doors. Well . . . times were hard, the Americas uninviting, so they would sell up or save, and cross the air or ocean to nestle at this broad maternal bosom. When they arrived, in tropical suits in winter, and with hard savings spent on fares, they found no one to greet them (except whores, rent-sharks and hostile journalists), and the first doors they knocked on, slammed. Even worse, having herself issued the tacit invitation by the nationality acts, when she found she was taken at her word, mother England (or her press and public) clamoured that the laws were wrong . . .[46]

This description of West Indians arriving in London is reminiscent of the opening of Samuel Selvon's *The Lonely Londoners*, a West Indian novel published shortly before *City of Spades*. Both these novels are already, by the mid-Fifties, filled with nostalgia for the good old days of the Paramount ('Cosmopolitan' in MacInnes's novel) dance hall in the Tottenham Court Road 'before the law clean up that joint' and the nearby Roebuck ('Moorhen') pub.

In *City of Spades*, when Montgomery Pew goes to the 'Moorhen', his lighter is expertly lifted by an African known as 'Mr Ronson Lighter' because of his penchant for these valuable objects. Here, as in so many of his delightful cameos of thieves, dope-dealers and assorted villains, MacInnes was drawing direct from life: Mr Ronson Lighter's real-life prototype was a Mr Parker Pen.[47]

These were the days before West Indian women came over in numbers to join their menfolk and keep them in order. By the end of the 1950s the women were 'firmly and domestically dug in with a great many of their own men'.[48] The men still outnumbered them by a considerable margin, but the golden age of the priapic male on the rampage was over.

In this sense, by the time it was published *City of Spades* was already dated; the situation of blacks in Britain was even then highly volatile. But in another, more important sense, the novel both was timely and remains timeless. 'Are we refreshed by optimism in the thought that we have only to be kind and understanding and full of brotherhood for the problem of an increasing coloured population to sort itself out?' Pamela Hansford Johnson asked in her *New Statesman* review of the novel, and answered:

No, we are not: and that is the strength of the book. Mr MacInnes sets out to show that understanding, in any deep and valuable sense, is pretty hard to come by and that there are no cosy answers. He is not directing this book at Virginian Colonels, Dr Malan, or bridling landladies afraid of the contamination of the lavatory: he is directing it at those people who, having accepted the proposition that all men are created equal, have now to find out what all men are like.[49]

For the most part, friends and critics alike – some of the critics *were* friends: Francis Wyndham, Charles Causley – responded enthusiastically to *City of Spades*, and Colin must have been surprised as well as pleased that he had achieved some measure of fame with a novel of which he had written dismissively, 'This Negro one will never be much more than picaresque . . .' The only time he was at all nettled was when an African woman, Femi Oyesiku, in conversation with him on a BBC book programme, criticised Johnny Fortune (whom Pamela Hansford Johnson described as perhaps 'a little too bright and shiny').

'Look,' he told her,

I think your – or the questions you've asked me so far seem to me to be prompted by an instinct to suppose that because this young African boy is set in a delinquent world, involved in a delinquent world, that the book implies that this is a natural thing to happen to any African coming to England – in other words, you're leaping to the defence of your people. I don't think it is necessary to do so as much as you seem to think because the whole point about this hero is this surely – and when I say hero I'm not saying it in a merely conventional sense like, say, the principal male character is the hero – I don't mean it in that sense; I think he is a heroic figure. He's brave at all times, even when he's alone and in great danger. He's faithful to his true friends, both African and European. He's entirely true to himself, completely free from humbug or pretence. And even when disaster comes he's quite undaunted – and also of his own people, if he feels his own people are slighted or misunderstood in any way, he speaks up for them instantly. Now set this – those qualities – which are, it seems to me, heroic qualities – beside the defects of laziness, of insouciance, of a certain delinquency [and the latter] seem to be much less important.[50]

It so happened, though, that at the time when the novel came out, 'the onlie begetter of J.M. Fortune', as Colin wrote to a friend, was in jail: 'No *Spades*, yet, for him.'[51]

However gratifying he found the – largely – favourable critical response to *City of Spades*, Colin really preferred, as Francis Wyndham puts it, 'praise from unknowns, blacks in a bar . . . [He] had the essentially rather romantic idea of breaking through and reaching the unliterary audience.'[52]

The story of Roy Kerridge and his mother provides as instance of this. Kerridge writes,

My mother divorced my father in 1950 and two years later fell in love with a West African, John Longmore. He was more political than most of the characters in *City of Spades*, with his own soapbox at Hyde Park Corner (where my mother met him), but essentially he belonged to the same world. He told my mother that he 'was married to her by African tradition', and after many vicissitudes we left our home in Middlesex for a basement in Islington, with Mr Longmore as my erratic stepfather . . . Our flat was full of Africans, unfortunate Cable Street girls and all kinds of such people. Eventually my mother, helped by her father, escaped to Ferring [near Worthing, in Sussex]. During the Islington years she had three children . . . and a fourth in Ferring . . . When we arrived in Ferring, my mother found the neighbours to be very stand-offish. Nobody was interested in the amazing ways of Africans and West Indians in London. Then *City of Spades* came our way. For the first time we saw in print things which we had hitherto only seen in real life. We felt we had an ally, someone who understood things we knew . . .

For Roy, in particular, the book was an eye-opener:

When I was in Islington, from the age of eleven to nearly sixteen, I lived in a mental fog, unable to understand what was happening around me. I had been accustomed to having an official, written-down view of life, as understood by teachers, and here I was in an uncharted world. So when I read *City of Spades* it was like a veil taken from my brain, and I knew what I had been living through. The immature question that had puzzled me – 'Are Africans good or bad?' – disappeared, as I read a tale of all different kinds of Africans with mixed motives, and none wholly good or bad at all! I hero-worshipped Colin MacInnes for thus revealing Truth . . .[53]

Roy Kerridge's mother wrote to MacInnes and a kind of pen-friendship developed between them, in the course of which he encouraged her to write a book. She tried her hand at a novel but, under the pressure of raising a large family single-handed, had to put it aside. Her son Roy carried on where she left off, but the novel eventually floundered between their very different styles, though Kerridge has since become a successful journalist, following MacInnes to some extent in his choice of subjects, if not in his political views.

8
The Road to Notting Hill

The year 1956 was a national and international watershed, with Britain's unilateral invasion of Suez and Hungary's brave rising against the Russians. But the impact of these events could only be measured in retrospect. In 1962 MacInnes wrote:

> . . . Then suddenly, from 1956 onwards, there came a crack in the social–political situation that released old allegiances and left conventional parties frozen into postures that ignored these changes. There came Poland, Hungary, Suez, death of Stalin, rise of Africa, the New Left, the teenage phenomenon, the race riots, the teacher strikes, Osborne and the new-wave writers, and, for what it is worth, CND . . .[1]

MacInnes was more aware than most people of the social upheaval he was living through; and in essays, as well as in his 'London' novels, he played no small part in forging our image of the era. If Holden Caulfield, in Salinger's *The Catcher in the Rye* (1951), epitomises the alienated teenage psychology of early 1950s' Americans which would find its apotheosis in the films of James Dean (who died in 1955), then the unnamed hero of MacInnes's *Absolute Beginners* is the pied piper of the more cheerfully anarchic British youth movement of the second half of the decade.

Although he was more than twice their age, MacInnes had no difficulty in identifying with the teenagers who flocked to James Dean films in the mid-Fifties. Peter Lewis, in his book on the Fifties, writes of Dean: 'In all three of his films adults, especially parents, exist to reject, hurt and warp the young.'[2] This was MacInnes's own heartfelt experience; and in the relationship between the Absolute Beginner and his mother – a most un-Angela-Thirkell-like character – there is all the fierce enmity of frustrated love:

> '. . . if you made up your mind to have me, you were supposed to love me. Mothers are supposed to love their sons.'
> 'And sons their mothers,' my mother said.
> 'If they get a chance. There's not one that doesn't want to, is there? But they must get a bit of it back, a little bit of encouragement.'

At this old Mum just sighed, and gave me a crooked smile, and looked very *wise*, I must say, in her way, though very nasty, too.[3]

The writer and broadcaster, Ray Gosling, who was himself a teenager at the time, saw the film *Rebel Without a Cause* three nights in a row. He was riveted from the opening shot: 'the teenage star, James Dean, is lying down in the road, drunk, cuddling a teddy bear, caressing and billing and cooing to it – going *aar, aaarrrh*, until his voice mimics the siren on the cop-car come to fetch him, *wow, wow, wow*.' And the film had a lasting effect on him. The fact that James Dean, so sensitively and moodily alive in the film, was already dead made it somehow 'religious'.[4]

James Dean died, and the legend grew; the other great Fifties male film star, Marlon Brando – mumbling, inarticulate hero-cum-victim of Elia Kazan's *On the Waterfront*, in which he topples his father-figure, a corrupt union boss played by Lee J. Cobb; and ur-Rocker in a film about teenage bikers called *The Wild One* which was actually banned in Britain – grew fat and middle-aged, and the legend died. As the jazz singer and critic, George Melly, comments: 'Death is the one certain way to preserve a pop legend, because age, in itself, is considered a compromise.'[5]

Along with the cult movies of Brando and Dean came a totally unmemorable film called *Blackboard Jungle*; but it contained a song – one song – which launched a movement. The singer, Bill Haley, was already fat and middle-aged, but the song, *Rock Around the Clock*, had the Teddy boys jumping in the aisles; and when a second film, named after the song, quickly followed, they ran riot and slashed the cinema seats to ribbons.

There were no soccer hooligans in those days; Mods and Rockers did not yet exist, let alone indulge in ritual battle at beach resorts on bank holiday weekends; the Teds were the first mani-festation of a now familiar phenomenon, and the press had a field day reporting – and enlarging upon – their outrageous behaviour. Readers of *The Times* solemnly debated in its corre-spondence columns the issue of whether rock 'n' roll heralded the end of empire, if not of civilisation itself, or was simply a flash in the pan, an example of young people letting off steam. Ray Gosling, like Colin MacInnes, later his friend and mentor, was something of an 'inside outsider' – a grammar school boy bound for university who was yet firmly on the side of the rebels. He found the whole argument patronising and disagreed with both points of view offered in *The Times* to such an extent that he wrote a letter himself (which *The Times* did not print), signed 'A Teddy Boy' (which he wasn't). For him, rock 'n' roll was 'never a safety-valve . . . but a clarion call'; it was 'a euphemism for sex, but not with the girl next door. We wanted to fuck the world . . .'[6]

George Melly, examining the phenomenon more dispassionately, concludes: 'The whole point of rock 'n' roll depended on its lack of subtlety. It was music to be used rather than listened to . . . crude and emotionally limited as it was, [it] established an important principle: the right of the underprivileged young to express themselves with a freedom and directness which until then had been the prerogative of their elders and betters.'[7]

Both Melly and Gosling are writing retrospectively and both pay tribute to the one man who saw what was going on *at the time*. Melly writes of Colin MacInnes's 'astonishing . . . empathy' with teenagers and his 'penetrating understanding of what pop was about' at a time when 'not many people over the age of 16 or so thought of pop as anything more than a profitable gimmick or an unpleasant epidemic.'[8] Melly himself took no interest in pop until he gave up jazz singing to become a writer at the beginning of the Sixties; he was quite as unprepared as anyone else, including his fellow jazzmen, when he first encountered rock 'n' roll in the person of an ex-merchant seaman called Tommy Hicks, but better known as Tommy Steele, who was England's answer to Elvis Presley:

The moment the curtain went up a high-pitched squeaking and shrieking started. I was absolutely amazed. After a couple of numbers I left and went back to the pub. The band was playing darts and Frank Parr was getting quite drunk. The orgiastic cries of worship inside the cinema were perfectly audible, and this moved him to prophesy.

'You hear that!' he announced as he swayed about, 'that's the death of jazz. We've had it. In six months we'll all be in the bread line!'[9]

Jazz was indeed knocked sideways for a while, though it bounced back into fashion with the trad boom of the early Sixties.

In the early Fifties there were, on the one hand, American singers like Guy Mitchell, Frankie Laine and Doris Day; on the other, there was jazz. In London a place of pilgrimage was 100 Oxford Street where the Old Etonian trumpeter and band leader, Humphrey Lyttleton, was the attraction; for those with cooler, more modern tastes there was Club Eleven in Carnaby Street with the Johnny Dankworth Seven. A very popular off-shoot of jazz in the mid-Fifties was skiffle: Lonnie Donegan's folksy *Rock Island Line*, for example, reached No. 1 in the charts in May 1956; and even after the arrival of rock 'n' roll Donegan continued to do well, selling more records than Tommy Steele himself. But however popular he might be, Donegan was not a 'pop' star in the sense – as defined by George Melly – that Tommy Steele was: 'Steele was the first British performer to receive the true pop accolade: the pubescent shriek.'[10]

The roots of pop, of course, were in American Negro music; what was new was having white boys sing it. It may have seemed to the uninitiated that one minute it was Doris Day bouncing along with *The Deadwood Stage* and the next, Elvis Presley pounding out *Heartbreak Hotel*; but in the background there were the likes of Fats Domino and Little Richard and, very much in the fore-ground, the enigmatic figure of Johnnie Ray, who delighted audiences with his highly emotional rendering of *Cry* and *What a Night*. But Johnnie Ray, though a precursor, was still not the real thing. For Ray Gosling, becoming a teenager meant 'drinking black-and-tans in the Criterion or the Horse and Groom and looking up at Johnnie Facer open his flick-knife and say, "Johnny Ray singing *Cry* – that's women's music, don't play it – right? – from now we've banned it".'[11]

At the end of 1957 and the beginning of 1958 Colin MacInnes published two essays dealing with pop songs and the teenage phenomenon. In these he 'discovered' (for an educated reader-ship) Tommy Steele. Steele was 'the Pied Piper from Ber-mondsey', a charmer with talent: 'The most striking feature of Tommy's performance is that it is both animally sensual and innocent, pure. He is Pan, he is Puck, he is every nice young girl's boy, every kid's favourite elder brother, every mother's cherished adolescent son.'[12] He could cavort about the stage with the best of them, but he came over so much *nicer* than Elvis, the American prototype.

By the time MacInnes wrote this, Tommy Steele was already on his way to becoming an all-round 'entertainer', and MacInnes was the first to suggest the direction in which he was likely to go. The title of his essay, 'Young England, half English', derives from the fact that pop songs on those pre-Beatle days were American imports and had to be sung, even by English performers, in the American idiom. 'Perhaps one day,' MacInnes speculated, 'Tommy will sing songs as English as his speaking accent, or his grin. If this should happen, we will hear once again, for the first time since the decline of the music halls, songs that tell us of our own world.'[13] MacInnes perceived the music hall link before it was at all obvious – even to Tommy himself.

What MacInnes instinctively grasped, though, was that music was the key to understanding the teenage revolution. On the basis of his familiarity with jazz clubs, his visits to coffee bars like the 2i's in Old Compton Street (where Tommy Steele began) and, above all, his friendships with youngsters, MacInnes came up with the view of teenagers which informs his novel, *Absolute Beginners*.

Teenagers were the 'new classless class'; England's two nations were no longer the rich and poor, or even the upper and lower classes – Marx and all that was old hat, passé – but teenagers and adults (tax-payers). Suddenly, teenagers were the ones with spending money; whole industries were geared to their needs – not just pop music, but the clothing, motor scooter, radiogram, travel, cosmetics and soft drinks industries as well. Like the Pied Piper himself, teenagers called the tune and, in keeping with their new economic status, they were more mature for their age than earlier generations had been, And just as they were classless, these new teenagers (MacInnes did allow that even in the late Fifties not all youths of either sex qualified as 'teenagers': the good news had not yet penetrated every corner), so they scorned national boundaries and were, in effect, an international movement.

Despite the all-powerful American influence they were '*not* "Americanised" ': 'The paradox is that the bearded skiffle singers with their Yankee ballads, and Tommy Steele with his "rock"-style songs, seem so resoundingly, so irreversibly, English.'[14] Teenagers did not drink alcohol, and they were cleaner as well as more joyful than earlier generations had been. Their sex life MacInnes characterised as 'promiscuity without pain'; but later he admitted that promiscuity had been the wrong word to use of teenagers and applied far more to their elders.[15] Judging by the fuss that was made when one of Tommy Steele's successors, Adam Faith, let it be known that he had had pre-marital sexual experience, that would certainly appear to be the case.

MacInnes's view of teenagers was essentially optimistic; it was his firm conviction that 'never before . . . has the younger generation been so *different* from its elders.' Yet in the midst of his celebration of youthful virtue he did sound a warning note: '. . . it would be equally possible to see, in the teenage neutralism and indifference to politics, and self-sufficiency, and instinct for enjoyment – in short, in their kind of happy mindlessness – the raw material for crypto-fascisms of the worst kind.' Nevertheless, his emotional commitment to the rising generation was so absolute that he could not seriously countenance such a possibility. 'I don't sense this myself at all,' he went on, 'though I may very well be wrong.'[16] Hence his reluctance to write about Teddy boys: they represented the crypto-fascist tendencies he deplored.

MacInnes regarded Christmas with particular horror: it was 'an annual nightmare' when everybody retired to the bosom of the family and those without families felt more excluded than ever. It was the one day of the year when it was not done to drop in on your friends; and when it was all over 'people behave as if a disaster had just overtaken the entire nation – I mean, they're dazed, and blink as if they'd been entombed for days . . .'[17]

Christmas 1957 was made additionally unpleasant for Colin through illness. He ran a high temperature which persisted in spite of treatment; and in the New Year he was obliged to go into the New End Hospital in Hampstead. There they diagnosed pneumonia and dosed him with penicillin. But no sooner had he come out of hospital than his temperature shot up again. He struggled to fulfil his various broadcasting engagements, including the first two programmes of a new series of *The Critics*, but in the end he was forced to admit defeat.

It occurred to him that his visit to Africa a couple of years earlier might have something to do with his illness, so he had himself admitted to the Hospital for Tropical Diseases.

At first the doctors there were baffled and put him through a series of extremely unpleasant tests. They extracted marrow from his bones; they threaded a tube through his nose and down into his stomach; and they used 'an embarrassing instrument known to patients as the "shuftiscope" ("We're very interested in the reactions to this thing," said the doctor, as he inserted it. "Some show marked signs of resistance, which we consider psychologically significant").'[18]

David Sylvester, who had replaced Colin on *The Critics*, visited him in hospital and gave him the Kinsey Report as suitable invalid reading. It was one of their best times together and Sylvester remembers Colin being very romantic about Africans.[19] Just then, however, he received the sad news that his favourite African, Richard Hawton Samuel Erizia, alias Johnny Fortune, 'who, two days before, had been entirely his life-loving, life-giving self', had died of double pneumonia in a hospital in Manchester. 'Friends by his bedside say that, as he left England, Africa and the world, he called for his compatriot, A——, and for me.' The irony of the situation – that this should happen at the time when he himself, who had been (wrongly) treated for pneumonia, was being 'despaired of' in a hospital for *tropical* diseases – was not lost on Colin.[20]

By 19 March Colin was able to report some progress in his case.

A month ago I tried this place [he wrote to Francis Wyndham] and after 14 days of gruesome 'tests', they discovered an amoebic abscess in my liver; and pumped therefrom 2½ pints of 'matter'. This leaves me recovering, with a hole the size of an orange in the 'organ', closing up. Temperature has dropped dramatically to normal.

The amoeba is tropical: therefore they conclude it lodged itself in me while in Africa, and retired throughout the years to the comfort of the liver. Why, at the end of last year, did it suddenly panic and create an abscess? Perhaps it was displeased at *City of Spades*? (or the reviews??)

The 'specialist' here is a god-like man (Dr Walters), courteous, modest, profoundly efficient – impossible not to trust him . . . The nurses are kind, competent and ugly. The ward sister scatty and wild-eyed. My fellow patients are mostly colonial administrators with bristling moustaches. We have two Africans, one of whom pleases all the Britons by moaning and keening by night. The food is atrocious, though substantial. Four to a ward – very select. People go off for afternoons and weekends – as in a Progressive Borstal . . .[21]

Nurses aroused in Colin deeply ambivalent feelings. To start with, they were women; and then, worse still, they behaved like mothers: 'Their tactic is to try to reduce grown men to cradle status ("Have you been a good boy? Come along now, beddy byes" – to middle-aged gents).'[22] This treatment did not go down well with Colin. His particular *bête noire* was the ward sister – 'Sister T, with a breast like Queen Mary's covered with medals. We took an instant dislike to each other, and battled . . . like a drill sergeant and a barrack-room lawyer.'[23]

Nurses' bullying ways, MacInnes believed, 'must be resisted at all costs – even if you have tubes in your arms and stomach, can't walk, and feel like the death you're close to. "Why did your visitor stay half an hour after the bell went?" Sister T cried, flourishing the book of rules before my blanched, unshaven face. "Because he enjoys the pleasure of my company," I shouted.'[24]

One day, however, there arrived a visitor who did not come to enjoy the pleasure of his company or to inquire after his health. This visitor was a small man with a bowler hat, denoting officialdom. He brought with him an Order in Bankruptcy.

'For some years . . .' MacInnes admits,

I had neglected to pay my Income Tax. Forms came, and the usual warning notices in black then red, next letter peremptory or pleading, then admonitions from legal departments at ominous south coast addresses (the greater the danger, the further away the menacing office), till at last I was waylaid in Camden Town by a stranger who handed me a summons. I was to appear at the High Court to explain my neglect of civic duty. I failed to do so, and the Inland Revenue set the bankruptcy machinery in motion.[25]

Yet just as the months in hospital and of convalescence, with alcohol and tobacco forbidden, cleansed Colin bodily, so the bankruptcy proceedings, culminating in a public examination in court, purified him spiritually:

. . . Fortified by an adequate dose of pep pills, I faced the presiding judge and the cross-examination of the Official Receiver (or one of his deputies, I believe). He took me remorselessly, yet courteously, from the time of my birth up till the present day, giving due weight to my achievements, and sparing none of my numerous follies. The total effect of this confessional was not, I must record, unpleasant – it had the effect of a psychological purgation, a sort of last judgment on a miniature scale.[26]

What made Colin's case unusual was that his debts (at least, the only ones that anybody was trying to recover) were exclusively to the Inland Revenue. The sums were not enormous and Mac-Innes's earning power was in fact increasing, so he was in due course able to clear these debts – as well as the hefty legal costs – in full. As a result he was not merely discharged, but annulled, his dossier destroyed and he free to walk out of Bankruptcy Buildings in Carey Street.

His relief, however, was tempered with regret. Being a bankrupt had hardly inconvenienced him. Due to the convention by which the sum allowed to a bankrupt person is commensurate with his financial status before bankruptcy, he was not badly off. And it suited him well that someone else should take responsibility for his affairs, especially as it meant that this official would chase up *his* debtors – those periodicals which owed him money; even the government, which still had not paid his war gratuity.[27]

Colin's financial behaviour, no less than his behaviour in other respects, was conditioned by his family and upbringing. There was a streak of meanness in his mother which derived, in turn, from her frugal parents. In Australia, Angela had been forced to be prudent by the circumstances of her life; but later, when she was earning considerable sums of money as a bestselling author, she preferred to live simply, even to deny herself warmth and comfort, and pretend that she was hard up. Colin liked to spend money. Friends remark on his generosity. Francis Wyndham, for example, says he was 'fantastically generous – the opposite of his mother'.[28] Yet Colin did not fool himself. 'Only he who is careful of money can be generous with it,' he wrote. 'To be a spendthrift is a form of meanness.'[29]

After his illness Colin had a brief convalescence at a hotel in the New Forest. He no longer had his flat in Regent's Park Terrace or his room in D'Arblay Street, so when he returned to London in April 1958 he moved into Bryan Robertson's flat just off Ebury Street in sw1. Despite the fact that they did not see very much of one another – Colin was never up when Bryan Robertson went out to work; and when Robertson returned he was generally on his way out for the evening – this arrangement did not last long.[30] But when MacInnes walked out of the flat some six months later, after a row, he had already written the bulk of *Absolute Beginners*.

Absolute Beginners was MacInnes's novel about teenagers, just as *City of Spades* had been his novel about Negroes. Only for better or worse (and reviewers would argue both ways) it was overtaken by events – namely, the Notting Hill race riots of 1958. In fact, the area affected by racial violence was not Notting Hill itself, which was only marginally involved, but Notting *Dale*.

'. . . this is the residential doss-house of our city,' says the Absolute Beginner of this London "Napoli" comprising chunks of W.9, 10 and 11 (this area 'that's got left behind by the Welfare era *and* the Property-owning whatsit'). 'In plain words, you'd not live in our Napoli if you could live anywhere else. And that is why there are, to the square yard, more boys fresh from the nick, and national refugee minorities, and out-of-business whores, than anywhere else, I should expect, in London town.' The Absolute Beginner chooses to live there partly because it's cheap: 'But the real reason . . . is that, however horrible the area is, you're *free* there! No one, I repeat it, no one, has ever asked me there what I am, or what I do, or where I came from, or what my social group is, or whether I'm educated or not, and if there's one thing I cannot tolerate in this world, it's nosey questions . . .'[31]

The authentic MacInnes speaks here as elsewhere through his teenage mouthpiece; his niece, Serena Thirkell, remembers that you were never to ask him questions like, 'Where are you living now, Colin?' If you did, he would instantly rebuke you, saying, 'That's a cop's question – don't ask me cop's questions.'[32]

In *Absolute Beginners*, the narrator first hears rumours of racial violence at a 'Maria Bethlehem' (Ella Fitzgerald) concert, thus enabling MacInnes to juxtapose contrasting images of racial harmony and disharmony:

They rose to her at the end – all those hundreds of English boys and girls, and their friends from Africa and the Caribbean – and they practically had to gouge us all out of that auditorium. Cats I didn't know from Adam said, hadn't it been great, and one cat in particular then said, had I heard about the happenings at St Ann's Well, up in Nottingham, last evening? I asked him, what happenings? not taking it very much in (because I was still back there with Maria Bethlehem), when I realised he was saying there'd been rioting between whites and coloured, but what could you expect in a provincial dump out there among the sticks?'[33]

This last remark, of course, is intended ironically, since the fighting which broke out in St Ann's in Nottingham on the night of Saturday 23 August was immediately overshadowed by even uglier events in the metropolis. That same Saturday night at closing-time a gang of nine white youths set out from the West London pub where they had been drinking on a 'nigger-hunting expedition'; they were armed with a bizarre assortment of weapons: wooden staves, pointed iron railings, the starting-handle of a car, an air-pistol, a knife and a wooden table-leg. Whenever they came upon a solitary black (once they were brave enough to take on a pair) they bundled out of their car and belaboured their chosen victim. Five people were taken to hospital; and three of them were detained for over a fortnight, so serious were their injuries.[34]

By the time the youths came to be tried at the Old Bailey three weeks later, the train of events they had precipitated had so outraged public opinion that they were given exemplary sentences of four years' imprisonment apiece.

The South African born novelist, Dan Jacobson, reported the trial for *Encounter*. What he found disturbing about these 'nigger-hunters' was their ordinariness: 'they weren't sunken nobodies; they were rather jaunty anybodies.' They did not strike him as being in the least depraved, dissolute, or dangerous, in spite of the way they had behaved. He concluded that they were themselves

victims of a complex of attitudes and beliefs which seem to be in the very bone and marrow of what we call 'our civilisation' . . . I believe that they – and a great many of those who followed their example – felt themselves in some special and terrible way *permitted* to attack the coloureds who were their victims; and that in their attitudes to what they did . . . there was an element of self-righteousness . . . These young men were trapped within a history; being both weak and violent they could not escape from it.[35]

Then, as now, there were fascist organisations only too willing to dignify racial prejudice with the name of politics. The White Defence League and the Union Movement were particularly active in Notting Dale and Shepherd's Bush during the last week of August and the first days of September 1958.

When MacInnes had written that 'it would be possible to see, in the teenage neutralism and indifference to politics . . . the raw material for crypto-fascisms of the worst kind,'[36] the race riots had not yet happened. He took no pleasure in seeing his worst fears confirmed. His portrait of 'the Wizard' in *Absolute Beginners* is made up of equal parts fascination and repulsion: to start with Wiz is the Absolute Beginner's 'blood-brother' and the latter is proud of this fellow teenager who, though even younger than himself, is so street wise; but by the end of the book he is metamorphosed into a weaselly creature giving the fascist salute and shouting, 'Keep England white!' He appears less than half-a-dozen times in the entire novel, yet on two of these occasions the Absolute Beginner ends up either slapping or punching him.

The Wizard is the dark side of the teenage dream, and *Absolute Beginners* itself is the author's valediction to the Fifties – 'What an age it is I've grown up in,' the young narrator thinks, as he prepares to flee the country after Notting Hill, 'with everything possible to mankind at last, and every horror too, you could imagine! And what a time it's been in England, what a period of fun and hope and foolishness and sad stupidity!'[37]

Of course the fun and hope that grew along with the increasing affluence of the late Fifties continued well into the Sixties; but something precious was lost along the way, and that something was innocence. That was the true significance of the Notting Hill race riot, as MacInnes instantly grasped. Even before the dust had settled he was suggesting to his publisher that someone should write an instant book – 'My guess is that it will seem, with Suez, the key event of the post-war period.'[38] Just as Suez spelt out, for the benefit of any lingering doubters, the end of the era of British world dominance, so Notting Hill put paid to the idea that we could still claim any kind of *moral* leadership.

'Editorial reaction since the riots,' he wrote disgustedly on 5 September,

has concentrated on considerations as to whether coloured immigrants should be here. That is of course a question to consider, but coming about 1,000 miles before that in importance is the immediate matter of condemning the riots absolutely.

There is a general tendency, too, in editorial comment to find alibis. There are vicious coloureds. Teds are frustrated psychopaths. This is a 'race riot', not a race riot.[39]

The question of when is a race riot not a race riot also exercised the sociologist, Ruth Glass, author of *Newcomers: the West Indians in London* (1960). She summed it up thus:

In London it was not [as in Nottingham] the retaliation of a few coloured men which sparked off the crowd outbursts, nor was there a definite chain of incidents during the turbulent days. 'Nigger-hunting' simply spread and collected an increasing number of partisans – active forces and passive spectators – simultaneously in several districts. And although no one was killed, the actual violence, and even more the cumulative threats of violence, produced an atmosphere of menace and fear which closely resembled that of a text-book race riot.[40]

Many of the incidents described in the final part of *Absolute Beginners* are based on reports in the *Manchester Guardian*. Throughout the riots MacInnes took notes from these *Guardian* reports, which he used extensively, but with fictional licence, in writing the novel. There was an account, for instance, of a young African student from Derby who came to visit friends in Notting Hill and was set upon by a gang of youths who punched and kicked him before he managed to make his escape. Pursued by his three attackers, he flung himself into the doorway of a green-grocer's shop. There he struck lucky: the shopkeeper's wife was equal to the occasion. She came out of the shop, locking the door behind her, and confronted the threatening toughs and the mob across the street who were calling for a lynching. Eventually the police arrived, dispersed the crowd and escorted the African to his destination; but it was the greengrocer's wife who had saved the young man from serious harm.

In *Absolute Beginners* MacInnes fleshes out the bare bones of the report and infuses it with moral indignation. In particular he pays tribute to the rare courage of 'that old vegetable woman (who I bet will go straight up to heaven like a supersonic rocket when she dies . . .)' 'Picture this!' he writes.

This one old girl, with her grey hair all in a mess, and her old face flushed with fury, she stood there surrounded by this crowd of hundreds, and she bawled them out. She said they were a stack of cowards and gutter bastards, the whole lot of them, but they shouted back at her, and I couldn't hear. But she didn't budge, the old girl, and her husband had got the shutters up inside, and by and by the law made its appearance . . .[41]

Ruth Glass was equally impressed. 'The "teddy boys" had the sanction of their own backstreet society,' she writes.

They rarely met white opposition. While there were many people who preserved their sense of decency in the turmoil of Notting Dale – some white housewives did the shopping for their coloured neighbours who dared not go outside – active defiance of 'nigger-hunting' was rare. There were not many who had the determination of the greengrocer's wife who stood outside her door facing a violent crowd.[42]

For MacInnes, as for the Absolute Beginner, the whole experience was shattering – 'as if the stones rise up from the pavement there and hit you, and the houses tumble, and the sky falls in . . . Your sense of security, and of there being some plan, some idea behind it all somewhere, just disappears.'[43] Coming so soon after his illness, it removed any lingering traces of complacency. He had just started a new stint on *The Critics*, his first since leaving hospital. On 28 August (five days after the riots began), he wrote to the producer requesting his release from the four remaining programmes he was contracted for.[44] He never again took part in a *Critics* programme. His attitude to the BBC henceforth is best summarised in a note he jotted down in his 'Thoughts' book: 'Extract max. loot from min. effort (BBC contracts).'[45]

In *Absolute Beginners* MacInnes marvellously conveys the latency of urban violence: how somebody has only to throw a bottle and what might otherwise have ended peaceably flares up into a fight. 'That milk that arrives mysteriously every morning,' he writes, 'I suppose it brings us life, but if trouble comes, it's been put there – or the bottles it comes in have done – by the devil. And dustbins, they get emptied just as regularly, and take everything away – they and their lids, especially, have become much the same thing: I mean, the other natural city weapon of war.'[46]

Another observation he makes about urban violence is its geographical containment, not just within the city but in one clearly delineated part of it:

Inside the two square miles of Napoli there was blood and thunder, but just outside it – only across one single road, like some national frontier – you were back in the world of Mrs Dale, and What's My Line? and England's green and pleasant land. Napoli was like a prison, or a concentration camp: inside, blue murder, outside, buses and evening papers and hurrying home to sausages and mash and tea.[47]

It was not a national frontier, of course, which defined the limits of the riot area, but a class frontier. With the coming of the new Teenager, who was anyway partly his own creation, MacInnes wanted to believe that the class war was obsolete: hadn't John Osborne written its epitaph in *Look Back in Anger*? What Colin envisioned was an across-the-board solidarity of right-minded and patriotic people. He was not like the historian, Eric Hobsbawm, who sees the jazz world as a 'neutral zone, one of those peculiar little islands where one can take a holiday from society';[48] he saw it rather as a blueprint for the society of the future. In this he was deluding himself, but the vision of like-minded individuals from all classes – the 'Horray Henries' and debs linking arms with the teenager hustlers and junkies in an anti-racist crusade – was a powerfully seductive one (not dissimilar to the Tory-radical, masonic ideal of Cousin Ruddy, for instance – not to mention B-P and the Boy Scouts).

'Colin's concern was for the *spirit* of things,' Victor Musgrave recalls.

After the Notting Hill race riots a committee was set up with lots of showbiz people like Johnny Dankworth and Cleo Laine, and it produced an eight-page newssheet [*What the Stars Say*] which was mostly showbiz stuff about Sammy Davis Junior – that sort of thing. Anyway, it had to be distributed in the riot area, it was no good just *producing* it. Conscience-stricken Colin felt obliged to make sure it reached the riot area, so he said to me, 'Do you know anyone with a car?' (I ask you – do you know anyone with a car? Who doesn't know someone with a car?) I said: 'Yes, Don Cammell (a painter) has a small Austin Seven.' Don agreed to do it, so we filled the car with mountains of these newssheets and set off. Colin made a big performance of this: he and I were to post the sheets through the letter-boxes; he wouldn't let Don help though Don volunteered to do so. 'You're our getaway man,' he told him. 'You're not to get involved . . .' Afterwards Colin said to me that we two between us had prevented a second Notting Hill race riot – and said it in all seriousness.[49]

Colin was a founder member of the Stars' Campaign for Inter-racial Friendship. Other members included the jazz critics Max Jones and 'Francis Newton' (the pseudonym under which Eric Hobsbawm wrote a jazz column for the *New Statesman*), the publicity man Leslie Perrin and the record producer Dennis Preston, as well as Johnny Dankworth and Cleo Laine. Most of the big names in British jazz and pop were on the list of sponsors – Humphrey Lyttleton, Chris Barber and Ken Colyer as well as Tommy Steele, Frankie Vaughan and Lonnie Donegan.

To Max Jones, Colin would emphasise 'the importance of going about and *bearing witness*' – a phrase that also crops up in *Absolute Beginners*. He took his involvement with SCIF very seriously. According to Jones, 'Colin was the best man to raise funds. He knew people like Howard Samuel [the millionaire socialist property dealer who, since he had bought MacGibbon & Kee, was Colin's publisher]; knew who the likely supporters were. He was shrewd about that, and about what to ask for – not £50 but £500, and then perhaps we got £100 . . .'[50] Colin was, of course, experienced in raising money for less altruistic purposes.

There were many other organisations and individuals who wanted to do their bit to prevent a repetition of the Notting Hill riots – so many, in fact, that the *Kensington News* asked in a headline: 'Will Too Many Do-Gooders Pave the Path to Notting HELL?'[51] Of the Stars' Campaign, Ruth Glass noted wryly in 1960 that while it had 'a rather energetic, "newsworthy" start (in 1958 it held an "inter-racial" children's Christmas party in North Kensington, which was televised), since then it has been rather quiet.'[52] Max Jones says the impetus faded when the judge meted out such stiff sentences to the original nine offenders; and Eric Hobsbawm recalls that the campaign just fizzled out after a month or two. It was not very well run and it was impossible to keep the stars – a case, perhaps, of too many generals and not enough troops.

Between the autumn of 1958, when he moved out of Bryan Robertson's flat in Cundy Street SW1, and the spring of 1959, when he rented the flat above Alfred Maron's tailor's shop in Hanbury Street E1, Colin was of no fixed abode. He informed a BBC producer that he had been unable to reply to his letter sooner because it had gone to the 'address before last (I really *must* settle down) . . .'[53]

He had long been fascinated by the East End. And to live in the heartland of the old London Jewish community appealed to him deeply. As 'an "English" London-born, Australian-reared Scot,'[54] he was drawn to localities with a foreign character which had yet managed, over the years, to become virtually indigenous. As an 'inside outsider' he felt an instinctive sympathy with other inside outsiders, be they black, Jewish, Cypriot, Maltese or Chinese.

The strength of his need to belong, to be part of a community, was in exact proportion to his nomadic impulse, his ideal of being able to fit all his worldly belongings into a taxi whenever he felt the urge to move on. Colin was both social explorer and social worker. He spent a substantial amount of time, over the years, in various courts of law going bail for blacks; and when he first went to live in Stepney, he told readers of the *Jewish Chronicle*, 'I did a little work for the Stepney Old People's Association, which involved entering dozens of rooms and tenements all over the borough, carrying "meals on wheels". Talking to these old people and learning in what absolute isolation so many of them lived, it seemed to me that this neglect of the old was one of the most shameful and callous features of our "new prosperity".' Jewish people, he opined, would never 'allow their grandparents to rot alone'.[55]

He never missed an opportunity to single out Jewish friends for special mention in articles and essays – Barney Greenman, who had been his solicitor at the drugs trial; David Sylvester, his old friend and fellow art critic; Irving Kristol, the former editor of *Encounter*; Howard Samuel, his publisher; Alfred Maron, the actor who was now his landlord; and Bernard Kops, the dramatist whose first play, *The Hamlet of Stepney Green*, he praised to the skies in an essay in *Encounter*.

Bernie Kops and his wife, Erica, are the models for the Jewish writer 'Mannie Katz and his spouse Miriam' in *Absolute Beginners*. Kops, like Maron, had an East End working class background. Erica Kops thinks that was 'one of the reasons why Colin liked Bernie – because of his non-literary background. He felt very ambivalent about his own advantages.'[56] He was delighted when Bernard once said, 'Angela Thirkell? Oh yes, one of the inner Thirkells, isn't she?' Yet, though Colin never had a good word to say for his mother, the Kops' sensed that he had a grudging respect for her.[57]

The Kops' lived in Blackfriars when Colin first knew them. They could not understand why Blackfriars was so full of romance for him. They decided it must be because he himself lived nowhere. Similarly, Bernard, who had grown up in Stepney, found Colin's feeling for the East End quite incomprehensible. They would be walking down Cable Street together and Colin would say to him, his voice husky with awe, 'You know, there are dope fiends here . . .'[58]

In the bustling life of Spitalfields, where the activity of the Jewish community precluded that Sunday paralysis which afflicted other parts of the city, Colin was to some extent seeking another bohemia, a second Soho. Soho itself had changed – for the worse. 'When the authentic bohemian world broke up,' says Bernard Kops, who also lived in Soho in the Fifties and used to trundle a barrow of second-hand books daily up to Cambridge Circus before his success as a playwright liberated him, 'Colin lost his home. When the world caught up, he lost his sense of adventure. The Soho world fitted him perfectly. He was anti-establishment. So when the establishment entered it all, he deeply resented it.'[59]

In the spring of 1959 MacInnes wrote for *Encounter* an article on British jazz, which was largely an interview, or distillation of several interviews, with Kenny Graham. Melvin Lasky, who took over from Irving Kristol as editor of *Encounter* in 1958, decided not to print the piece as it stood but, in the hope of salvaging something from it, agreed to pay for MacInnes and Graham to visit Poland. The idea was that they should contrast the jazz scene in the two countries. This article never appeared either.

To Kenny Graham, Colin was 'a don – he had a don's mentality. He was really out of place in the jazz world; he used to embarrass himself like mad . . . it was going on all round him, but he couldn't grab it. He was all calculated; everything he did, said, etcetera, was thought out. He couldn't understand how people just acted on instinct.' In jazz, Graham thinks, Colin sought 'all the things he wasn't'. He might claim that all musicians were illiterate, yet he was always picking Kenny's brain

for it – music, jazz; it was definitely a problem for him. He wanted you to explain. But I wasn't explicit enough. It was the jazz attitude . . . He couldn't understand Negroes and jazz musicians, their total disrespect for everything. He would flatter, cajole, bribe all the Spade musicians. Yet they used to call him 'Mr Collins' while they called me 'Kenny my brother' . . . He couldn't understand it. But he never *gave*, you see. He wasn't a mean man, but he couldn't give – he was taking all the time. He couldn't cope with love relations . . .[60]

Kenny Graham's originality as a bandleader was in combining a bebop frontline with African drums; thus he evolved his distinctive Afro-Cuban music, which he played first at the 51 Club in Little Newport Street and then at the Flamingo Club, off Shaftesbury Avenue. Graham shared with MacInnes an admiration for Africans:

We got all the characters with get-up-and-go, perhaps, but they were characters. They all want to be the guv'nor, too. They have no sense of time: if an African says, 'See you Tuesday,' he means one Tuesday, not necessarily the next one. There was a nice story of Colin's: he comes to the Downbeat in Newport Street to meet this young African who's supposed to be there at eight. It's gone midnight when this chap finally arrives, very harassed, and he says: 'Colin, Colin, I'm terribly sorry but my watch disappointed me.' Colin was absolutely fascinated by the way they spoke. I murdered the language, according to him; they invigorated it. So I used to play on this and I'd get coarser and coarser while Colin got more and more prim.[61]

The Poland that these two unlikely ambassadors set out to visit had been arousing considerable curiosity, particularly among

1 Portrait of Angela Thirkell by John Singer Sargent.

2 The Thirkell family at 4 Grace Street, Melbourne, 1924.
Left to right: Graham, Angela, 'Thirk' with Lance, Colin.

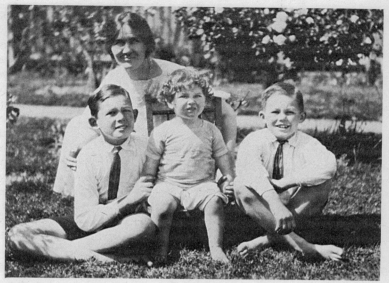

3 Angela and the three boys, Melbourne, 1922.

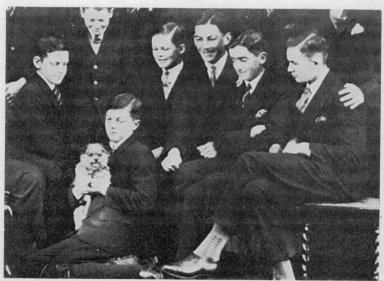

4 Part of the cast of Ian Hay's *A Safety Match*: Scotch College, Melbourne, 1928. Graham is on the extreme right; Colin – who played Lady Strathrea – is fourth from the right.

5 Graham with his father, James Campbell McInnes, Toronto, 1934.

6 Colin in Bonchurch, Isle of Wight, 1948. His ex-boss, Eric Dadson, is on the right.

7 Colin, 1948.

8 Tommy Steele, who started his career at the 2 i's coffee bar, 1956.

9 Colin in the late 1950s.

10 The Notting Hill race riots. On 1 September 1958 white youths set upon a West African student; he found sanctuary in a greengrocer's, where he remained until the police arrived and escorted him to safety (see page 135).

11 Michael X speaking at a Black Power meeting in London shortly before his arrest in July 1967 (see page 196).

12 Colin MacInnes.

intellectuals, ever since Gomulka had come to power in 1956. There had been something of an artistic renaissance: Polish cinema was beginning to attract international audiences; and Polish jazz, which had been – literally – an underground activity, being played in caves, now flourished in the open.

MacInnes writes,

The only mistake we made – but it was a very big one – was to set forth, like two huntsmen venturing to rich game pastures from Nairobi, without pausing to enquire from anyone when the rainy season might happen to be. The Polish musicians . . . were there right enough . . . But in late August, the moment we very cleverly chose for our expedition, they were scattered on holiday all over their great country. Our ten days in Poland accordingly turned into a frantic pursuit, by air, rail, road and even by sea, of the migrant Polish jazz artists – no doubt all very ready to bid us welcome, but entirely unaware that we were desperately searching for their elusive spoor.[62]

Kenny Graham remembers this trip as

the only time I'd felt foreign. Colin's French and German got us through. He'd put them on like another jacket; he'd use them, they were just tools to him. He wasn't drinking then, only fruit juice, and that made him unbearable. One night we ended up in Hel (spelt H-E-L), a little isthmus with sea on both sides. A team of students had this traddy jazz band – it was just a holiday lark for them. But Colin and I gave them Armstrong records and, a little while later, one of them came back with a litre bottle of 'Vodka Anglais', which made me legless. Colin was envious. He was sullen most of the time, which made me go over the top. Each of us would sail off on his own, then we'd meet up later. Colin always had to wash his white cotton socks and do his rituals. There was a hotel where the water coming out of the taps was brown; we had crates of 'limonada' sent up . . . But it wasn't all crazy. We met publishers; there were Sunday picnics, pleasant occasions; we went to Chopin's birthplace; we tried raw fish, visited schools . . . The two of us had a similar apolitical attitude, which helped: you pick what you like out of each system; you don't attack or defend either one entirely . . . Colin could never *belong*.[63]

MacInnes's return to London coincided with the publication of *Absolute Beginners*, just one year after the Notting Hill riots. It had enthusiastic, though not uncritical, reviews. He would have to wait three years, however, for the most penetrating and challenging critique. This was written by the philosopher, Richard Wollheim, and it formed part of a long essay on the modern city called 'Babylon, *Babylone*'.

Colin first met Wollheim in September 1958. 'I can't wait to tell you . . .' he wrote to their mutual friend, Francis Wyndham, 'but guess what . . . RIGHT first time! I've met R. Wollheim! And not only that, but we clicked! Imagine us standing on the rather windy (and rickety) balcony of the Irving Kristol apartment, vying with each other in singing your praises to the moonlit wastes of S.W.7, like two oriental civil servants in a snowstorm talking about the Emperor . . .'[64]

MacInnes and Wollheim met perhaps thirty times in all over the next four or five years, but their relationship seemed special to them both. The Wollheims' invited Colin to various dinners and parties they gave; occasionally they went to the theatre together (Wollheim remembers going to a Japanese Noh play with Colin); and once Colin invited them to Hanbury Street. Yet Colin remained 'the man who came from nowhere, and when he left he was going back to nowhere.' Wollheim attributes his Spartan mode of living to the desire to have nothing that could be taken from him. Similarly his wiry, austere appearance was a front he deliberately cultivated: 'He had a sweet and affectionate side struggling to get out of this Grenadier persona he'd imposed upon himself.'[65]

Wollheim thinks of MacInnes as a very 'dandified writer'; and Colin was delighted when Wollheim compared him to Ronald Firbank, who was an admired model, a favourite writer of his. Wollheim writes:

. . . For the highly aesthetic, almost Firbankian, attitude that MacInnes adopts towards the London scene is something that to a large extent he shares with those who have made it as it is and who are the heroes and heroines of his books. Supremely this is true of the Teenager . . . For the Teenager has rejected the conception of the city as a solid three-dimensional environment that shapes and enfolds his life, and instead regards it as a kind of highly coloured backcloth against which he acts out, and upon which he projects, his fantasies . . .[66]

The poignancy of the Teenagers' world 'is that what is begun in reality has so often to be completed in fantasy.' They may plan to turn life into 'one great ball', but they lack the means to achieve this aim; their 'nomadic, rootless existence' is 'a kind of institutionalised form of the manic life'. Pursuing the psychological strand of his argument, Wollheim writes:

Freud has used the term 'feast' in connection with the manic ideal: wishing, amongst other things, to contrast the immense assiduousness and energy with which objects of pleasure are pursued and accumulated and the comparative indifference with which they are enjoyed, squandered, spoilt. When the Absolute Beginner expresses his desire to make a ball out of life, the kind of ball he has in mind, I suggest, is a feast.[67]

Wollheim is careful to stress at this point that 'in none of this am I talking of individual psychology', but only of 'certain general factors . . . that tend to encourage, to facilitate, certain defences to which the individual, in dealing with his private anxieties, might be inclined to resort.'[68] I have already suggested that Colin's astonishing empathy with the 1950s' young was due to a fortuitous psychological kinship based on a sense of rejection; and he himself admitted there was more of him in *Absolute Beginners* than in any of his other novels, including the autobiographical *To the Victors the Spoils*.[69] So when Wollheim goes on to say that 'there is an only too projectible path that runs from the sense of rejection, through the reactivation of anxiety, to the attractions of the manic state,'[70] the application of this to Colin's particular case is at once obvious and inevitable.

But there is another strand to Wollheim's argument. The teenagers who get their clothes at Cecil Gee's, hang around Ronnie Scott's jazz club or go jiving at Manor House, who buy their LPs and take their holidays abroad, who are 'great consumers in the Common Market of juvenile taste', may not be very numerous, but 'they fulfil an exemplary role within the society of their contemporaries.' They form an 'aristocracy' and manifest traditional aristocratic attributes – namely, loyalty to one's peers, the pursuit of pleasure, 'indifference to general moral considerations and the substitution for them of a complex, labyrinthine, and ultimately arbitrary code of correctness', and, above all, 'the detached contemptuous attitude towards anything in society or the environment which thwarts or frustrates one.'[71] This contemptuousness expresses itself in an icy scorn.

'Nowhere,' Wollheim continues, drawing a parallel with Baudelaire's 'Dandy' of a hundred years earlier, 'does the Absolute Beginner show more clearly *his* aristocratic descent than in his "*air froid*", in the cult of "coolness".'[72]

In the late Fifties and early Sixties the cult of 'coolness' spread across national and class barriers; no doubt it was partly a by-product of affluence, but for a while it did seem that it might undermine the class war and render it obsolete.

'You poor old prehistoric monster,' exclaims the Absolute Beginner:

I do *not* reject the working classes, and I do *not* belong to the upper classes, for one and the same simple reason, namely, that neither of them interest me in the slighest, never have done, never will do. Do try to understand that, clobbo! I'm just not interested in the whole class crap that seems to needle you and all the tax-payers – needle you all, whichever side of the tracks you live on, or suppose you do.[73]

Wollheim shrewdly asks: 'But is this really the end of class, or just of class-consciousness?' And he answers: 'I cannot help feeling that the base upon which the Absolute Beginner stands as he hurls his message of scorn at society is too narrow for us to hope for much from his gesture.'[74]

The world of the Absolute Beginner, he suggests, is 'that of the unconventionally successful: is it not a piece of unjustified social optimism to identify this, unreservedly, with the world of the conventionally unsuccessful?'[75]

Apart from the question of eligibility to enter the classless society, there is the age factor: how old is the oldest teenager? MacInnes himself often wrote that the test of the 'teenage revolution' would come when today's teenagers became tomorrow's parents. With hindsight we can see that most of them conformed and that nothing really changed. The teenagers of the late Fifties and Sixties, whose revolt was anyway so largely a matter of style, were as easily assimilated as their culture was commercialised. After their brief hour of near-autonomy they slotted back into the niches society had pre-ordained for them; the class war continued as before, uncircumvented.

However, *Absolute Beginners* did have an almost cult appeal to the young who read it when it came out. Roy Kerridge went 'wild with joy' and

tried to base my life exactly on that of the nameless hero. The preoccupation with clothes, or 'schmutter', in the novel had a great appeal for me then, and I remember going into a hairdresser's and, with great trepidation, asking for a 'college boy' hairstyle like the Absolute Beginner. Luckily, there *was* such a style! Basing my life on the Absolute Beginner led me into all kinds of trouble, but that wasn't MacInnes's fault – he never thought his book would be used as a Bible![76]

Roy Kerridge at eighteen or nineteen was neither one of the 'unconventionally successful' like, say, Terry Taylor, nor one of the 'conventionally unsuccessful'. He describes himself then as 'timid and bookish'.[77]

When he made the pilgrimage to Hanbury Street shortly before his transformation into a hip teenager, he had a thoroughly uncomfortable time. He was wearing an old grey duffle coat and he could feel MacInnes's disapproval of his appearance. Working-class lads went in for sharp schmutter – duffle coats and scruffiness were the mark of middle-class youth. Nevertheless MacInnes invited him up to his attic, 'one enormous bare room with a tiny hard bed and no other furniture', only two books (one of which was the autobiography of Tommy Steele).[78] In order not to be disturbed when he was either working or asleep, Colin had replaced the doorbell with a fish-eye which lit up instead of ringing. Kerridge seated himself on the bed and tried hard to think of something to say while Colin shaved, eventually blurting out, 'I've got an electric razor myself.'

'I don't care *what* the fuck you've got,' [Colin] roared back, terrifying me into fits! Perhaps he thought I was boasting. He seemed remorseful and took me out to a seedy Indian restaurant, where they knew him, and treated me to a meal. I annoyed him again by saying, 'Africans–West Indians, it's the same thing.' He controlled himself a little better then, and gave me a kindly farewell, slipping me a ten shilling note like a benevolent uncle! Within a year I was in sharp schmutter myself, and trying to work in tailoring factories where I was very much out of my depth. I wrote to MacInnes, but did not dare meet him . . .[79]

Absolute Beginners, whatever else it might be, was a popular success. On 23 September Colin wrote triumphantly to Eric Dadson: 'New book, for a giddy week, hit the Top Six. I feel like Tommy Steele (wish I had his energy, though).'[80]

9
Success and Failure

The two years which followed his illness were productive ones for MacInnes. He not only composed two of his three most memorable novels – *Absolute Beginners* and *Mr Love and Justice* – during this period; he also wrote the majority of the essays collected in *England, Half English*.

Taking stock at the beginning of 1960, in a memo to his publishers – the purpose of which was to extract yet more money in the way of advances – he ventured to 'assess his own status' as a writer.

'The quality I think is there,' he wrote.

I don't dare to estimate its level (I mean by comparison, for instance, with other admired literary names, present and past), but I think it's exceptional enough.

The reputation. There have so far been two stages. First, that reached by the first two novels and by radio/article work: not much, but quite something. Second, the shape of events since *City of Spades*, developed by *Absolute Beginners*, and by the 'key' essays of 1956–59. This has lifted me (thanks more than I can say to MacG & Kee) up to a quite different level. Not 'fame', or anything like it; but to having a *small* but I think *attached* reading public, and, what I think matters much more in the long run, quite a lot of influential, strategically-placed supporters in the whole English cultural scene.[1]

This last remark in particular suggests that MacInnes approached his literary career like a general contemplating an extended military campaign; and certainly his 'Thoughts' book for the years following his spell in hospital is filled with scribbled injunctions to himself to abjure this and develop that in order to live better and/or work harder. It is as though he were deliberately whipping himself up into a frenzy of activity for fear he might otherwise go to pieces.

In late November 1959 Colin had gone to Lincolnshire to pay a visit to his old Nanny for the first time since 1950. He wrote to her on his return, 'It was lovely seeing you again, and I am indeed an idiot to have left it so long before I came: I shall not make the same mistake again.'[2] In fact he never went back there, though he incorporated the early memories refreshed by this visit in his introductory essay to the photographic book, *London, city of any dream*, where he tries to give the impression of a continuing relationship with Nanny: 'When I *sometimes* visit her in Spalding, Lincolnshire, I am *always* touched to see . . .'[3] (my italics). It was his brother, Graham, who kept in touch.

Between 1958 and 1963 Graham and Joan McInnes were living in London. They had expected to resume their old relationship with Colin but found him increasingly tetchy and difficult to entertain. At one family dinner where Nanny was the guest, Colin made no attempt to conceal his boredom and irritation and left immediately the meal was over. He became aggressive and quarrelsome with Graham, who said, when Joan asked him why he stood for it, that Colin had always been able to bully him.[4]

Yet Colin remained proud of Graham and mentioned him in articles and letters. To his wartime friend Hudson Smith, who was thinking of returning from abroad to settle in London, he wrote of his own enthusiasm for the city, adding however that it was a bit short on 'poor man's pleasures' – 'whereas for the rich, it's a fine playground, I imagine; at any rate, my diplomatic elder brother tells me that among his colleagues, it's the No. 2 choice when they're threatened with a change of posting.'[5] And in an article on the dreadfulness of service in England, he describes how Graham, having once been ticked off by a salesman in Harrods for asking for something in the wrong department, overcame his initial irritation and 'grew to be fascinated, till he encouraged, by additional artfully obtuse questions, the salesmen –preachers to prolong [their sermons]; so that he can now give, at diplomatic parties to his colleagues, a vivid imitation of these dialogues which foreign emissaries find hilarious, and the English guests rather painful.'[6]

To his younger half-brother, Lance, who had aspirations to be a writer, Colin gave every encouragement. He wrote him a letter suggesting possible subjects and setting out how many words he should aim to write daily, given that he was a family man with a full-time job at the BBC.[7]

With his mother, who celebrated her seventieth birthday on 30 January 1960, Colin had no contact whatsoever, though there was a story of her in old age he would tell several of his friends. Each of these friends remembers it slightly differently (such are the pitfalls of oral history), but the gist of it is this: that Colin went to help an old lady on to a bus, and it was not until he had done so that he realised the old lady was his mother. What happened next depends on the storyteller: either they proceeded to embrace or – rather more likely – they parted without a word.[8] As with the story of his father's attempted seduction of him in a taxi, the point is not whether this meeting actually took place, but that Colin and his mother should have become so estranged that they *might* meet without even recognising one another.

Throughout 1960 MacInnes bombarded his publishers with lengthy memos on this, that and the other. Most of them were requests for loans or advances, but there were also his thoughts on being 'Angela Thirkell's son' (his ambition was that she should be remembered as Colin MacInnes's mother, rather than he as her son), his reflections on the relationship between writer and publisher ('in spite of inevitable frictions and exasperations, it is so satisfactory, so organic, so entirely *natural*')[9] and his 'Wild Glance at the Book Trade', which he later recycled as an article, exhorting publishers and booksellers to follow the example of trendier leisure industries and market their wares more aggressively.[10]

In one memo he asked (rather in the manner of the BBC's *Any Questions*: 'Does the team think . . .?'): 'Does the firm think that 1960, with two books (plus quite a few more "key" essays) coming out, on top of the initial breakthrough of the others, is going to be the most critical of my career, and of their sponsorship of it?'[11] Among the 'key' essays published in the first half of 1960 were 'The Other Man' (an offshoot of *Mr Love and Justice*, outlining his attitude to the ponce), 'The Englishness of Dr Pevsner', 'Hamlet and the Ghetto' (a defence of Bernard Kops's play), and a self-confessedly Orwellian analysis of cartoons by Giles, Appleby and Osbert Lancaster in 'The *Express* Families'. His enthusiastic essays on the writings of Anthony Carson ('The Game of Truth') and Ada Leverson ('The Heart of a Legend') came later. What Mac-Innes says of Pevsner, in his tribute to this 'thoroughly inside outsider' – that his 'natural instinct is to praise'[12] – is also true of the author of these essays. Colin's generosity of spirit, so blocked in life, poured out in his critical writings. In this respect he matches his own estimation of Orwell, whose 'critical imagin-ation', he reckons, 'was as superb as his "creative" imagination was defective'.[13]

The irony is that at precisely the point at which he felt (justifiably) that 'something biggish is bubbling just under the soil (and even a bit above it) about my writing reputation here in England,'[14] his career – as an imaginative writer, at least – was about to go into a decline from which it would never recover. Of the two 'creative' tasks he had set himself in 1960-61, the jazz play he was writing with Kenny Graham and the *Angus* saga (the novel based on his father's life), neither would see the light of day – *Angus Bard* because he was unable to complete it, and *Cousin Mixed*, as the play was called, for reasons beyond his control.

What precipitated, if not caused, his decline was alcohol. After two years' abstinence as a result of illness, MacInnes had started drinking again. He was not an alcoholic like his father, who had only to touch a drop in order to descend into some subterranean world of his own. Colin was more of a bad drunk: he drank out of self-disgust; he drank to forget. However successful his professional life, his personal life was more or less a blank: no love, only sex – as often as not by arrangement. There were one or two West Indians – not Africans – in London who understood the masochistic desires of certain white men and would, for a consideration, arrange 'scenes' in which fantasies of pain and humiliation could be acted out without anyone getting too seriously hurt. Of course, Colin's sexual experience was not confined to orgies; he went to bed with a variety of people – white, as well as black; occasionally even women. He could be affectionate, but it was sex he wanted, not love; and as he both snored and ground his teeth when he slept, he was not the most restful of bed companions. His ideal lover, according to Victor Musgrave, 'was a black man, preferably a ponce'.[15] He told Terry Taylor that what he liked was to be raped by a black. And he enjoyed shocking friends, particularly women friends, by taking them to seedy bars in places like Paddington and pointing out the pimps. He once took Elaine Bromwich, the sister of a friend who had died of muscular dystrophy (the ballet designer, Hugh Stevenson), to a club in Soho and introduced her to 'a beautiful Muhammad Ali-like black' who had just returned from the Caribbean, where – he told them – he had a string of lorries. Colin said afterwards that he might indeed have a string of lorries in the Caribbean, but in London he had a string of girls.[16] This may have been true, but, as Alexander Weatherson points out, where blacks were concerned Colin was prone to fantasise on their violence and would describe perfectly ordinary people as 'rapists'.[17]

A ponce did not have to be black; it was the activity, not the colour of the man's skin, which fascinated MacInnes. This is the subject of *Mr Love and Justice*, the last of his London novels – or rather, half the subject. The theme of the novel is crime *and* the law, the ponce *and* the copper. It is a highly schematic novel. Frankie Love is a ponce who lacks the ability to love but has a well developed sense of justice; Edward Justice is a copper who loves his woman so much that he compromises himself with the police force, but his sense of justice is defective. The novel moves with an almost mathematical precision towards the inevitable confrontation between Mr Love and Mr Justice. This is not a shoot-out, Western-style, but a recognition or reconciliation: the two protagonists become, as it were, one – hence the title, *Mr Love and Justice*, and not – as it is often thought to be – *Mr Love and Mr Justice*.

'Superficially,' MacInnes writes of the novel,

this is a realistic portrait of the worlds of the police and prostitution, and as such it was kindly acclaimed by not very acute reviewers for its factual accuracy. But my true intention was to write a morality, or religious allegory . . .

The final scene of this novel takes place in a hospital, where both men lie wounded and where each man finally becomes, as the result of his material fall and inner illumination, identical with the other . . . I had hoped this hospital scene would be read in two ways, on two levels, both as what it is, realistically, and also as an allegory of purgatory . . .

That everyone (so far as I know) entirely missed the point of my endeavour may prove artistic incompetence, or perhaps that the religious instinct I thought I possessed was unconvincing . . .[18]

To my mind, *Mr Love and Justice* is a poorer novel than its predecessors to the extent that it is more ambitious. If the two protagonists are to become identical, they must be adequately differentiated to begin with; Mr Love and Mr Justice both lack a human dimension – they have attributes, not souls. MacInnes, like his Frankie Love, is prey to 'that most delicious of intoxications, the excitement of an *idea*'.[19] He is at the opposite pole to Henry James who, in T.S. Eliot's memorable words, 'had a mind so fine no idea could violate it.' This may explain why, whatever his ambition, MacInnes's literary future lay with the essay rather than the novel.

An ominous note in MacInnes's 'Thoughts' book, under 1960, confirms the (mis)direction his imaginative writing was taking: 'Now abandon social scene (for writing, not observation) & pass on to *forms* & essentials.'[20] In his essay writing, however, he remained blessedly free of formal preoccupations. In the summer of 1960 he paid a six-week visit to Nigeria, shortly before that country's independence. While he was still there, staying in Kano – in 'the "dream hotel" travel writers seem so often, and so happily, to discover on their professional ecstatic journeys'[21] – he set down his impressions in the long essay, 'Welcome, Beauty Walk', which forms the centrepiece of *England, Half English*. This essay remains among the best and most vivid things he ever wrote.

Colin was no ordinary traveller and this 'scamper round Nigeria' was no ordinary journey. To start with, his desire to go there was deeply rooted in his London experience of the previous decade, and particularly in his relationship with Richard Hawton Samuel Erizia, whose Ijaw countrymen he made a point of going to visit on his arrival in Lagos. But when he reached Lake Street on the waterfront, even he faltered: 'I passed several times before the house wondering how, or whether, to announce myself. I knew Hawton's mother lived there with his elder and younger brothers Easter-day and Eugene, but not if they knew of my existence or would welcome memories.' His dilemma was resolved by a chance meeting with another London acquaintance, who greeted him with a shout of 'Collins!' and proceeded to act as go-between with Hawton's mother. Still 'it seemed I and my story had scant reality, did not connect up with the reluctantly believed and unproved fact of her son's death in that place "England" ' – which MacInnes, with a neat inversion, denominates 'the Black Man's Grave'.[22]

Through Hawton's two brothers Colin met a cousin who was a seaman, who was finally able to vouch for him – as he explains: 'Eyeing this mariner I suddenly recalled that Hawton once brought home to Camden Town a relation from a ship who saw I was limping with a dislocated toe, asked leave to look at it, and had immediately (and without permission) seized it and set it straight: an incident I could scarcely have invented and he fail to remember. It was indeed the same man . . .'[23]

Once he was accepted by the family, Colin was taken by the brothers to meet their sister, Rose, of whom Hawton had often spoken to Colin as of a 'guardian angel'. When he died Hawton left behind him a baby daughter born in Manchester, and his sister and brothers alike were now determined to enlist Colin's aid in having the child brought out to Nigeria. MacInnes remarks on 'the paradox of this family's instinct to retrieve part of their flesh, and of their neglecting, for two years until my arrival, any practical measures to ensure this.' He pointed out to them that, even if they disregarded the mother's feelings, the girl herself – 'an infant Mancunian suckled on telly, cold rain, and rock salmon with soggy chips' – might not want to come to Africa. But they politely brushed aside such objections and begged him to organise the removal of the child.[24]

What MacInnes does not remark on is the extraordinary way in which life was imitating art. At the end of *City of Spades* (published three years earlier), Johnny Fortune's sister, Peach – 'a guardian angel' – comes to London to train as a nurse. Practically her first words to her brother's English friend, Montgomery Pew, are: 'I come to speak to you of Johnny's baby . . . I tell him he must take it home to Africa.'[25] And Pew, like MacInnes himself, is expected to make the arrangements.

Colin visited the Africanists, Ulli Beier and his wife Susanne Wenger (whom he had met briefly in London), at their home in Oshogbo. He pays tribute to their penetration of Yoruba culture, their willingness to learn from the Africans whom they had originally come to teach. But his day there was spent 'almost entirely in disputations with my hosts'. MacInnes's position, or 'obsession', as he calls it,

happens to be to try, insofar as a writer can at all hope to do so, to stick to the lurching European ship and help it by self-awareness to find courses that may keep it off the reefs among fresh trade winds and new currents; and not to wave it a censorious farewell from the refuge of any enchanted isle. Susanne Wenger, if I understand her, thinks our continent is doomed, and that such real life as may survive can best be re-found in old religious wisdoms. Ulli Beier's position, I believe, is somewhat intermediary, since his encouragement of modern African arts is as active as are his investigations of the old ones.[26]

MacInnes might contrast some African and European customs to the detriment of the latter, yet he never lost sight of the fact that other comparisons might go the other way. 'What one must try to keep in mind . . .' he writes sensibly, 'is that if one admires any quality a people has, one must accept any defect that is its natural companion: one cannot just pick and choose. Thus Africans, divinely unselfconscious, can be inconsiderate to a degree; generously affectionate, they can also be oppressively possessive.'[27]

Intercultural influence was not necessarily a good thing – as he discovered one day when he flung open the window of his room in Enugu and saw,

on the concrete open-air dance floor of the hotel, an exclusively male class of [Victor]Silvester addicts . . . in session: some sailing round in pairs, some moving with solo preoccupation holding an instruction sheet, others being admonished and encouraged by a plump instructor. They performed these ghastly gyrations, I must say, very prettily indeed . . . And yet I shuddered: will the day come, I wondered, when Africans in white tie and tails, and with numerical placards plastered on their backs, will twirl dark belles in leg-revealing tulle and flounces around a huge palais, as may be seen in English temples of the Silvesterian art – occasions which resemble a vast terpsichorian congress of head-waiters and female hairdressers? Will this be the new English cultural penetration to carry on, in even more insidious form, the ground-work of the missionaries and of the British Council?[28]

Such a prospect might horrify MacInnes, but he was enough of his mother's son to relish the absurdity of it as well.

Colin's own behaviour did not always measure up to African expectations. On one occasion he walked eight miles to a village where he hoped to catch a glimpse of the elusive Fulani, the very tall nomadic tribe of cattle-breeders in the far north of Nigeria. When he arrived at the village he was presented to the Ardo, or chieftain, whose 'Old Vic entrance' elicited from Colin a Shakespearean response:

> MacI: Worthy Ardo, I am a traVeller
> Who to famed Shuni's mart has come,
>   seeking
> The wild Fulani.
> ARDO: And where is your cook?[29]

For a white man to travel with nothing but a plastic bag, containing raincoat, underpants and miscellaneous pills, was unheard of in those parts. Colin had brought nothing to drink either, imagining the ubiquitous Pepsi Cola would be available. When he found there was nothing but well water and remembered the amoeba that had lodged in his liver with near-fatal consequences following his previous African trip, he abandoned all thought of seeing the Fulani that day and, 'like a character of P.C. Wren's', tottered out in the midday sun. 'Three miles from a Cola bottle, a huge limousine drew up and I found myself exchanging small-talk through parched lips with an affable minister of education, Northern Region; who told me, with impeccable lack of accent, of his pleasurable sojourns in "the UK", and that himself several times a pilgrim (but by air surely?) to Mecca, he appreciated the English passion for "a trek".'[30]

Colin was a good traveller, in the sense that he relished casual encounters and untoward events. He also enjoyed freedom from the constraints of his life in England – the tyranny of deadlines, the lack of money, the importunity of the Inland Revenue. But above all, he was fascinated by Africa and the Africans. He concludes his Nigerian essay thus: 'Africa is Eden: loved for what is lost, hated because we have lost it: longed for by distant recollection, despised because by ourselves rejected. Out of the Garden, its last inhabitants now make themselves ready to come forth forever. May they carry into the world a closer memory and warmer gratitude than ours.'[31]

'Welcome, Beauty Walk' was published in October 1960 to coincide with Nigerian independence. In mid-September Colin got together an 'illustrious and selective roll' of writers – Charles Causley, Dan Jacobson, himself, John Mortimer and Francis Wyndham – to telegraph best wishes to Chinua Achebe and all Nigerian writers for the occasion.[32] By this time, of course, the unscrambling of Africa generally was proceeding apace. Western liberals averted their gaze from Nkrumah's Ghana and the war-torn Congo and looked instead towards Nyerere's Tanganyika. There, if anywhere, was hope for the future; and the future of Africa was the topic of the hour. In June 1961, *Encounter* published two articles on the subject; one was by Elspeth Huxley, who took the opportunity to mock progressive, anti-colonialist attitudes:

The wickedness that warps humanity in other lands, and especially in your own (you must consider), has passed the darker brethren by; somehow they are purer, simpler, deeper, better than Europeans steeped in mean, self-seeking, self-destructive vices. Somewhere, if no longer in our own behaviour, the golden rule can be realised; somewhere, if never in our own country, the golden age can dawn. Rousseau's fantasies, in short, go marching on. 'The world apprehends,' suggested Laurens van der Post, 'that Africa may hold the secret of its lost and hidden being.' . . . Utopia has been Africanised, like the civil service in Ghana.[33]

Yet, Mrs Huxley suggested, 'far from standing in pristine innocence upon the brink of enlightenment, African society may well be like the soil on which it lives, immeasurably old.' So the question had to be asked: 'Is African culture decadent rather than nascent?' She likened the end of colonialism to 'the end of a frost: it reveals all the burst pipes and leaking valves.'[34] The image is striking because it suggests as unflattering an attitude on her part towards colonialism as to anti-colonialism: it is the frost, after all, which damages the pipes, not the thaw – which merely exposes the extent of the damage. In typecasting Elspeth Huxley as Cassandra, those readers of *Encounter* who rushed into print to challenge her gloomy prognostications, missed this crucial point. She was not denying the inevitability of change; only taking a cool look at the likely outcome.

Colin wrote her an enthusiastic letter, praising the 'power and passion' of her essay but challenging some of its assumptions.[35] In the course of the ensuing and lengthy correspondence between them, Elspeth Huxley remarked, 'I think the perfectibility of human nature impossible.'[36] To which Colin replied: 'So do I. And it is not for *that* I hope: it is that the destruction of human nature should also be impossible.

'Though disillusioned about almost everybody (including, and perhaps specially, myself),' he went on,

I nevertheless greet each newcomer in my existence as if he were quite free from the defects that have made me lose hope in others. This is by no means a 'virtue', rather a sort of built-in and rather absurd faith, of whose disadvantages I am very much aware. Nevertheless, to date it has subsisted. And I feel much the same about Africa. Comes the Congo. Very well – there are Nigeria and Tanganyika. Same thing happens there: very well, there is something else. I am extremely aware of evil and its power, perhaps too much so – in nations as in individuals. But I know evil cannot exist without its opposite; and if the one is eternal, so is the other.

On this splendid note, I bid you an affectionate adieu . . .[37]

Unlike Elspeth Huxley, Colin would not pitch his hopes lower 'in an African way,' hoping 'not for the future of humanity but for particular things for particular people.'[38] His life being devoid of a domestic dimension, he felt public issues in a personal way.

Elspeth Huxley thought that perhaps she lacked 'the didactic impulse normal in most who take an interest in public affairs.'[39] In Colin, the didactic impulse was paramount. As Richard Wollheim remembers, 'He always gave out information in a magisterial way; you simply had to take it from him. He was a great instructor really. Like travellers' tales, except that you never had any idea of the evidence: not, "I went into the village and they do such-and-such," but "They *do* such-and-such." '[40]

Elspeth Huxley was able to admire, if not to share, Colin's 'wonderful summary of hope and faith'. She called it 'the Miranda vision' – that 'feeling one had when young on entering a room or going to a party, that within lurked *the* fascinating character, the perfect man, the instant friend . . .' The vision for her, she admitted, had become 'a bit attenuated'.[41]

The 'Miranda vision' is essentially youthful. In a man approaching fifty it might be less becomingly labelled the 'Peter Pan vision'. Indeed, when Elaine Bromwich sent Colin a specially drawn Christmas card, which included in its design the figure of Peter Pan, Colin reacted suspiciously 'Well, thank you,' he wrote back, '– much flattered; though not so sure I like P. Pan . . .'[42]

Angela Thirkell had been ailing for some time. She had a rare blood disease and had to undergo frequent blood-transfusions. She spent part of the summer of 1960 in St Thomas's hospital and was moved from there, first to a convalescent home near Godalming, and then to another nursing home in Surrey. Cold, lonely and unable to work, she read Gibbon, Proust and Stendhal, complained bitterly of her fate and sent out urgent requests for rum, which was her 'tipple'.[43] She died on the eve of her seventy-first birthday. Parsimonious to a degree, she had amassed a small fortune from her writing and left over £80,000 – but none of it to Colin.

His brothers, Graham and Lance, agreed to offer Colin a third share of the legacy; but he refused it. Whatever she was like, he told Lance, she had given him birth and they should respect her wishes.[44] When they suggested that he might like something out of her Chelsea home, he replied:

'Unless there should be a crate of champagne secreted at Shawfield Street, I most truly cannot dream of *any* thing I'd be anxious for. Thank you most truly: but my own kind of "luxury" (a very real one, and no less egotistic than the dream-house alternative) is to be able to move everything in one taxi.'[45]

The brothers took the hint and sent Colin a crate of champagne. Geoffrey Lawson, who had been an assistant at the Institute of Contemporary Arts in Dover Street and was at that time Colin's chosen literary executor along with Graham McInnes, was with Colin when the champagne arrived: 'He had a few friends round and it was very pleasant. He was much fonder of his mother than he ever admitted.'[46] But the story that Colin liked to tell was of how, when he and Graham took their mother's ashes to Rottingdean to be buried, they stopped for a drink on the way and, entirely forgetting the purpose of their journey, left them behind in the pub.[47]

Colin's refusal of a share of his mother's legacy did not prevent him from immediately 'borrowing' £500 from Graham, who was obliged to get an advance from the Canadian government on the strength of his expectations in order to let Colin have the money. Graham never saw either Colin or the £500 again. He continued to send Colin cigars and champagne at Christmas and on his birthday right up till he left England in 1963 to become Canadian High Commissioner in Jamaica, but Colin never even acknowledged these gifts. Nor did he reply when Graham sent him a copy of his first book of Australian reminiscences, *The Road to Gundagai*, in 1965.[48] Whatever precipitated the breach, Graham's emergence as a fluent and skilful autobiographer did nothing to heal it. While Colin was happy to acknowledge his brother's success as a diplomat and continued to speak of him warmly in that capacity, he could not tolerate the thought of him as a rival writer. When he caught a young friend in the house where he was living reading one of Graham's books, he would not speak to him for days.[49] Quite simply he was jealous: his brother's achievement as a writer, he must have felt, diminished his own. However seriously Graham took his writing it would still seem like a hobby, something he turned his hand to when he wasn't being a diplomat; whereas for Colin writing was the justification of his life.

First there had been his mother; and now, just when the field seemed to be clear for him at last, along came his brother and threatened to overtake him both in terms of output and of popularity. Add to this the fact that Graham's writings cover a territory which Colin had come to regard as his own and his silence becomes more comprehensible, if no less reprehensible.

When his 'junior brother', as Colin told Lance the Nigerians say, completed his novel, *A Garden Full of Weeds*, Colin behaved quite differently. He took a proprietorial interest and gave Lance every assistance, even to the extent of writing – of his own initiative – an enthusiastic letter to their mother's publisher, Hamish Hamilton.[50] But he could afford to be more generous towards Lance because Lance was younger than himself and was not trespassing on what he thought of as his patch.

Of his mother's death, Colin wrote to Hudson Smith, 'Such events put one in the front line, don't they?'[51] and to Eric Dadson, who also sent condolences: 'Thank you for thinking of my old Mum – she and I agreed about nothing, but she put me here on the globe and that was a great tie . . .'[52] In the article he wrote about her two years later (was it chance, or a calculated insult to her memory, that the article appeared in the *New Statesman*, which had always given her books such bad reviews?) he acknowledged that he had 'perhaps been influenced by her indirectly – as we all are by parents of strong character who repel us. Some of the themes I have chosen – or which have chosen me – may have recommended themselves precisely because they were ones that would disgust her. Her example also reinforced an inherent dislike for writing as an end in itself – instead of as revelation, however modest.'[53]

He claimed in the same article that 'as a writer' he found her death 'a liberation'.[54] But such freedom as he gained was more than outweighed by the motivation he lost. Without his mother to shock with his familiarity with the underworld and his rejection of the values she espoused, the urge to write – imaginatively, at any rate – waned. His failure to complete *Angus Bard*, in which his mother was to play so central a role, may not have been unrelated to her demise. The desire, Hamlet-like, to set her up a glass where she might see the inmost part of her, was bound to die with her.

Another death affected Colin more immediately than his mother's had done (mother and son had been estranged for so long that she was, in a sense, already dead to him). On 10 May 1961 he wrote to Kenny Graham: 'Howard Samuel, my millionaire publisher, died last weekend (which I enormously regret since he was a very good man as well as a wonderful man to work with) . . .'[55]

Colin's relations with his publishers at this point were not of the best. He had complained bitterly that the American edition of *Mr Love and Justice* (which had just been brought out by Dutton) was riddled with errors, having followed the first, and very faulty, British edition rather than the corrected second printing. The managing director of MacGibbon & Kee, Reg Davis-Poynter, replied at uncharacteristic length, and with unwonted exasperation: he regretted the errors, of course, but pointed out that speed was of the essence in publishing. Colin's style and themes made his book difficult to place in the United States and the firm had done their best to promote him there – an uphill task, Davis-Poynter wrote, 'in view of the scant success of your American publications hitherto'. Goaded by the 'intemperance' of some of Colin's statements, Davis-Poynter raised the matter of his 'indefatigable importunity as regards finance' and suggested that he would be wise to concentrate his faculties 'upon the work in which you are at present engaged, and for which we have entered into contract with you (and in anticipation of the receipt of whose MS I venture to remind you we have taken unusually generous dispositions for your benefit), so that we may, at the earliest possible moment, produce this volume to our joint advantage.' He addressed the letter to '5 (we are led to believe) Hyde Park Crescent.'[56]

Colin had moved out of Hanbury Street more than a year before and had lodged 'here and there' until he went to Nigeria. In this matter, too, he had importuned his long-suffering publishers. He wrote to them before he left for Africa, asking if he might leave a box of manuscripts in their office for safekeeping. 'And could I,' he added, 'please use the firm's address till I get a new one?'[57] – thereby initiating, with an apparently innocuous request, what was to become a lifelong arrangement. From then on Colin's ever-changing address was a more or less closely guarded secret; even his accountant, trying to agree with the tax inspector on the amount of money to be disallowed for private residence, wrote in exasperation: '. . . if we are to charge any rent . . . I am unable to say you sleep on the embankment and have your letters addressed to MacGibbon & Kee . . .'[58]

Howard Samuel's death, immediately followed by Davis-Poynter's rebuke, meant that Colin had to look elsewhere for funds. He turned once more to his friend in the City, Eric

Dadson. His prospects as he outlined them (books to be published, film rights sold and a contract for the jazz play on which he was collaborating with Kenny Graham being negotiated with the Royal Court Theatre 'at their request') seemed dazzling enough; but he still needed to 'buy time'.[59] Would Dadson consider lending him £500? Dadson would not; but he sent Colin a gift of £100.[60] Colin, when he thanked him, said he would still like to be allowed, on his side, 'to regard this as a debt'.[61] That was the last Dadson heard from him, though the debt – if unrepaid – was not forgotten; it figures on a list of his debts which Colin kept meticulously right up to his death.

The summer of 1961 was largely taken up with negotiations for the staging of *Cousin Mixed*, the music drama about rival black and white African States for which MacInnes had written the libretto and Kenny Graham the jazz accompaniment. George Devine was to direct it and Sidney Nolan to design the sets (the Thames & Hudson book on Nolan, with an introduction by MacInnes, appeared that summer). In July, MacInnes and Graham received an advance from the Royal Court and all seemed set for a production at Christmas or thereabouts. But by the autumn an element of uncertainty had crept into Colin's letters to Kenny Graham. He took the line that they had done all they could and, should the Court pull out, they would be free to offer the show elsewhere. In the event, when George Devine fell ill – he died not long after – all hopes of staging the play faded.

MacInnes and Graham used to fantasise about the opening night. Colin would make up newspaper quotes, such as 'Kenny Graham was seen rushing from the stage door. When asked by a reporter what he thought of it, he said, "They've fucked it up." '[62] When it became clear there was not going to be an opening night there were no recriminations between the collaborators. 'We were right,' was their attitude; they were defeated by external events. They remained friends, though Kenny Graham noticed that after the collaboration Colin 'started going strange; he forced himself to work. Before, the introvert bit was calm and nice. After, he got hard, bitter – not to me personally – in his attitude to the world. What did it, I don't know, because nothing happened. He got more recognition than he expected . . .'[63]

Indeed, the publication of *England, Half English* in September

1961 set the seal on MacInnes's reputation as a perceptive and humane commentator not just on London in the 1950s, but on an impressively wide range of literary and cultural subjects. V.S. Naipaul, reviewing the book in the *Listener*, said of his essay on Nigeria that it rescued the travel writer's art 'from the magazine degradation into which it has fallen'. He went on: 'Here all Mr MacInnes's gifts are displayed, and all his personality. He is shrewd, analytic, at times amused, always tender. Most important, he is capable of delight, and capable of transmitting this delight. This is a rare ability . . . Mr MacInnes is important to half English England, and she is lucky in him.'[64]

Colin returned the compliment when he reviewed Naipaul's novel, *A House for Mr Biswas*, in the *Observer* less than a month later. West Indian novels, he wrote, 'have hitherto remained mere "regional" studies, comparable to those of lesser Scots or Irish authors. What hadn't yet appeared was any total Caribbean portrait which, while still firmly rooted in its island source, might soar to universal meaning. This book has now been written . . .'[65]

As ever Colin's literary enthusiasm spilled over into life and on 19 September he was writing anxiously, nanny-like, to their mutual friend, Francis Wyndham, about arrangements for a dinner at the Café Royal for 'Vidia and Pat' – Naipaul and his wife.[66]

A couple of months later, on 18 November, he arranged, in conjunction with Wolf Mankowitz, a lunch for another literary figure, the poet Robert Graves. This was an act of pure hero-worship. Graves had a special place in the MacInnes pantheon. In 1957 Colin had sent him the catalogue (with his introduction) of the Sidney Nolan exhibition at the Whitechapel; Graves had replied that he was sorry he had missed the exhibition, that Nolan's Australia was about as 'flinty-hearted and bloody' as he had imagined it and that he wished Nolan would do a picture of Mr Micawber prospering in Australia at the end of *David Copperfield*.[67] When Colin sent him another of his works, the poet replied with words of praise and encouragement – 'Keep it up. So few writers do. And there are so few writers anyway' – and expressed the hope that they might meet some day.[68] Colin, though he spurned possessions, framed this fragment and kept it ever afterwards.

When he invited Kenny Graham to attend the lunch he and

Wolf Mankowitz were 'tendering' to Robert Graves, Colin wrote: 'He is (in my own un-humble view) the most top splendid writer of the English scene: in his sixties, young as a lark, bang-on, "professor of poetry" at Oxford (for kicks), wonderful triumphant artist and human person.'[69] Graves, outwardly at least, was just the kind of free spirit Colin adored.

Of the lunch itself, another guest, Richard Wollheim, recalls that 'Graves filled the role assigned to him, came in with his enormous hat, his entourage – like Augustus John.'[70] Charles Causley, who sat on Graves's left, was too nervous to say a word.[71] There were about twenty people there in all, a select gathering to pay homage to the great man. It was not a special occasion, a birthday or anything of that sort. 'What was beautiful about it,' according to David Sylvester, 'was its gratuitousness.'[72]

In an essay on 'Hosts and Guests' (1918), Max Beerbohm wonders at the Romans for using the same word to cover both these social functions. Though they are, of course, interchangeable he suggests that 'in every human being one or other of these two instincts is predominant: the active or positive instinct to offer hospitality, the negative or passive instinct to accept it. And either of these instincts is so significant of character that one might well say that mankind is divisible into two great classes: hosts or guests.'[73]

On this reckoning – as Bryan Robertson, for one, recognised – Colin was 'really a host, never a guest'.[74] Much of his social *gaucherie*, whether deliberate or otherwise, may be attributed to the fact that, though by nature a host, he was by circumstance almost invariably a guest. As Beerbohm points out, 'The host as guest is far, far worse than the guest as host . . . The host . . . is a guest against his own will. That is the root of the mischief. He feels that it is more blessed, etc., and that he is conferring rather than accepting a favour. He does not adjust himself. He forgets his place. He leads the conversation . . .'[75]

Even as host, though, Colin's behaviour was quite unpredictable, as the story Tony Parker tells of his one and only meeting with him amply illustrates:

'In 1961 I wrote my first book,' Parker recalls.

It was called *The Courage of His Convictions* and it was a joint effort, a series of tape-recorded conversations with an habitual offender, a man called Robert Allerton, whom I'd met when I was a prison visitor. The publishers, Hutchinson, had – unknown to me – sent a proof copy to Colin MacInnes. Not long afterwards I got a long and enthusiastic handwritten letter from him, saying how much he'd liked the book and would it be possible for us to meet.

I was very thrilled, flattered in fact that an author of his stature should respond in this way, and I wrote back and said, yes – by all means. He then asked me to lunch and suggested we met at the offices of his publishers, MacGibbon & Kee. I went along and said to the young lady at the reception desk that I'd come to see Mr MacInnes, and she said she didn't know anything about that, he didn't work there, he was one of their authors. But perhaps if I'd like to hang on a bit he would turn up.

Well, I waited and waited. The young lady then said she was going out for her lunch but if I wanted to I could sit there and hang on. A few minutes later the door from the street burst open and there was this very tall, iron-grey haired man in an open-necked shirt, looking rather wild. He said, 'I'm Colin MacInnes, and we're going to have lunch, aren't we?' I said yes. He said. 'Well, hang on a minute. Er, you'd better come with me.' And we marched upstairs to some little office to collect his mail.

There was quite a pile of letters waiting for him. He said, 'Just sit down for a moment while I look through these.' So I sat down, and he went through about twenty envelopes, I suppose it must have been, that were addressed to him. He just looked at the outside and said, 'Ooh, I don't like the look of that one,' and tore it up and threw it away. Then he'd look at another and say, 'That looks like a bill to me,' and he'd tear that up and throw it away. And he'd look at another and say, 'Well, I don't feel like reading this at the moment, but it might be important.' So he'd stuff it in his hip pocket. He went on like this through all twenty letters; he never opened a single one.

Then he said, 'Okay, let's go and have lunch now.' We went downstairs into the street, where he hailed a taxi. I hadn't the remotest idea where we were going. He said to me suddenly, 'Do you like red or white?' I said, 'I'm sorry, I beg your pardon?' He said, 'Do you like red, or white, wine?' It really did seem to me an extraordinary question to be asked in a taxi on the way to lunch. Anyway, he hammered on the glass partition separating us from the driver – this was somewhere in Soho – to make the driver stop. He jumped out of the taxi, said to the driver, 'Hang on,' and dashed into an off-licence. He came out a couple of minutes later with two *enormous* bottles of white wine and jumped back into the taxi, having given the driver the address he wanted to go to – which, to my utter astonishment, was the address we had just come from: MacGibbon & Kee's offices.

So back there we go again, with these two enormous bottles of wine. Back inside, upstairs to the little office. He said, 'There was one of those letters, it might have been important'; and he started rooting through the wastepaper basket looking for one he'd torn up. Then after a bit, he said, 'Oh fuck it, never mind,' and gave up. He took the other letters out of his pocket and said, 'I'll just see what these are about. You open the wine.' He passed me a corkscrew, which he'd fished out of a desk drawer some-where, and a couple of mugs.

I opened the wine and he read his letters, muttering, 'Huh . . . huh . . . huh,' like that. And then proceeded – he did, at least – to drink the wine as though it were water. When I'd opened one bottle, he took that for himself and kept drinking out of it, leaving the other one to me. I only had very little because I'd had nothing to eat and I was still under the – er – misapprehension that we were going out to eat somewhere. Also I was working in an office and I didn't want to go back reeling drunk.

Anyway, Colin chatted away about *The Courage of His Convictions*, this book which he said was so good – the first book he'd *ever* read that was really true to life and how criminals were. I said, 'Well what about your book, *Mr Love and Justice*?' He said, 'Oh, if only I'd known you before I wrote *Mr Love and Justice*, or if only I'd read your book, it would have been a very different book indeed. It's only half right, and what's right about it are the parts you'll know about.' Then he jumped up and went to a shelf, where there were copies of his new book, *England, Half English*. He took down a copy and scribbled something in the front of it, and handed it to me and said, 'Here you are, and I hope you'll accept that as a sort of apology.' I'd no idea what he had written and I really did wonder what he was on about.

Then he said he had to go off somewhere, if I'd excuse him. So I left, clutching the copy of *England, Half English* he'd given me. When I got outside, I read what he'd written in the front – I've got it in front of me now, and it says: 'For Tony Parker, joint author, if he will accept the description, of' – and he'd drawn an arrow across to the title, *Mr Love and Justice*, which was listed on the opposite page – 'with all best wishes from Colin MacInnes, Salisbury, WC.2'. I wondered what on earth he meant by 'Salisbury, WC.2'. It was only several years later that I found out. Some-body told me that Colin had told him about our meeting and said, 'I meant to take him to the bloody Salisbury' – which is a pub, I think, in St Martin's Lane.[76]

When Norman Mailer's *Advertisements for Myself* was published in England, and the BBC producer, Philip French, invited Colin to interview the author, Colin leapt at the opportunity. Towards Mailer his attitude was reverential. In a passage which was edited out of the broadcast version of their interview he told Mailer that his book had revived in him the feeling that 'to be a witness, a worthy witness, of your time is a worthwhile thing.'[77]

The author of 'The White Negro' preached a kind of living which Colin had been practising, to a greater or lesser extent, for a decade. Colin was a hipster almost before the term was invented; he belonged with the 'new breed of adventurers, urban adventurers who drifted out at night looking for action with a black man's code to fit their facts'; he too had 'absorbed the existentialist synopses of the Negro, and for practical purposes could be considered a white Negro.' He might stop well short of the ultimate, but he had something of the hipster's ambition 'to exist without roots, to set out on that uncharted journey into the rebellious imperatives of the self . . . to encourage the psychopath in oneself, to explore the domain of experience where security is boredom and therefore sickness . . .'[78]

Philip French recalls that Mailer, for his part, took the trouble to get hold of a copy of *England, Half English* and read at least some of it before the interview.[79] If he read the essay on 'Pop Songs and Teenagers', he must have been struck by the identical fears voiced both by MacInnes in respect of his teenagers – 'the raw material for crypto-fascisms of the worst kind' – and by himself with regard to the hipster: '. . . it is possible, since the hipster lives with his hatred, that many of them are the material for an elite of storm troopers.'[80] (A further parallel is that both writers reject this scenario in favour of a vision of fulfilment.) The first question MacInnes asked Mailer was about God. They got on famously.

When MacInnes came to write his essay on religion more than a year later, he referred back to this interview with Mailer – who, he said, far from being 'a roaring boy and intellectual hipster', seemed to him to be 'an almost rabbinical moralist'. He was attracted to Mailer's existentialist view of religion. 'According to Mailer,' he explains, 'God is not omnipotent, but dependent on us as we are on Him. Satan was not thrown down from heaven – he tore himself out of it by the force of his own evil, and God could not prevent this. The whole universe – as each human life – consists of a creative and a destructive force. The meaning of our lives is to add to the positive, and repel the negative. Insofar as we do so, we survive eternally in essence. If sufficient of us fail, we help drag the whole cosmos into destruction, and all life, physical and spiritual, comes to an end.'[81]

Yet Colin's spontaneous religious feeling was less apocalyptic, more introspective: it had to do with a consciousness

of an *otherness*, of a reality both in and outside all our lives, in function of which [one] also lives even if, by his deeds, he may deny it. This 'otherness' I can best define as a perpetual sensation that life exists in ways the brain and even imagination cannot apprehend – but of which a powerfully intuitive instinct (which I expect is what the orthodox mean by 'soul') is constantly aware despite itself, and by no act of conscious volition . . . Nor . . . is this a matter of 'belief' at all. To me, this very word is suspect, since it implies blind effort of a desperate will. I would rather say, not that I 'believe' these things, but that after 48 years of thinking, reading and questioning . . . the concept is so real as to impose itself, and thus be beyond belief.[82]

Colin's admiration for Norman Mailer was such that some years later he reproved Roy Kerridge for a remark Kerridge had made in a letter with the words: ' "I don't get on with writers", indeed! I bet you'd like Norman Mailer!'[83]

10

Anarchist Sympathiser

Towards the end of 1961 MacInnes began to take a serious interest in anarchism. Sometime earlier the then editor of the anarchist journal, *Freedom*, Colin Ward, had written to him asking if he realised that he was an 'unconscious anarchist' and suggesting that he might like to write for the paper. But MacInnes did nothing about it at the time. What attracted him to the anarchists now was that, instead of inviting him to join a party, they invited him to come to one. On 20 October he went along to the Anarchist Ball at Fulham Town Hall to celebrate *Freedom*'s seventy-fifth anniversary. He offered there and then to write both for *Freedom* and for Colin Ward's new monthly magazine, *Anarchy*.

From an anarchist point of view, however, Colin did his most useful work not in the pages of the anarchist press (where he published a rare poem on the sentencing to nine months' imprisonment of the Committee of 100 anti-nuclear protester, George Clark),[1] but in *Queen*, the *New Statesman* and *New Society*, where – as an 'anarchist sympathiser' rather than a true believer – he argued the anarchist case.

The limitation of anarchism, as he saw it, was that it was really 'a religion without a god'; there was 'an unconscious deception – or self-deception – about [anarchists'] belief in the innate goodness of man.' Such goodness as individual anarchists themselves exemplified was exceptional; societies were made up of bad men as well as good.

'So, what then?' he had his hypothetical anarchist reply. 'Must we have churches to correct the evil? Dictatorships to coerce [people] into proper conduct? To this I answer no, but also that the anarchist message seems to me incomplete as a total understanding of the human situation. To coerce men by politics or religion is to destroy them. But to appeal to their natural good is not enough.'[2]

MacInnes remained an anarchist sympathiser, happy to promote the politics of the unpolitical from a sceptical distance; and anarchists still count him as a friend. 'We have always had some prominent sympathisers,' Nicolas Walter remarks, 'and they have sometimes done us more good than harm. Colin MacInnes probably did more than any other writer in this country outside the formal anarchist movement to turn the general libertarian revival into a specifically anarchist direction during the early 1960s.'[3]

In politics, though he flirted with anarchism, MacInnes remained essentially a liberal, or even Tory radical. He was happier with specific issues than with philosophies or ideologies. He once impressed Bernard Kops with his handling of a racist priest from Stepney, with whom the two of them were invited to debate the racial issue on the BBC radio programme, *Today*. Kops was all set to castigate this priest, but MacInnes was surprisingly conciliatory in his approach:

He said, Father So-and-So has done very good work, he's done this and that . . . And lulled the priest into a sense of security. He sat there beaming while Colin listed his attributes. Therefore, Colin went on sweetly, it's quite incredible that he should believe in this rubbish about sending the blacks back, etc., etc. – catching the man right offguard! Afterwards he said: 'Bernard, always use the Swiftian approach. Build up the edifice and then remove a single matchstick and the whole lot will come tumbling down.'[4]

Colin himself did not always use the 'Swiftian approach'. When John Sparrow, the Warden of All Souls College, Oxford, made his notorious intervention in the argument over *Lady Chatterley's Lover*, following the 'Regina v. Penguin Books Ltd.' trial, sniffing out heresy in D.H. Lawrence's sexual gospel, and teasing the eminent literary critics among the defence witnesses for their lack of perception in not spotting – or, more charitably, their coyness (or even deviousness) in now drawing attention to – the element of buggery in the novel, MacInnes weighed in with a 'plague on both your houses' argument. He castigated the defence witnesses for 'being trapped, by ignorance, vanity, or fatal good intentions, into appearing in a court of law at all'; and he chided the Warden of All Souls for his 'bold candour about an irrelevance', his attempt to draw 'yet another shabby veil over Lawrence's artistic and human achievement'.[5] Colin may have been especially touchy about accusations about buggery, but he was surely right to defend Lawrence's genius from legalistic sniping.

As a result of this altercation in the pages of *Encounter*, the

Oxford Union invited MacInnes to debate the issue of censorship with John Sparrow – a debate which almost did not take place because of the Cuban missile crisis. The Warden of All Souls, Colin found, was 'as able and deadly as would be expected [and] I reflected I would not like to have him against me in a real court.'⁶ The motion against censorship was carried – but only just. Colin's adolescent experience of debating at Scotch College in Melbourne may have helped; more likely the vote went according to preconceptions. Yet Colin's theory, that 'you are for or against censorship according to whether your temperament is authoritarian or libertarian,'⁷ is a little too pat. Few temperaments are wholly one or the other – certainly Colin's was not. His attitude towards authority, as Kenny Graham points out, was thoroughly ambivalent.

Graham considers himself to be naturally anarchistic: it makes no difference to him where he stands in social terms. He is genuinely contemptuous of authority. Whereas Colin, he believes, was 'the opposite: he wanted to be on top in a situation; but he also accepted that there should be someone telling you what to do.'⁸ Perhaps this was a residue of his army service; he retained a military air about him. When Kenny Graham told him about his desertion from the army after VE Day, Colin was impressed – he could never have done that. The writer, Paul Potts, sums it up most aptly. 'Colin,' he says, 'was not an anarchist; he was an alternative authority.'⁹

MacInnes was by now something of a public figure. His byline appeared in just about every 'intellectual' weekly and monthly in the country, as well as the posh Sundays; and occasionally he even pontificated on the BBC radio *Any Questions* programme – a certain measure of celebrity (for non-politicians). When Timothy Raison founded *New Society* in October 1962, he created a column called 'Out of the way' especially for him. For the first six months of the magazine's existence MacInnes wrote a weekly essay, until the strain of recurring deadlines became too much for him and he opted for a more flexible arrangement – which was better suited to his temperament, if not his purse.

Inevitably there was considerable overlap among articles produced at different times for different papers. But he always tried to suit the subject to the potential audience of whatever journal he was writing for. Thus it was in the *New Left Review* that he took up the cudgels on behalf of Tommy Steele and his manager, John Kennedy (who had just published a book): 'It is this *ignorance* [on the Left] of how show-business works at all – this failure to realise that, within it, authentic art and commercial ballyhoo have always moved together . . . that makes so much Leftist criticism of pop art nagging, sterile and defeatist.'[10] And it was in the pages of the *New Statesman* – where else? – that he defended another favourite pop singer, Helen Shapiro, as well as promoters and impresarios in general, against the Marxist strictures of 'Francis Newton'. Once again he complains that 'writings of the Left about pop arts reveal little real liking for these arts at all; and I do not believe you can "improve" anything unless you are, in some sense, fond of it.' This was the core of his argument with the Left, which he saw as radiating 'disapproval of enjoyment, almost of imperfect life itself'; whereas the much maligned impresarios were 'emotionally involved in the adventure whatever their other motives may have been'[11] (Colin's sympathies, as George Melly acutely remarked in his obituary notice, 'were always on the side of feeling: that was the point').[12]

Colin may have had in mind his relations with his publisher, the late Howard Samuel, when he continued:

Myself, I see nothing reprehensible in this fact, nor in this kind of person. Artistic promotion is so chancy – as it ought to be – that none but a gambler by temperament can really help an artist, and there cannot be an artist, pop or otherwise, who has not been helped on his way, at many critical moments, by intermediaries of this kind: by persons organically involved in discovering artists in the first place, and then in advancing their careers. And for anyone who knows by experience how this relationship operates, it is a crude error to suppose that the impresario temperament can ever be artistically disinterested.[13]

MacInnes, of course, was a bit of an artistic impresario himself, discovering, or re-discovering, and promoting talent. Sometimes the artist to whom he appointed himself PR man was already well known, as in the case of the playwright, Brendan Behan; but still Colin interviewed him on television and wrote a lengthy critique of his work. Like Norman Mailer, Behan had the reputation of being a 'roaring boy': 'The ex-Borstalian, the rebel in trouble with two governments, the interrupter of his own plays in London and New York, the drinker, the singer, the "broth of a boy" persona, have been a gift to columnists and the shame of those who expect of artists that their loftiest aim be the Order of Merit . . .' But MacInnes prophesied that 'of all the writers of my generation . . . the only one who I am certain will be read a century from now, is he.'[14]

In the late summer of 1962 MacInnes was invited, along with Norman Mailer, Henry Miller and others, to the Writers' Congress organised by the publisher, John Calder, at the Edinburgh Festival. There, he writes, 'we all made fools of ourselves for the delectation of the multitudes.' Henry Miller 'was with difficulty coaxed towards the microphone. "What are we all doing here?" he asked of the alarmed McEwan Hall. "We should all be out watching dancing, or painting, or looking at pretty girls. And what's the use of talking about the novel, anyway? It's been dead for thirty years." '[15] All Norman Mailer remembers of Edinburgh is being drunk for two days.[16] It was that sort of occasion, very Sixties – a 'happening'.

After the Edinburgh Festival, Colin went on to visit the home of a new friend. James Campbell is the younger son of the fifth Earl of Cawdor. He was a student of ceramics in London and had friends on the Soho bohemian fringe, including Henrietta Moraes, who was then living in a house in World's End in Chelsea left her by the painter, John Minton. MacInnes and Henrietta Moraes were old friends – though there was, as James Campbell recalls, 'considerable mutual irritation'. It was through Henrietta Moraes that James met Colin. He was only nineteen when they first met, and theirs was 'almost the relationship of a teacher and a pupil'. James was the youngest in his family by about ten years, so he was used to being with older people. Colin was exceptional in that he was the first older person James had met with interests similar to his own.[17]

Colin stayed three or four nights at Cawdor Castle. When he arrived, he asked James where he might buy a bottle of whisky. James, not thinking, replied that he could always help himself from the sideboard. Colin explained, very patiently: 'James, I'm a *secret* drinker – I want a bottle on my bedside table.'

At the time of Colin's visit, James's father, step-mother, elder brother and a step-sister and her husband were all there. At first they were suspicious of Colin, but he succeeded in charming everybody. He wanted to know how a Scottish estate worked: 'He was interested in the whole situation because of his interest in history – he wanted to see the remains of the tribal, feudal thing.'[18] Colin still had a driving licence, and though he could no longer trust himself to drive he could sit beside James, who had a provisional licence, and be driven about by him. They went to Culloden, for instance, to see the battlefield. Ten years later, when MacInnes was preparing an article on Scottish nationalism, he contacted James's elder brother, the sixth Earl of Cawdor. Even Angela Thirkell would have approved.

The early Sixties saw the rise of what Colin contemptuously dismissed as 'wittery' – the stage show, *Beyond the Fringe*, with Alan Bennett, Peter Cook, Jonathan Miller and Dudley Moore, at the Fortune Theatre; the opening of the nightclub in Soho called The Establishment; the launching of the journal, *Private Eye*; and, characteristically bringing up the rear in November 1962, the BBC's bold experiment in satirical television, *That Was the Week That Was* . . .

'The gift of the early Sixties to our country,' MacInnes wrote, 'is said to be that of satire. Great heavens! Swift, La Rochefoucauld or Voltaire understood – and so, to our shame, their readers also did – that satire arises from a tragic sense of life, from a castigation whose inner motive was a horror of society's corruptions and an implied vision of a finer world.' *Private Eye* – for which Colin inaccurately predicted a 'fleeting day of favour' – 'never stands outside the rottenness of the society it purports to flail: it is itself part of this decadence . . .'[19]

But then MacInnes himself – homosexual, alcoholic and radical – was precisely the sort of person that *Private Eye*, in its snobbish, prurient and often reactionary way, despised and pilloried. Instead of being flattered by its attentions, though, Colin reacted hysterically. 'A stout stench of loot on the make,' he wrote, 'surrounds the whole charming enterprise . . . A private eye is a hired spy. We're all hired partly, one way or another; but no one need be a nark save by necessity of cash, or desperately absent talent.'[20]

In his attack on 'wittery' in general, Colin was on safer ground. He pointed out, for instance, that it was deplorable that The Establishment should mount 'a necrophiliac display of photomontages concerning the late Robert Colquhoun', a London-Scottish painter whose behaviour had often led to his being barred the club's doors during his lifetime:

The display seeks to create a legend, profitable to The Establishment, irrelevant to Robert Colquhoun. This is the legend of Soho and of a 'Soho figure'. Both these existed until places like The Establishment moved in.

Now Soho is dead, except commercially. Soho, at one time, owed its reputation to its people: now, the area bestows a bogus reputation on almost anything.[21]

Nonetheless, Colin still liked to live as near as possible to Soho; and towards the end of 1962 he moved into Monty Haltrecht's flat near the British Museum. Haltrecht was initially reluctant, but he eventually 'succumbed', as he puts it, 'to the literary attraction': 'Colin was very experienced at moving in on people. He was always very careful about whom he was nasty to, and then he'd make up for it by being nice to you . . .'[22]

The way he made it up to Monty Haltrecht was by recommending his first novel to various publishers (it was accepted by André Deutsch). But when he did you a favour, Haltrecht found, 'he made such a performance of it that you'd think it was his own achievement.' Haltrecht could not forgive him for being 'untactful in his help'.

In fact, he grew to dislike Colin so much that his second novel, *A Secondary Character*, had to be changed because the publisher thought it potentially libellous – though Colin would have been unlikely to sue. His attitude was, as Haltrecht knew, that 'writers shouldn't sue each other; they should use their pens.'

To Haltrecht, Colin was a 'succubus': 'At first this huge man, so light on his feet, seemed considerate. But he didn't adapt. Gradually the bottles piled up, the black boys came and stayed the night . . .'

Whatever he might write about race, Haltrecht reckons, he was not liberal in his attitude. His treatment of blacks was 'exceedingly peremptory and colonial'. He had 'a blanket contempt, but at the same time he glamourised them. He was always patting blacks on the shoulder and saying, "Look at those wicked eyes." He would go to Cable Street, which was then the place to pick up black boys. He liked an atmosphere of violence. He liked being brutalised.'

Yet he was personally fastidious. He

primped like mad – would spend hours in the bathroom and come out with his wrinkles miraculously smoothed away. I don't know how he did it. He was incredibly meticulous about his clothes. He would go to Cecil Gee's to see the latest fashions. Visiting gay clubs he would know exactly the right thing to wear – I remember how meticulously he would roll up his sleeves so that they came to just below the elbow.[23]

Ray Gosling, who became friendly with MacInnes at this time, agrees with Haltrecht about the meticulousness of his appearance:

. . . he would emerge, white, close cropped hair, a John Wayne of a man, with beautiful skin, in a white T shirt and blue slax like a football coach, with white socks, fine Italian shoes one day and pumps the next. 'Always wear one article of class about you.' He dressed with the same exactitude and style with which he used our common English language.
And then would come the lecturing, hectoring games . . .[24]

Gosling remembers a pub conversation in which Colin remarked in his usual way, admitting no contradiction, 'You have to have read all the classics by the time you're twenty-five, or you never will.' When Gosling countered with a pert question about what constituted a classic, Colin erupted: 'The Classics – you know: Homer. H-O-M-E-R!'[25]

'He enjoyed me,' Ray Gosling recalls,

because I was Provincial and he loathed provinciality . . . He was a Scot, colonial, Australian, world citizen. I remember with what glee he threw at me John Prebble's history of Culloden. Colin was helping give the British Empire back to the natives and make them proud of their own history. I remember his explaining and then pressing upon me a bundle of reprints of an article pleading for a return of the Parthenon ('Elgin') Marbles from the British Museum to Greece. 'Distribute these to your Provincial bores . . .'[26]

MacInnes's earliest attempt 'to initiate a campaign for restoring to their owners the Parthenon marbles at present lodged, like stolen goods at the receiver's, in the British Museum' was a dialogue he wrote in 1957 called 'Greeks and Vandals'. In this an impertinent 'Oriental' interrupts the lecturer in the Elgin Room at the British Museum to challenge him on the legitimacy of Britain's claim to possession of the pride of the Parthenon, and then disposes of all the lecturer's arguments to justify the retention of the marbles. MacInnes included this piece in *England, Half English* along with an introductory note in which he admitted failure in getting a campaign going, but proudly recorded the fact that the Greek newspaper, *I Kathemerini*, had reprinted his article under the title, 'The Loot of the Scottish Lord'.[27]

At the beginning of 1963 he tried again to get a campaign going, this time in the pages of *New Society*, whose editor sent Colin to Athens to test his assertion that the Greeks really cared about the Parthenon marbles: 'I arrived in Athens knowing not a soul nor a word of Greek, but within 24 hours all doors at all levels swiftly opened.'[28] From the Mayor down, every Athenian Colin met endorsed his feeling that the marbles should be returned. In addition to moral considerations the Greeks emphasised an aesthetic one – that the marbles, which were yellowing in the British Museum, would soon be bleached by the sun once they were returned to the Parthenon. He came away more than ever convinced that the marbles were 'a prime national symbol: the Ark of the Covenant, so to speak, of the Greek people'.[29]

This brief visit to Athens – and another to Israel in March for the *Sunday Times* Magazine – provided Colin with a temporary respite from the bitterly cold English winter of 1962-63. By now he had taken over the front room of Monty Haltrecht's flat, in addition to the room he rented, and he kept the gas fire on all night. Haltrecht himself had gone away on holiday. When he returned he gave Colin notice. Colin seemed pleased to encounter opposition at last and left in a matter of days.[30]

For Monty Haltrecht, Colin was a domineering influence he had to escape. For Ray Gosling, he was a mentor he is still happy to acknowledge. But Gosling never had to live with him: 'I was but one of many protégés – he loved taking people up. Moody, petulant, he loved seeing how far disciples would put up with him . . . but his temperament could never stand anyone for very long. Colin was the tall cat who walked on his own.'[31]

The visits to Athens and to Israel provided MacInnes with locales for the opening of a new novel, to be called *Children of Eve*. This was to combine his two current obsessions – anarchism and the Parthenon marbles. The idea was simple: to write a novel which, by dramatising an attempt to steal one of the marbles from the British Museum as a form of 'direct action', would once again draw attention to the anomaly of their presence there. What survives of this project is a few hundred pages of manuscript, top-heavy with contemporary references, dedicated to Colin Ward.[32]

When he was writing *City of Spades* and *Absolute Beginners*, MacInnes had immersed himself in the world of Africans, Caribbeans and teenagers not simply because he saw a good subject in them, but out of a deeper psychological need. By the time he wrote *Children of Eve* he had come to believe his own press cuttings: his reputation as an acute observer of the 'scene' was such that he may have felt all he needed to do was to drape his social observations on a skeletal plot and, hey presto, a novel would emerge. But without the underlying experiential compulsion, the novel did not begin to transcend its journalistic origins.

As journalism, though, the same material provided excellent copy. MacInnes's essay on 'The New British', which the *Spectator* published in June 1963, takes as its text Kipling's 'allegory', *Puck of Pook's Hill*.

'Puck's message to the young,' MacInnes writes,

is that England's essential nature, throughout its history, is to be constantly invaded by new races which the older settlers first resisted, and then accepted once the genius of each race became fused in a fresh form of the English soul. Puck's lesson is that hostility to the invading race is natural, but equally so the wholehearted acceptance of its presence once it has lost its alien nature and is contributing to the mongrel glory of the English people.[33]

The purpose of MacInnes's essay, of course, is to provide a framework for racial tolerance in the new situation of the peaceful invasion of our shores by thousands of Caribbeans, Cypriots, Pakistanis, Chinese and others at a time when the Tories, sensitive to the popular mood, had introduced immigration controls. These peoples, he says firmly, are here to stay; and their offspring, born in Britain, are as British as you and I. Their presence he sees as a marvellous opportunity. 'No one can doubt that England in so many ways is jaded, needing new vitality. Without our wishing it – let alone, God knows, planning it – Puck's voice has summoned from every continent of the globe new races whose chief common characteristic is a grim will to survive. They came here to use us but, in doing so, cannot fail to force us to use them if we are willing.'

If we deny them, MacInnes warns, the future is bleak:

. . . the more I think of racialism . . . the more it seems to me this wretched folly is most dear to most of mankind . . . In race hatred, there seems psychological security; in the lack of it, a freedom that terrifies most souls.

Well, the choice is to be terrified and be; or cling to safe hatreds, and destroy ourselves as no bomb ever will.[34]

This is MacInnes at his rhetorical best. His strictures on racialism have become more, not less, urgent with the passing of the years; and his use of Kipling to make his point is inspired. Kipling, prophet of Empire, dreamed of a federation of the 'white' dominians – Canada, Australia, New Zealand, South Africa, as well as Britain itself – giving the world a moral lead. MacInnes wishes to 'steal Puck from his inventor' and extend, if not subvert, his message. By looking forward rather than backwards (Kipling 'was a backward-looking prophet, as most prophets are'),[35] he offers the reluctant English a vision of a new 'mongrel glory' undreamed of by Puck's creator, with his cast of Romans, Danes and Normans, safely mellowed in the mists of time. The key word is 'mongrel'. A mongrel dog may not look as pretty as the pure breed, but is often more vigorous and intelligent. Kipling, who wrote whole stories in dog language, knew all about that.

In the Fifties Colin had boasted to the BBC radio producer, Richard Keen, that he was the 'best off-beat journalist in London'.[36] This remained true. His range was wide and, more important, he was always extending it. Sport generally had little appeal to him, and cricket in particular struck him as the epitome of tedium. He had suffered as a boy in Australia both because he was no good at the game and because he was English: 'In every street after school hours the kids play with a petrol-tin for wicket, and the Tests arouse frantic passions – of which, when a lad, I was the victim since, as an expatriate "Pommie", I supported the visiting English teams and suffered more "stoushings" when they won a game than when they lost . . .'[37] Yet he could go along to Lords on the last day of the Second Test between England and the West Indies in June 1963 and produce as riveting an account of that titanic struggle as any accredited sports writer.

His opening sentence sets the scene beautifully: ' "They won't be playing," said the taxi-driver, gazing at the windswept skies, and with that joy-in-gloom so characteristic of our island race . . .'[38]

First the weather; next the crowd.

Fearing the elements, only 6,000 of the faithful were now scattered round the wet cold darkening ground. To the west, cossetted in mackintoshes, sat the members, like senators at some Roman spectacle. To the east, the Caribbean contingent were massed enthusiastically as if preparing for

some Birmingham or Little Rock. The displaced clergy wandered pur-
posefully, very gentlemanly chaps mingled with gnarled provincials and
hearties from the Tavern, and dotted here and there were rare members
of the sorority of female fans. 'If a woman was hard pressed for a man,'
one of them said to me, 'this might not be a bad spot to look around in.'

And finally the contestants: 'The West Indians now re-
appeared [after tea], loping, elegant, casual and dynamic . . . The
embattled Close, looking stocky, reassuring and prodigiously
English, stepped calmly on to the ground . . . England were 171
for 5, and had to make 63 to win before stumps were drawn at 6, or
the rain fell, or the light vanished . . .'[39]

The stage thus set, the drama is enacted. Against the lethal
bowling of Hall and Griffith, 'Close was now lashing out, hitting
impossible fours off balls that must have been invisible to any
naked eye but his, and sometimes carrying the war into the enemy
camp by charging down the wicket before the ball had been
delivered. This so disconcerted Hall that, on one occasion, he
stopped, as if in acute physical and mental agony, before hurling
his ball, and began his 80 yard safari all over again.' Brian Close
was running out of partners when he finally fell to Griffith after
he had made 70. With his dismissal the game swung towards the
West Indies. But the result remained in doubt until the very end,
with a one-armed Cowdrey (the other arm was encased in plaster)
coming in to join Allen for the last wicket. There were two balls to
go, and England still needed six runs. Allen was facing Hall; if he
took a single, Cowdrey would have to face the final ball. 'If this
had happened, would Cowdrey (against Hall) have hit a one-
handed six – like Harry Wharton at one of those crucial matches
at Greyfriars School?' In fact, Allen shielded Cowdrey from the
bowling and the result was a draw.[40]

As he 'tottered into St John's Wood Road', MacInnes wondered
how he could ever have described cricket as dull. True, there
could be long periods of boredom, but

when grace descends upon a game, cricket is *mathematically* exciting as well
as physically: it's like a game played by champion athletes who are also
Grand Masters at chess. Additionally, there is the battle against time, and
the correct use of it, which is an allegory of the part time plays in all our
lives . . . A final appeal is that the game is both so polite and yet so
ferocious . . . Cricketers are brave men and, at the same time, so casual, so
apparently unexcited; and when they are locked, as in this match, in a
really vital struggle, and yet behave so coolly, they restore one's faith

in human dignity; for to be valiant and calm is a marvellous human combination.[41]

Such writing brings to mind C.L.R. James's description of Hazlitt (whose account of the fight between Bill Neate and the Gas-man is, of course, a classic sporting essay): 'He takes his whole self wherever he goes; he is ready to go everywhere; every new experience renews and expands him.'[42] MacInnes was no cricket enthusiast but he responded to a dramatic situation. Like Hazlitt, too, he could switch from high art to popular culture and back again without any sense of strain.

In August, *Encounter* published his long critical essay on the writings of James Baldwin. Towards Baldwin, as towards Mailer (and Brendan Behan), Colin's attitude was reverential: 'He is a premonitory prophet, a fallible sage, a soothsayer, a bardic voice falling on deaf and delighted ears.'[43] So that while Baldwin might be criticised as a writer – particularly as a novelist – as a man Colin put him on a pedestal:

If I have called this study, rather romantically, *Dark Angel*, this is not simply because its subject is a Negro, and his temperament and character one of the most lovable of any I have yet encountered . . . It is because my words have also a double meaning: *dark* being not only coloured, but used in the sense of 'dark irony' (*humour noir*) – an insidious, mocking, dangerous, challenging, seriously subversive tone that may be felt in all Baldwin's writings. And when I think of *angels* I think, certainly, of guardian ones, and of visitants from heaven who bring tidings of joy and comfort to mankind, but also remember that angels are perilous creatures, often appearing with a sword to warn, admonish, even scarify and scourge.[44]

In a sense it matters little what MacInnes wrote about Baldwin's work – though he was acute enough to recognise that the author of *The Fire Next Time* had reached a similar impasse to that which Baldwin himself had detected in his precursor, Richard Wright: that 'on the "colour question," he had said his say but did not realise it.'[45] Nor does it matter what Colin had to say about the preoccupations he shared with Baldwin: that same 'colour question', homosexuality, and essay and novel writing. He said similar things elsewhere – and repeatedly. What does matter is how he himself related to James Baldwin. Monty Haltrecht thinks that what Colin liked about blacks was that they represented no intellectual challenge. In this he does Colin an injustice, though it is an understandable one. Colin's psychological make-up was such that he had either to look up or down to people – not only blacks, of course. It was a case of 'bully or cringe', as he admitted to himself in the privacy of his 'Thoughts' book, now long since abandoned. Whereas a measure of equality is possible for most people in their relations with one another, Colin had to go to one extreme or the other. He might indeed be contemptuous of the 'black trash' he picked up in Cable Street, but he worshipped James Baldwin.

One evening when they were having a drink together, the BBC radio producer, Philip French, mentioned to Colin that he and Michael Sissons were editing a book of essays on the immediate post-war period in Britain, called *The Age of Austerity*. Colin expressed interest and, after asking French's permission, got hold of a proof copy of the book from the publishers.

'The next thing I knew,' French recalls,

was that an article appeared in *Queen* [' "An Unrewarded Virtue": Britain 1945–51'] which was nothing more than a summary of the book, with a couple of personal anecdotes thrown in. Colin claimed that I had given him permission, but there was no way I could give him permission to do what he liked with other people's work, and without any acknowledgment. The matter nearly went to court. Lawyers were brought in and *Queen* said they'd fight. In the end, I didn't want to sue; and Sissons reluctantly agreed, though he had no doubt we would have won. That was the end of one – and nearly two – friendships, so far as I was concerned; though when I did later meet Colin again at some do, it was clear that he considered himself the injured party and expected an apology from me! Obviously he was in desperate need of money . . . He must have had a kind of lunatic innocence about what you could do with other people's work.[46]

Colin always needed money; but both his own publishers, MacGibbon & Kee, and Thames & Hudson, with whom he was contracted to produce a text on the Music Hall, had paid him advances and were still awaiting the promised books. So he had no alternative to journalism as a means of earning a living, and journalistically he cast his net as widely as possible.

In a 'Letter from London' published in the *Partisan Review*, he entertained his American readers with a description of high summer in England, known as 'the Silly Season'. He told them about the Great Train Robbery, the Stephen Ward trial and English justice (with a side-glance at the Vassall tribunal and our secret services), and the iniquity exposed by the Profumo affair and known as 'Rachmanism'. Peter Rachman, whose intimacy with Mandy Rice-Davies brought him unwelcome publicity, had in the Fifties bought up slum properties in the Ladbroke Grove area and evicted poor white tenants from their rooms in order to instal immigrants paying three or four times as much rent, thereby making his contribution to the race riots of 1958.

MacInnes ended his 'Letter' with the now obligatory plug for anarchism. In the new-found 'libertarian and egalitarian moral climate', he detected

a growing disenchantment of all kinds of people with party government. Often, of course, this attitude is cynical and irresponsible, and falls into the fatal fallacy of supposing that the government are They, and the public We, and that neither is responsible for the other. Certainly, the glee with which the British nation has gobbled up all the muck that has been raked over in the past few months is far from reassuring. For comment on these scandals has suggested that the patient does not seem to have recognised his own malady; and that many English men and women see these events as if they were happening not to ourselves, but to some imaginary alien country.[47]

Wayland Young subtitled his Penguin Special on *The Profumo Affair*, which came out at the end of 1963, 'Aspects of Conservatism'. The affair, he wrote in the final sentence of the book, 'was the natural fruit of a period of government when convenience was set above justice, loyalty above truth, and appearance above reality.'[48] (It is perhaps a sign of the present times that one now wonders which period of government was *not* like that.) And in 1970 Vernon Bogdanor and Robert Skidelsky wrote in their introduction to *The Age of Affluence* 1951-1964: 'Today we . . . remember the whole period as an age of illusion, of missed opportunities, with Macmillan as the magician whose wonderful act kept us too long distracted from reality . . . Already by 1964 the appeal of the slogan 'Thirteen Wasted Years' was strong enough to give Labour a tiny majority.'[49]

MacInnes offered his thoughts on the condition of England in an article published in *Encounter* in November 1963. It lists those aspects of national life which he found sterile – Lament for Empire; Monarchical Magic; Worship of Law; the Torment of Secrecy; 'Anti' attitudes (anti-American, anti-communist); the Curse of Class; Sexual Straitjackets; and 'Great Men' and 'greatness': 'What we want is not "great men" but that more men shall behave greatly.' In view of how the Sixties turned out, MacInnes's prescription seems remarkably prescient:

We should stop trying to teach, and begin to learn again: from Africa and Asia as much as Russia or America. We should begin to like ourselves, and less our grandfathers. We should banish anyone who says 'Don't' (whatever his authority, and even if he is right) and hearken to anyone who says 'Do', however crazy. We should be gay, libertarian, serious, and energetic, intoxicated with life, not stopping all the time to pick its nose. We should mock smug naysayers, applaud the adventurous. We should stop being 'English', and become English men and women.[50]

In 1964 Colin took the opportunity provided by Time Life Books to revisit the antipodes. He had left Australia in 1930 and though he had written about the country intermittently during the intervening years – most notably in *June in Her Spring* and his essays on Sidney Nolan – he had never been back. Now, armed with a commission to write the 'LIFE World Library' volume on Australia and New Zealand, he spent six months updating and extending his knowledge of Australasia.

He visited Adelaide, scene of a biennial arts festival. 'In theory,' he writes, 'one might think it the last place to welcome thousands of peculiar aliens and exotic artists, but Adelaide rises to the occasion with surprising fervour. Handsome girls pin flowers in visiting button-holes at the airport, wine companies leave discreet gifts in hotel bedrooms for astonished Filipino dancers and Czech actors, and there is a veritable orgy of lavish private entertainment . . .'[51] But according to reports which reached his brother Graham's old schoolfriend, the Australian columnist, Ross Campbell, Colin 'ruffled people' at the festival.

When he went to stay in King's Cross, the Sohoish district of Sydney, Colin invited Ross Campbell to have lunch with him. Campbell had not seen Colin since the famous family reunion of father and sons in Belgium in 1934, but he had read – and admired – some of his books. 'I found him interesting,' he writes, 'but disliked an offhand insolence in his manner – not towards me, but as I recall he was rude to a waitress.'[52]

In Alice Springs, Colin was taken into custody by the local police for 'consorting with Wards of the State'. He had been drinking with an aboriginal. This was against the rules: state wards were not allowed to drink – in theory. An aboriginal, he explains, can opt out of being a ward of the state, but if he does he loses 'protection'. Colin took advantage of the confusion over categories of aboriginals – wards of the state; detribalised and semi-urbanised workers; and half-castes, usually in menial jobs – to turn the tables on the policeman who had arrested him.

Under interrogation, I asked him how on earth a tourist was supposed to know which abo was which? I further asked him – if it's illegal for state wards to drink, why do the publicans all serve them? (The abos *are* very bad drinkers, by the way, and the authorities have certainly got a point there; though I might add I have seen plenty of punch-ups among white Australians, as well as among abos.) I finally asked him, weren't these men Australians – in fact, the very first Australians – and didn't he feel ashamed at treating his fellow-countrymen like pariahs? The fact is that, though I am usually highly circumspect with the police, I wanted him to bring a charge against me so that I could defend it and attack, in court, the whole aboriginal policy of the Federal government . . . Unfortunately, the detective-constable dismissed me with a caution – and I immediately went back to the bar and drank, illegally, with the aboriginals . . .[53]

After he had sent off the draft of this book from Australia, MacInnes was invited to spend three weeks at the offices of *Time* in New York revising the text – a prospect he did not relish except insofar as it gave him the chance to reacquaint himself with New York City after a thirty-year gap.

He arrived on a flight from Hawaii at 7 o'clock on a Sunday morning only to find that the New York hotel he was booked into was not expecting him until the evening, and because of the World's Fair he was unable to get in anywhere else. 'So faced with a homeless Sunday in the city, I dug out my address book and looked up names.' The one he hit upon was 'Minnie W, a coloured dancer' whom he had known in London. He explained his predicament to her on the phone, and she invited him over. She lived in Harlem.

He began to wonder if he was doing the right thing when the cab-driver asked him if he really wanted to go to *that* address. He said yes, so the driver took him to Harlem, dropped him off and did not hang about.

Lost in a host of black faces – 'not the affable, if menacing, dark faces of Africa, nor even the crafty ironic features of Smethwick or Ladbroke Grove. These faces were shut, locked and hostile' – Colin hesitated to ask directions. He approached an old woman, who 'pointed vaguely and said nothing'. Even the children, he noticed, looked at him coldly.

When he found the right building, he entered the lobby and pressed the button to summon the elevator: 'It came down with three large men inside. I stood aside for them to exit, but they didn't: they stayed in the elevator saying not a word. Breathing a prayer, I got in and pressed the floor. Up we went shakily, I waiting for the blow that didn't fall.'

By the time he reached Minnie's door, even the intrepid Mac-Innes, veteran of many interracial incidents, was ready to collapse – and not merely from fatigue.

' "Hullo hon," she said. "How you been keeping?" "Minnie," I answered in severely trembling tones, "you live in a peculiar neighbourhood." She gave me that Negro "will they never learn?" look, sighed slightly, offered me a triple gin, and said, "Well, Collins, you had to find out for yourself." '[54]

MacInnes tells the story of 'this totally minor incident' in order to demonstrate in reverse 'what millions of Negroes have known for centuries in circumstances that were not minor at all . . .' It is the occasion for a familiar – though perhaps none the worse for that – sermon on the need for full racial equality, not mere 'tolerance'. Yet the true significance of this personal experience is expressed earlier in the article.

'Thirty years ago,' MacInnes writes, '. . . the white could go slumming up in Harlem, and the Negro came down town off-duty at his peril. But today, despite the accumulation of white magnificence, and even despite the ghetto conditions of Harlem and Bedford Stuyvesant, New York has become a Negro city.'[55] With a white shirt, a tie and ten bucks in his pocket, the black can wander where he will; whereas whitey cannot. Things have changed – that far, at least.

The purpose of Colin's visit to New York, however, was to work on his book for Time-Life. He anticipated trouble from his editors; therefore he was 'agreeably surprised' to find that they regarded as sacred any flight of fancy, or opinion, or criticism . . .' They were not, like Dickens's Mr Gradgrind, concerned only with facts; but such facts as there were had to be accurate, and the meaning of each sentence clear to their putative reader – 'who is thought to be a Ford car salesman in Wicheta (though some believe he may be a Cadillac salesman)'. There was also 'the convention that the writer doesn't say "I", but uses some abstract formula like "the visitor" when describing his experiences.' Colin spent hours with the 'bright and highly literate' girl researchers, who 'checked remorselessly' on every date and statistic – and thereby saved him from many errors, large and small. His judgments they scrupulously left alone.[56]

Although he was impressed by their rigorous approach – and suggested to his English publishers on his return to London that they might profit by their example – he was 'rather haunted by the relentless pursuit of meaning by these sharp girls'. What, he found himself wondering, would have happened if the poet Shelley had gone to work in the Time-Life Building. And he composed a dialogue, a copy of which he handed to his hosts before leaving New York. A year later he published it under the title, 'Life with Time':

RESEARCHER: May I come in, Percy?
POET: Certainly. Take a chair. What's your worry?
R: No worry, Perce. It's just this line in your copy. I quote:
I am the eye with which the universe
Beholds itself, and knows it is divine.
Well, we feel that needs some little clarification . . .

Needless to say, the clarification it gets transforms the couplet into total gibberish. But in the course of this fragment of dialogue, the brightly literal approach of the researcher, who is polite, efficient, a bit governessy, yet pathetically eager to show respect for a real writer, is established with wit and economy:

RESEARCHER? . . . So to date we have
People in general are the left blue eye . . .
You okay that?
POET: Sure.
R: I'm not harassing you?
P: Not a bit.
R: You want me to clear it with Grace? Oliver? Norm? Anybody else?
P: No, no. You're doing fine. What else?
R: 'With which' – that strikes me as ill-phrased.
P: What do you suggest?
R: 'Through which'. Our researcher on the optical nerve establishes that you don't see *with* the eye, but *through* it.
P: You sure of that?
R: Sure we're sure. We've checked with a professor at MIT . . .

And so it goes on until the poet, goaded beyond endurance, asks for his '$100,000,000,000' and runs.[57]

Working for Time-Life, though, meant that for once in his life

Colin was flush when he returned to London – as the late Frank Norman had good cause to remember. Norman had first met Colin six years before, when *Encounter* had printed an extract from his prison memoir, *Bang to Rights*, and thereafter frequently came across him in Muriel's or at the French pub. Although Norman had a West End success with *Fings Ain't Wot They Used T'Be*, his second play, *A Kayf Up West*, was a flop and Norman himself was close to bankruptcy. He wrote in his obituary of Colin:

. . . Shortly after my play had been thoroughly roasted by the critics he sidled up to me one lunchtime in the French pub and tucked ten, unasked for, ten-pound notes into the top pocket of my jacket.

'Just a little present,' he said. 'Don't hate me.' Before I could utter a word he fled and I didn't see him again for weeks.[58]

What amazed Frank Norman was that Colin did not expect the £100 back. But Colin gave (when he had the money) in the same way as he took. 'Don't pay me back,' he would say to Ray Gosling when he handed him cash, 'unless you become rich, but remember when you're older to do the same for your youngers.'[59] In his attitude to money, at least, he was consistent.

11

Michael X's Pale Pink Friend

Shortly before he went out to Australia and New Zealand, Colin had moved into the basement flat at 43 Harrowby Street, just off the Edgware Road, north of Hyde Park and Marble Arch. Soon after his arrival the area underwent a sudden transformation: the Victoria Sporting Club, one of several casinos to spring into being as a result of the Betting and Gaming Act of 1960, which liberalised gambling, opened on the corner site at the end of the street. The immediate vicinity, which had until then been quietly residential, now reverberated with the sounds of night life – taxis arriving, car doors slamming, shouts and laughter. In self-defence the residents formed an association. At first Colin's sympathies were with the club: 'I strongly suspected that the tenants' committee [was] motivated not so much by the public weal as by a puritanical objection to gambling in itself and, in particular, to people enjoying themselves late at night.'[1] But when the representations of the tenants' association led to the withdrawal of the club's dancing licence and there were dark tales of anonymous threats over the telephone, Colin switched his allegiance and wrote an article in support of the residents.

At Harrowby Street Colin took to giving regular Sunday lunch parties. These were mainly for blacks, but generally included a sprinkling of sympathetic white friends. There would be chicken and rice and peas to eat; and those of Colin's friends who, like Frank Norman, were used to seeing him in the context of street life, were surprised at his fastidiousness over the food and seeing that the ashtrays were emptied and so forth. He also kept cats at Harrowby Street. He was perhaps more domesticated there than he had been at any time since the early post-war days at Regent's Park Terrace, when he had cooked for himself and hung strings of onions in his French-style kitchen.

Even so, there were disruptions. He phoned Frank Norman one morning at 9 o'clock and said, 'You must help me – and bring some money.' When Norman arrived, Colin opened the door a fraction, then came out, pushing Norman back up the steps and into the street. He took his money, went straight to the off-licence and bought a bottle of gin. Only then would he say what had happened. It appeared that 'a young Negro had dumped his blonde, sluttish wife and two kids at his flat: "Only for one night," the man had promised. But they'd been there a week and he had disappeared . . .'

Colin and Frank Norman phoned various agencies – 'it took us all day' – and eventually located a place in the City which took destitute mothers and children.

So we got a taxi. Colin was getting more and more pissed – we were taking slugs straight from the bottle. By the time we got to the place he was having a go at the girl. She never said a word. At the place there was this bloke with a bristly moustache who wanted to take down our particulars. Colin wasn't have any: 'If you didn't spend so much time growing that stupid little moustache, you might be able to do something useful . . .' We simply dumped the girl, the kids and all the chattels – pram, etcetera – we'd loaded into the taxi. Then Colin took me on a walking tour of the City . . .[2]

When the husband (who had been off with another woman) returned after several weeks' absence, he was not at all pleased to discover that Colin had evicted his wife and family.

MacInnes's long visit to Australia and New Zealand had re-awakened his interest in the country of his upbringing. On his return to London he dug out an early attempt at a radio play, *The Baileys*, which the BBC had rejected nearly twenty years before, and rewrote it as a novel. In October 1965 MacGibbon & Kee advanced him £500 for *All Day Saturday*.

The most striking thing about this novel is how it resembles an Angela Thirkell novel turned upside down: not only geo-graphically, with the Victorian 'squattocracy' replacing the English aristocracy – or county folk (each, though, having the characteristics of a closed society or charmed world) – but also in the treatment of the subject-matter. *All Day Saturday*, like a Thirkell novel, is about love, and young love in particular. But whereas the older women in Angela Thirkell's novels are poised and know just how to deflect the 'calf-love' they inspire, in *All Day Saturday* it is an older woman who makes a fool of herself in pursuit of a young larrikin. In Thirkell novels the older people are wise and tolerant of the foibles of youth; in *All Day Saturday* the situation is neatly and precisely reversed: the false wisdom of the older people is tellingly contrasted with the instinctive good sense of the young – in this instance, of Maureen, a girl not unlike June in *June in Her Spring*:

'. . . surprising herself at rebuking a man she had hitherto held somewhat in awe, and realising yet again (as she had come to do more and more) that those older than herself were not always so "wise" as they had so often implied to her they were . . .'[3]

Yet this novel is also a kind of back-handed tribute to mother: there are echoes of Thirkell in the whole treatment of the mating-game as well as in particular snatches of witty dialogue, such as this exchange between the young Nancy and the middle-aged Mrs Baxter:

"Nancy, I think you're a slut."
"And what are you?"
"An older woman is never a slut – she's just a misfortune."[4]

All Day Saturday is less sensuous and idyllic than *June in Her Spring*, but it is also less flawed. There is no equivalent to the 'madness' theme which mars *June*; and there is, in addition to the taut drama which culminates on a tiny square metal platform at the summit of a radio mast hundreds of feet above the ground, a sustained attempt to get at the essential 'Australianness' of Australians. This is where *All Day Saturday* overlaps with the Time-Life book on Australia and New Zealand, and this is where the essayist takes over from the novelist.

MacInnes concludes his non-fiction account of Australia thus:

Traversing this splendid country, with its sun and joy and sports and riches, one may sometimes feel oneself to be in a kind of paradise before the Fall, amid a people committed to a life of mindless beatitude. One cannot imagine Cassandra getting a hearing in Australia, let alone a Moses or a Dante. One cannot even really imagine the existence of a Romeo and Juliet. For in Australia, Cassandra would become a 'personality' on television – her warnings treated with tolerant condescension – while Romeo and Juliet would simply tell their Montague and Capulet elders to stop 'going crook' about the situation, and themselves go off to Manly beach to join a surf carnival. These countries [Australia and New Zealand] have no tragic sense because they believe they have bypassed tragedy . . .[5]

In his novel, too, MacInnes presents Australia (as elsewhere he presents Africa) as a kind of Arcadia:

As is the Australian custom, the men soon drifted together and if they addressed the women, were matey to them as if they were males of a different sub-species; for though their country is uninhibited about sex, it has no conception of sexual mystery, glamour or romance.

And yet, these people *were* in a sense glamorous. They had a vigour, a physical perfection, a confidence, a youthful hope despite their cynicism, that have vanished from the ancient world. At rare moments in history, by a series of accidents never to be repeated, there flower societies in which the cult of *happiness* is paramount: hedonistic, mindless, intent upon the glorious physical instant! And such a benison had fallen, for a decade or so (and despite the recently remembered horrors of Gallipoli and Ypres), on this generation protected by the seemingly fixed radiance of the kind sun and the nocturnal brilliance of the Southern Cross.[6]

In a review of *All Day Saturday* the writer D.A.N. Jones thought he detected an ambiguous attitude on MacInnes's part towards 'European "culture", piano-playing and fancy talk' in the sporty Australian context. 'After reading Graham McInnes's autobiography,' he wrote, 'it's possible, if unfair, to relate this hearty-aesthete conflict to the McInnes family history.'[7]

By an ironic coincidence Graham McInnes's second volume of Australian reminiscences, *Humping My Bluey*, which came out only a few months before *All Day Saturday*, contains an account of the incident on which the novel is plainly based.

'Back at Ballan,' Graham writes of the time when he was sixteen and Colin just fourteen,

the parties went further afield. Sunday tennis now alternated between Bungeeltap and the Lanes' Station, Moorac, about eight miles across the plateau . . . To reach [Moorac] one passed the spidery three-hundred-foot tall lattice towers of the 'beam wireless'. This, together with its twin at Rockbank down on the plain, was the Australian end of the ambitious globe-girdling 'All Red Route' whereby wireless communication was to be ensured between 'the Great Dominions' from Daventry in Britain to Yamachiche in Canada and Ballan in Australia . . .

. . . Colin and I had once been invited to spend a weekend at 'the beam' with the engineers and as a special treat mounted to the top of one of the enormously tall towers. I horrified them all, including myself in retrospect, by crawling out along the lateral beam which capped the tower like the cross-bar of a T and there singing 'It Had To Be You' suspended three hundred feet over the iron-hard grass . . .'[8]

By 1965 the number of immigrants to Britain was said to have reached a million. Popular anti-immigration feeling was reflected in the 1964 general election result at Smethwick where, against the national trend which saw Labour returned to power, a Tory called Peter Griffiths who had conducted an anti-immigration campaign won the seat from the Labour front-bencher, Patrick Gordon-Walker. The new Labour government, however, proved to be just as anxious to control immigration as the Tories had been. Richard Crossman wrote in his diary for 8 July 1965, 'We can't digest the numbers who are now arriving in the Midlands.'[9] But at the same time it sought to alleviate discrimination (as well as salve its conscience) by legislation, and the first Race Relations Bill became law in October 1965.

While successive British governments pandered to popular anti-immigration feeling, from across the Atlantic came unmistakable signs of a black awakening – manifest not only in the writings of James Baldwin, Ralph Ellison (whose novel, *Invisible Man*, though it was first published in 1952, was rediscovered in the early Sixties) and, later, Eldridge Cleaver, George Jackson and Angela Davis, but also in rioting on the streets of Harlem, Chicago and elsewhere in 1964, and Watts in 1965. The political and religious leaders, Martin Luther King, Elijah Muhammad and Malcolm X in the first place, then – in a second wave – Stokely Carmichael, Huey Newton and Bobby Seale, channelled the new militancy in reformist or revolutionary directions according to their respective beliefs. Black Power was the slogan of the hour.

In Britain, following the visit of Martin Luther King in December 1964, the Campaign Against Racial Discrimination (CARD) was set up; and then in February 1965, when Malcolm X arrived, the so-called Racial Adjustment Action Society (the initials, RAAS, spell out a Jamaican swearword) came into being. The founder and leader of RAAS was one Michael de Freitas, better known as Michael X and, later, Michael Abdul Malik – the same Malik who was hanged in Trinidad ten years later for the murder of an English girl called Gale Benson.

In view of what happened in Trinidad, it requires an effort of historical imagination to see Michael de Freitas, ex-seaman and rent collector for the notorious slum landlord, Peter Rachman, as others saw him when he emerged from obscurity in 1965. The event which launched him as a public figure was the assassination in the United States of Malcolm X by Black Muslim extremists not long after Malcolm's visit to England during which the two men had got to know one another. The *Sunday Times* used the occasion to print a story about the 'X brothers'. 'Call me Michael X,' de

Freitas had told the journalist Lewis Chester when they had met in an Indian restaurant in Birmingham during Malcolm X's visit – and Chester did. Malcolm was dead but his 'brother' Michael was alive and living in England. When the article appeared, Michael commented: 'We are in business.'[10]

MacInnes first wrote about Michael in December 1965. 'Michael and the Cloak of Colour' is not one of his better essays, but it does give the impression of an initial wariness, as of two dogs sniffing around each other before deciding whether to fight or be friends.

'For some time,' the article begins,

messages had reached me that Michael wanted to see me, but I hadn't done anything to make contact . . .

I did not want to meet Michael because I don't want to have anything to do with Negro politics . . .

At last Michael himself called me on the telephone and said he wished to see me . . . So far as I can judge, by asking other Negroes what they think of Michael, opinions vary between a cynical assurance he is on the make, and an equal certainty that he is, if a rough diamond, a reliable political animal.[11]

Despite his doubts, MacInnes seems to have accepted at face value Michael's self-identification with Malcolm X, which turned to advantage his hustling background – his pimping and his unsavoury record as one of Rachman's bully boys (though there is some ambiguity in his relations with Rachman: as well as working for him he had also, at one stage, joined forces with social workers who were trying to expose him). If Malcolm, 'by self-education and discipline, became one of the most effective leaders of militant black Americans,'[12] then why shouldn't Michael do likewise for British blacks? The fact that he lacked discipline and in the matter of self-education mistook the wish for the deed was less evident than the superficial resemblances to Malcolm X: both were part-white, both had a hustling past, both became political leaders. That Michael never really changed, but remained a hustler even while playing the part of a militant, was not immediately apparent. What *was* apparent was the need for the kind of political leadership in the black community which Michael seemed to personify. As the Trinidadian film-maker, Horace Ové, says: 'Michael was *hope*.'[13]

The 1958 race riots had exposed the vulnerability of blacks to racist attacks and, though the crisis failed to throw up community leaders, it was then that Michael had his first taste of leadership: he interrupted a peaceful gathering of worried blacks, who were intent on lobbying their MP, to demand a more aggressive vigilante-style response, meeting violence with violence (the applause which greeted his outburst showed that he had success-fully gauged the mood of the meeting).[14] That and his brief opposition to Rachman suggested to him that he might have a political future, and the example of Malcolm X clinched it. Even so, RAAS might never have got off the ground but for an opportune strike of mainly Indian workers in a Lancashire textile factory; whether or not Michael had any influence on the out-come of the dispute, he used it to put himself and RAAS on the political map. He struck the right poses and the newspapers did the rest. It was almost as if, had not Michael so obligingly come forward, they would have had to invent him. They needed him for quotes just as he needed them for publicity; in giving him a measure of notoriety, they were also establishing his credibility. They gave currency to his wildly exaggerated claims of influence and membership and in their pages he emerged as the leader of a national organisation of over 45,000 members, whereas in reality RAAS never at any stage had more than 200 members.[15] To dignify it even so far as to call it an organisation was to misunder-stand the nature of the beast: RAAS was a confection of words, not of deeds; it was a triumph of rhetoric, not accomplishments.

In addition to RAAS, however, Michael X and a few others (MacInnes was the only white involved) formed themselves into a body called Defence, following increased police activity in the Notting Hill area in 1966. The idea was to give blacks better representation and protection in courts and in prisons through the arrangement of legal aid, sureties' to stand bail and prison visits. Although this was locally based, and limited in its ambition to practicalities, Defence too suffered from having – to use a suitably ethnic metaphor – too many chiefs and not enough Indians.

Another founder-member of Defence was the proprietor of a Notting Hill café called El Rio in Westbourne Park Road, in which the initial discussions took place. Frank Critchlow, like Michael, came from Trinidad. When the Rio closed at the end of the Sixties, he opened the Mangrove round the corner in All Saints Road. For two decades these cafés have served as meeting-places for the West Indian community in West London. 'The achievement of the Rio,' Critchlow believes, 'was to get people from all the different islands under the same roof.'[16] Although the Rio became a fashionable place for whites to go in the hippy era, acquiring a certain glamour even from its connection with the Profumo affair through Christine Keeler's association with a West Indian called 'Lucky' Gordon, Critchlow's primary objective was not black-white integration but West Indian integration.

'Out of the Rio,' he says, 'came many things – it was a kind of school, a university. It just happened. It got a lot of hustlers, and it attracted all sorts of West Indians – from Jamaica, Trinidad, Barbados, all the islands. It attracted people who were rebellious and a bit smart, those with street intelligence, those for whom the factory was not their speed.'[17]

In the early days, Critchlow remembers, West Indians in London felt like Englishmen in Africa: they wanted to club together – especially after the race riots. The Rio provided what they needed; it was open seven days a week and through the night as well. 'Frustration and boredom are the enemies for a stranger in a foreign country: what to do with all this energy?' People came twenty-four hours a day and the Rio inevitably became the focal point of tension between the police and the West Indian community. For Frank Critchlow it was a nerve-wracking, as well as exhilarating, time; he carried a heavy responsibility and it drove him near breaking point. 'It was like running a hostel for "bad boys," ' he says. 'You had to gain the respect of a cross-section of West Indians from the different islands.'[18]

Although Critchlow and Michael had a common aim, they did not agree about everything and once even came to blows. The occasion was the big fight between Muhammad Ali and Henry Cooper in 1966. Michael was busily seeking links with the black Muslim movement in the United States and, to that end, had already visited Sweden in order to make friends with both Ali and his business manager, Herbert (son of Elijah) Muhammad (in addition to taking the Muslim name of Abdul Malik). When Ali came to London, Michael supplied him with a bodyguard for the night of the fight (for which he was rewarded with the blood-bespattered shorts the champ wore during the contest – the blood, of course, was Cooper's – which were then paraded in triumph up and down Ladbroke Grove). But Michael wanted to do more than provide a bodyguard; he tried to persuade Frank Critchlow to let him take over the Rio for a week and serve only halal food. Typically, he gave no thought to Critchlow's regular customers; he was only interested in making an impression on Ali and, through him, on the rich and powerful American Nation of Islam. When Critchlow refused, Michael turned nasty. A scuffle ensued; but, fortunately for Critchlow, Michael's henchmen kept out of it and Michael beat a hasty retreat.[19]

Yet Frank liked Michael and in some ways respected him, though he never took him entirely seriously. In Trinidad, he explains, class difference depends on the colour of your skin – the lighter the better. Michael's father was Portuguese, his mother very black. She had aspirations for her pale-skinned son, but he snubbed her. He was ashamed of her – she was an *obeah* woman and, when she came to London in the wake of her son, she turned brothel-keeper. According to Critchlow, 'No real tough has to prove his toughness: Michael was the nice boy who had to show that he was tough – he had to be the *biggest* hustler. He got carried away by his own rhetoric. He was clever (though not clever enough). He was attracted to villains and became one himself.'[20]

In those days, though, as Horace Ové recalls, 'people took Michael pretty seriously. He was a Jekyll and Hyde personality. He was very bright, but he had to kick down his castle after building it up . . . He got worse, angrier and angrier. He was always a hustler, but he got things done. Colin was impressed by this, his ability to organise a demonstration, build a house, start a newspaper . . .'[21] And Critchlow himself says that

Michael was like a general in an army; he liked to organise and plan everything. For instance, when we wanted to set up a place in Reading, we got the place [a barber's shop which was turned into a community centre] but there was some last-minute hitch, some trouble with the agents, and we went down there. But we didn't just go down there. Michael phoned the press and everyone, so when we arrived there they all were, waiting for us . . . The visit became an event.[22]

This was the heyday of 'happenings' and Michael was adept at staging them. Manipulating the media was his forte, not the slow, unglamorous work of building up an organisation. He had no patience for that.

When MacInnes wrote an article on the pros and cons of committees, he did not let on that the particular committee he had in mind was Defence; but some of his frustration comes through. The disease which afflicts the committee, he writes, generalising his experience, 'is the supposition that the object of a committee is to hold meetings, instead of to decide at these meetings what to *do*.'[23]

In 1967 Michael X finally fell victim to his own publicity. The American, Stokely Carmichael, on a visit to Britain, had been thrilling radical audiences and alarming the authorities in about equal measure with his advocacy of black liberation and the revolutionary struggle; he was due to make a speech in Reading on the day – 24 July – that he rather precipitately left the country, and Michael spoke in his place. By Carmichael standards the speech was a disappointment, but Michael did his best to emulate the American and the press response, if not that of the small audience who actually turned out to hear the speech, was gratifying: it was widely described as 'inflammatory'. Among other things, Michael, who himself had a white mistress (as well as a black wife), urged his black brothers to kill any white who so much as laid hands on a black woman. As a result of the publicity the speech received, rather than the speech itself (other black demagogues were saying similar things at Hyde Park Corner and elsewhere and were getting away with, at worst, modest fines), Michael was charged under the Race Relations Act and sentenced to a year's imprisonment. His appeal against the sentence was dismissed and Michael, who was already familiar with the inside of a prison from his earlier hustling days, was sent to Swansea gaol. Only this time, in his own mind at least, he went there as a political martyr, not a common criminal.

MacInnes defended Michael, even after the Reading speech, from the charge of racialism: 'I think a racialist is a neurotic who hates men of another colour *whatever* they do, good or evil. What I think Michael hates is what we do, not what we are. This distinction seems to me crucial . . .'[24]

Colin was not the only white to be charmed or conned by Michael X; but his longstanding familiarity with the West Indian world meant that he was in a position to know better – and in a sense, of course, he did. When he first interviewed Michael he realised that, 'to use a delightful Trinidadian term . . . he was trying to "mamagai" me (that is, delude, give me the soft soap) throughout most of the conversation.'[25] But like many of the blacks who initially supported Michael, he allowed his objective judgment to be overruled by his passion for the cause he represented.

There was another, less creditable reason, though, and that was his susceptibility to the flattery of being singled out by militant blacks as the only trustworthy white. His suspicions of the motives of other whites who cultivated blacks throw his own into question. Frank Critchlow says that though Colin was quite genuine in his desire to improve black-white relations, he did want to be the only one. When a girl reporter from the local paper came to the Mangrove, for instance, Colin was so rude and aggressive that he soon reduced her to tears: 'He made her feel guilty and said things like: "You should thank these people for allowing you to come in here." ' And he would go up to other whites who ventured into the restaurant and tease them, saying, 'Are you enjoying your meal? Do you feel safe in here?'[26] The way in which he made use of his privileged position, not to put others at their ease, but to exacerbate their uneasiness, reveals his own bad conscience.

Colin and Michael had much in common. Both were 'Jekyll and Hyde' personalities who were charming one moment and could turn the next without the slightest warning. Both were fascinated by crime and the criminal mentality – though in Colin's case admiration stopped well short of participation. The essential difference between them was that while Colin might indulge in fantasy, he never let go of reality; whereas Michael, particularly after his prison sentence, lived increasingly in a fantasy world.

MacInnes went to Swansea, along with Horace Ové and others, to meet Michael when he was released from gaol; but after that their friendship quickly cooled. The Michael Abdul Malik who emerged from prison was an altogether tougher proposition from the X whose indulgence in fashionable radical politics had put him there in the first place. And when Michael started systematically conning money out of whites, ostensibly to set up the Black House in Islington (his chief benefactor was Nigel Samuel, the son of Colin's former publisher, Howard Samuel), Colin had the good sense to keep well away. Horace Ové says that Colin 'admired two sorts of black: the militant and bright, and the tough gangster/hood type.'[27] But the two rolled into one was too much even for him.

In the game of bluff and double bluff that Michael played – the

hustler who dealt in drugs pretending to be a political and
religious leader who had *once* been a hustler but had seen the
error of his ways and was now only concerned with the welfare of
'his' people – he got deeper and deeper into fraud, larceny and
threatening behaviour so that eventually he had to flee the
country to avoid prosecution.

The story of what happened when he got back to Trinidad has
been told more than once – the setting up of the Arima
commune; the arrival of a black American con-man called Hakim
Jamal, second only in plausibility to Michael himself, with his
English girlfriend, Gale Benson; the murder of Gale at Michael's
instigation to create a blood bond among his retinue, followed by
a second killing, of an unemployed barber named Joe Skerrit, by
Michael himself; the subsequent discovery of the corpses;
Michael's flight into the Guyanese jungle; his capture and return
to Trinidad; the trial and death sentence; the years in a condemned cell, punctuated by fruitless campaigns and appeals
against his sentence; and then, finally, on 16 May 1975, his
execution.[28]

There can be little doubt that by the time he went back to
Trinidad Michael was a megalomaniac, and that part of his
megalomania, at least, is traceable back to the heady days of the
mid-Sixties in London when this half-white, small-time hustler
was transmogrified into the 'X' – the great black hope of the
English immigrant community – and lionised by all those artists
and writers (MacInnes among them), those pop stars and rich
dilettantes who thought it chic to claim acquaintance with a black
rebel, especially one who was known to have been a hustler in his
unregenerate days.

In September 1966, Roy Kerridge called on Colin at his basement
flat in Harrowby Street. He noticed that, by comparison with
Colin's East End room, it was sumptuously furnished. On the wall
there was a photograph of Prince Charles in short shorts – 'meant
satirically' – and another of a black footballer; Kerridge sank in
his host's estimation for failing to recognise Pele (the 1966 World
Cup having just been staged in England). Colin proudly showed
off a gift he had received from Michael X, which was inscribed:
'For my pale pink friend, Colin'. The reference, Kerridge
explains, would be to the colour of his skin, not his politics.

'As of old,' Kerridge writes,

he was acting as a one-man Council for Civil Liberties for Negroes in 'law trouble' . . . He explained his methods of work to me as follows, to my amazement: 'Every afternoon I go to Hyde Park and pick up a boy. I bring him back here, and later get some sleep. In the morning at about five, I awake and sit at my typewriter until about half-past ten, in an intense, alert frame of mind, sleep being out of the question. My work done I sleep for several more hours, have a meal and go to Hyde Park again.'
. . . When he told me this, stressing that he went with a boy every day, he looked at me keenly and almost defiantly, as if to see whether I was shocked. I was, but I may have concealed it, as he went on in a most cordial vein, inviting me to stay and pointing out a spare divan, saying, 'I don't mind *who* you bring back.' Evidently he assumed my sex-life was as uninhibited as his own![29]

Roy Kerridge declined his invitation, as Colin must have known he would. No doubt Colin deliberately set out to tease him with an exaggerated account of his own promiscuity in order to draw him out or, failing that, to frighten him off. Whatever his intention, he succeeded in the latter objective.

The hippy era, love generation and drug culture were not really to MacInnes's taste, though he welcomed libertarian initiatives. In November, for instance, he went to Holland to write about a gathering of Provos – the self-styled 'last rebellious group of the welfare state' – celebrated for their tactic of leaving white bicycles all over Amsterdam for anyone to use (the purpose of which, though it was largely frustrated by police promptness in confiscating the bikes, was to protect the centre of the city from the 'tyranny of traffic', while at the same time giving 'a moral lesson of individual social responsibility').[30] In January 1967, he interviewed the young editor of a new publication in London called *Oz*, Richard Neville, whose brushes with the law over censorship in his native Australia had given him a certain advance notoriety.

With its large format and riotous colour, which often obscured the print, *Oz* (like its rival, *International Times*, which was also started in 1966) was instantly recognisable as an underground magazine, opposed to conventional politics, of the left as much as of the right, and preaching revolution by 'obscenity, blasphemy and drugs'. The traditional patterns of work and leisure – the nine-to-five job and telly in the evenings – were the targets of the long-haired young whose standard-bearer Neville was: the counter-culture was very much an attitude of mind, a reaction against industrial slavery at a time when, still cushioned by affluence, people started to question where the endless chain of production led and to talk of post-industrial society.

Neville's pronouncements vis-a-vis his intentions were, in the contemporary manner, vacuous enough. 'I would like to produce a magazine that I would read,' he said; and, 'I question the assumption that a magazine must have a policy at all' – though he went on to say, almost in the same breath, '*Oz* should have the courage to attack its own convictions.'[31] MacInnes was mildly critical of the first London-based issue of *Oz* (and of his own contribution to it) but he was instinctively on the side of rebellious youth in its recurring battle with sanctimonious age. In addition, he had a natural affinity with Australians.

The libertarian atmosphere that spawned the likes of *Oz* and *IT* also affected attitudes to other journals. In the spring of 1967 Stephen Spender's resignation as Consultant Editor of *Encounter* sparked off a public row over the funding of that magazine with CIA money via the Congress for Cultural Freedom. Although *Encounter* had found other sources of support, the subsidy it had received from the CCF was a skeleton in its cupboard. In the Fifties most people (with the exception of Marxists like John Berger and Eric Hobsbawm, who never wrote for *Encounter* as a matter of principle) neither knew nor, if they did, cared about CIA funding – the Cold War mentality meant that it simply was not an issue. The climate of the Sixties, however, was so different that some people, like Richard Wollheim, who had previously written for *Encounter*, ceased to do so when this source of revenue was revealed – in the first instance by Conor Cruise O'Brien. Wollheim, who was deeply opposed to American foreign policy, felt that while *Encounter* might be free of overt censorship, there was negative censorship of a kind with regard to such sensitive areas as Latin America and Vietnam.[32] The editor, Melvin Lasky, denies the charge of censorship and points out that *Encounter* was not afraid to criticise American policy over the Bay of Pigs invasion, for example. He says, 'Where the money came from never determined editorial policy.'[33] But there was another aspect to the row, and the resignation of Lasky's co-editor, Frank Kermode, along with Stephen Spender, had less to do with politics than with the invidious personal position in which he found himself when, called upon to defend a libel action, he received contradictory information about the financing of the magazine.[34]

Colin MacInnes was one of the contributors who took the line that it did not matter where the money came from so long as what they wrote was published without editorial interference. He even wrote a letter to *The Times* in which he defended both Lasky and his predecessor, Irving Kristol. In gratitude, Lasky offered him the co-editorship of *Encounter* after Kermode's resignation. But Colin declined it, saying, 'I would be too troublesome – you only know the nice side of me.'[35] He continued to contribute occasionally to *Encounter*; but its great days as 'the foremost social-intellectual-political magazine our country has produced in the last decade,'[36] as MacInnes described it, were over. It can be no more than coincidence, but the fortunes of MacInnes the writer and *Encounter* the journal describe a parallel course, peaking around 1960, then going into a slow decline.

12

Travels Abroad and Trials at Home

On 9 December 1968 MacInnes received a £300 advance for the completed typescript of the first of his two published historical novels, *Westward to Laughter*. He later described this novel as a satire on Stevenson's *Treasure Island*:

> not only because it introduces all the essential elements Stevenson omitted from his Caribbean study (the blacks, to start with), but because it also uses, satirically, the conventional machinery of the blood-and-thunder pirate story. Its narrator, a lad like Stevenson's, is a sort of Candide whose humourless account operates (so I hope) on two inter-connected levels: that of factual description of the horrors he encounters, and yet of a double-take whereby he views them with the eyes of our own day. It is not, in fact, a 'historical novel' at all – at any rate by intention; but a critique of an eighteenth century slave society in terms of the apprehensions of our times, and a satire on the conventions of the Jolly Roger historical novel itself.[1]

Westward to Laughter, like its Shakespearean successor, *Three Years to Play*, was better received in the United States than in Britain. Robert Kiely, a professor of English at Harvard and author of the book, *Robert Louis Stevenson and the Fiction of Adventure*, gave it a long and enthusiastic review in the *New York Times*. 'It is the peculiar and remarkable achievement of *Westward to Laughter*,' he wrote, 'that MacInnes takes an old and popular literary genre in which cruelty is often the custom and uses it to explore the cruel customs of a historical phenomenon, attitudes and effects of which extend into our own midst.' Kiely also admired the eighteenth-century style which, he said, was 'neither a dull, pedantic copy nor a barbarous and artificial mixing of thous and thines. It is the invention of a disciplined mind and a sensitive ear, an imitation not so much of the detailed habits of one or two writers but rather of the rhythm, tone and usage common to a number of British writers in the first half of the eighteenth century.'[2]

In this respect, *Westward to Laughter* is not so much a radical departure as a continuation from *City of Spades* and *Absolute Beginners*, in which MacInnes also 'invented' languages, in the first instance for blacks, and then for teenagers. In other respects, too, the novel is recognisably a MacInnes production: the picaresque form, the emphasis on types rather than individuals, the peculiar relationship of innocence and sleaziness, as well as that inescapable didactic impulse. Yet, for an admirer of the earlier, contemporary moral fables, this latter exercise is a disappointment, remarkable only for its ingenuity. The satire, if such it be, is at best intermittent; for the most part it is merely pastiche. The intention to provide a critique of eighteenth-century slave society in terms of twentieth-century apprehensions amounts to little more than making the escaped slave rebel leader into a kind of eighteenth-century Michael X. Without first-hand knowledge of the phenomena he purports to describe MacInnes is too far removed from any reality other than a purely literary one.

Three Years to Play, for which he signed a contract in January 1969, is a more substantial work than *Westward to Laughter*. MacInnes invents not only a pseudo-Shakespearean language, replete with puns and stylish word-play, but also an entire fictitious background for Shakespeare's *As You Like It*, rooted in the Elizabethan equivalent to the London of *Mr Love and Justice* and in Epping Forest. The Arcadian setting of *As You Like It* and the Elizabethan theatrical custom of having boys play the female parts (given an additional twist in this play when some of them disguise themselves as boys) had an obvious appeal for MacInnes.

For his tale of intriguing nobles, jealous authority, Shakespeare and his Dark Lady, he did some research. An unpaid bill from the High Hill bookshop in Hampstead records that he purchased *Shakespeare and the Earl of Southampton* in August 1968 and Hollis's *History of the Jesuits* in November. His notebook for the novel contains extensive notes from A.L. Rowse. (In 1973 he wrote a letter to *The Times* in response to Rowse's claim to have discovered that the Dark Lady of the Sonnets was one Emilia Bassano: 'Sir, Two joys are mine: of Will to be near-spouse,/And now to be laid bare by Dr Rouse' – signed 'E.B. per Colin MacInnes.')[3]

Yet the novel lacks the dimension which would transform it from historical fiction into literature that merely makes use of the historical mode. MacInnes's Dark Lady remarks of Shakespeare's Rosalind: 'She is his dream, of a world that he would wish. But when he speaks true, 'tis through Jaques that rejects this sylvan world, knowing it is not real.'[4] In the novel there is no such infusion of reality; it remains a seductive fantasy, an essentially lonely man's yearning for companionship.

According to MacInnes's contract, *Three Years to Play* was to be delivered to the publisher by the end of March 1969. The £300 advance was paid in six monthly instalments and, on 23 April, Reg Davis-Poynter authorised a further loan of £600, to be paid to Colin over twelve months. The novel was published in 1970.

By the end of 1968 Colin had left Harrowby Street and taken a room in a house in Stanlake Road in Shepherd's Bush. Among the other residents there was a young man whom he nicknamed Monsieur Mustard-seed, from *A Midsummer Night's Dream*. Iain Campbell had read *Absolute Beginners* at boarding school, when he was fifteen, and had wondered how Colin had managed to get it so right. Yet though they were both now living in the same house and shared a love of Shakespeare, among other things, it was some time before they became friends. Campbell blames himself for this; he thinks he was too young and giddy to win Colin's approval at first.

'Colin never lived his life round anyone,' he says, 'you had to live your life round him.' Even then he would only tolerate so much: 'He was totally a loner. You were like an earring – when you began to itch, he took you off. Mind you, he'd hate that remark. He wouldn't have stood for it if you'd said anything like that to him.'[5]

Colin's relationship with Iain Campbell developed along classic MacInnes-and-acolyte lines. Campbell had aspirations to be a writer, and Colin was the only person he'd ever met who gave him any encouragement. But he also put him through a terrifying catechism: 'He'd give you a plot and you had to provide motivations. There was to be no *deus ex machina*.'[6] This was all part of teaching Campbell to be a writer.

Conversations with Colin, Campbell recalls, 'often went like this: "Do you know? No, you don't. Well, I'll tell you . . ." Then he would impart information. Even if you did know, it was better to keep quiet about it and let him tell you.'[7]

Iain Campbell was amazed at the paucity of Colin's belongings: all he had was a typewriter and a trunk to live out of. He never cooked for himself, never so much as boiled an egg at Stanlake Road. But he did have a weekly account at the local café. The off-licence down the road opened at 7 a.m. and when he was drinking Colin became so aggressive that the only thing to do was to keep out of his way. Occasionally he would get Iain to bring in his record-player, but he was only allowed to play Billie Holiday records – nothing else. 'He would give you a lecture on the lack of need for personal possessions. So I once asked him: "What if there was no-one around with Billie Holiday records?" To which he replied, "There always will be someone".'[8]

One day two large West Indian women came to the door. They were Jehovah's Witnesses. Iain was about to send them away when Colin, who was standing in the hall talking to someone on the phone, indicated that he should let them in. 'He had that lovely little smile on his face which meant you were in for some fun. This was all right as long as you weren't on the receiving end.' Colin's room was on the ground floor and it was devoid of furniture except for an enormous double bed:

The two women parked their fat bums on the bed and started in with their Bible quotes. But Colin knew the Bible better than they did and was able to cap their quotes with others. He said to them, 'Think of it: there was this young man, with twelve other young men, out there in the *desert*, in the hot sun . . . Well, you know what they're like at home . . . Now let me ask you a question: what do you think they were up to?' One of the women was so indignant that she called him the Antichrist and an agent of Beelzebub and heaven knows what else. To which Colin sweetly replied: 'And you, dear Madam, are full of Christian brotherly love.' And they ran! Afterwards Colin wondered if, like tramps, they would mark the door with an 'X'.[9]

Just as Colin had no compunction in getting rid of you if you started to bore him, so you were perfectly at liberty to run off if he became tiresome – there was no rancour about it, no recriminations. But there was a sinister side to him. His patronising attitude towards blacks could be dreadful: 'His Lady Bountiful act and his sexual abuse of them did a lot of people a lot of harm.'[10]

Among Colin's intimates at this time was a young part-South American Indian called Patrick Persaud. Persaud had ambitions to become an actor which Colin helped him to realise, and his career was launched when he got a small part in a Marlon Brando film. Colin felt romantically about Amerindians, and to achieve a closer acquaintance with them he determined to visit Peru. In November 1969, by way of preparation, he wrote to the Peruvian embassy in London for names and addresses of Peruvian writers he might contact. The embassy gave him the name of Mario Vargas Llosa and his address in London.[11]

But before he got any further with his plan to visit Peru, he received an invitation from the British Council (much to his surprise, in view of the adverse impression he knew he had created on his East African tour of 1955) to do a lecture tour of South Africa in the summer of 1970. Never one to miss an opportunity to visit Africa, Colin accepted with alacrity. But just then, in January 1970, he learned that his brother Graham was dying of cancer in Paris – where he was the Canadian delegate to UNESCO. Despite the fact that there had been no communication between the brothers for years (and Colin still owed Graham the money he had borrowed from him after their mother's death), Colin was deeply distressed. He borrowed more money from friends for his fare and instantly flew to Paris. He arrived ten days before Graham died but never got to see him. Graham was so ill that he had seen no one other than his wife Joan for weeks; and Joan thought that the shock of seeing Colin after so long might have an adverse effect of him. She believes that Graham probably would have seen Colin but she was not prepared to risk it. Though Colin made fearful scenes, Joan remained adamant and he returned to London without seeing Graham.[12] If the relationship between Colin and his sister-in-law had not been soured by growing mutual antipathy, a happier resolution might have been possible. But Joan could not forgive Colin his neglect of Graham over the years, and she probably felt that his presence would be altogether too explosive for her sadly reduced husband.

Whether as a result of Graham's death or not, Colin himself became ill in the early spring of 1970. Towards the end of April he was obliged to telephone the British Council to inform them that he had recently had phlebitis, now had pleurisy and might also have an abscess on his lung. By mid-June, when he was able to report a clean bill of health, it was too late to go ahead with the tour that year;[13] so it was rearranged for the following year and Colin took advantage of the postponement to revert to his original scheme of visiting Peru.

'The prime event of 1970 for me,' he wrote to Hudson and Margaret Smith at the beginning of 1971, was my excursion to Peru. Among the many obsessions of which I am possessed, is one for the American Indians . . . One has to go up into the Andes, and this I did, to a height of 16,000 feet, nearly killing myself, since I am subject to altitude sickness, or *suffocación*, as the Peruvians cheerfully call it. Very nasty. But not the Amerindians: they fulfilled all my hopes – aloof, stately, withdrawn and glamorous . . .[14]

The Andean ascent, on the highest railway in the world, the FC Central del Peru, was the subject of an article in which MacInnes described

the ghastly experience – and the incredible folly – of Señor Don Colon Martinez (as he invariably became known in Spanish). He had been warned not to attempt the eight-and-a-half-hour journey from Lima to Huancayo in a day, but to take the trip in two or three stages to allow for acclimatisation; above all, he had been warned against starting the journey with a hangover, or eating and drinking anything much on the way up . . .

All these sage counsels Señor Don Colon (renowned for his knowing better than anybody) most presumptuously ignored. The consequence was that, about halfway up (at a mere 7,000 feet possibly), I became afflicted by one of the nastiest sensations I have ever felt. Have you ever dived too deep into water and run out of air on the way to the surface? Flown in an unpressurised aircraft at 10,000 feet or more? If so, you know what *suffocación* is like: for when you breathe in, *nothing happens at all*; nothing, that is, save for a ghastly groan as you suck at non-existent air.[15]

The Peruvians, of course, treated such an everyday ailment lightly. On his arrival at Huancayo, Colin was taken to the municipal hospital where, instead of the oxygen he yearned for, he was offered pills. With the help of his Amerindian guide, Juanito, he staggered from the *farmacia* to his hotel and up two flights of stairs: 'I collapsed on to the bed, "*Muero, Juanito!*" I cried with my expiring breath.' Juanito, however, went out and returned with a sympathetic doctor who rushed Colin to his clinic. There, for two luxurious day, Colin sucked his fill at an enormous tube of oxygen, ate hearty meals and drank the wine that Juanito smuggled in to him. Rather than risk another eight-and-a-half-hours on the spectacular FC Central del Peru, he chose to return to Lima by car.[16]

'. . . one can see why the Latin American poet-novelists are so good,' he wrote to Charles Causley. 'Scenery and all that apart, the social climate is 17th century, if not 16th; providing them with splendid raw material, and the impulse to define the wicked gorgeous chaos.'[17] And to Hudson Smith he wrote:

As for Lima, it is as I suppose most Latin American cities are – viz, wild
extremes of affluence and poverty, and hardly any middle class at all
(though quite a lower middle). Their Spanish is Andalusian (not surprisingly since so many of the invaders came from Cadiz), their manners
affable, and their beauty sensational: everyone is under 25, and I have
never seen so many Romeos and Juliets. Nice to us, too – I mean *los
Ingleses*, since they know we can no longer rob them. Secret police everywhere (even one on duty at the modest hotel I stayed in, and quite openly
– *'Buenas dias, Señor: siempre trabajando?'* *'Si, hombre, y porque no?'*) but if the
foreigner shows no sign of busying himself politically, no trouble. I also
plucked up courage to visit the *barios* which even the Lima police enter
only in tanks. Once was quite enough, even for the intrepid Señor
Colon.[18]

Colin's letters to Charles Causley and the Hudson Smiths were
occasioned by the beginning of another year. As he wrote to the
former,

A New Year duty is to cannibalise last year's address book, and make a
fresh one. Those eliminated are either persons whose identity is totally
mysterious (as Freddy Jswx, 38 (or 9)A, Heftn St, Fulham); or those one
thought one liked, but doesn't now; or those one is ashamed of keeping in
any longer, the initial motive therefore being spurious (as OSBORNE, Jn,
something Chelsea Sq). There remain the Elect: who are mostly business
addresses – also some friends who, though one may not have seen them in
ages, must remain as talismans. So I am dropping a line to some of them,
encouraged by the feeling that, there being no post, I am like Capt Scott
sending postcards from the S. Pole.[19]

Another reason for his sense of isolation was that he had now
moved out of his beloved London. 'I surprised myself a year and a
half ago,' he told Charles Causley, 'by coming for a week to the S.
Coast, and then staying here ever since.'[20]

In an article he claimed he had moved to the country as a result
of a self-imposed journalistic assignment to write about it –
'having set out to scan the country for a week I stayed there for
nearly eighty; so that like Henry Morton Stanley, despatched to
Africa by Gordon Bennett, my life has been altered by this casual
assignment.' He added, though, that 'I strongly suspect the real
and unadmitted [reason] is that weary retreat from urban battle
which often afflicts writers of middle age when, lurching
dreamily among cowpats, they attribute to mature serenity a
move conditioned by exhaustion and defeat.'[21]

Bryan Robertson remembers Colin phoning him to say that he
was in trouble, even that someone was trying to kill him, though

that may have been an exaggeration; it could have been simply that he owed money he was unable to pay back. Whatever the cause, he sounded scared. He said he needed to get out of London for a fortnight or so, and did Bryan think he might go to Hythe and stay with Bryan's sister there?[22] Peggy Little agreed to his coming, and what began as a temporary respite turned into a more or less permanent arrangement: though he was loath to admit that he had found a home, the house on the sea-front at Hythe ('where no one is over 20 or under 60,' as he described the town) became precisely that for him in his last years. Now in his late fifties he had booked his bed, as it were, in the south coast 'geriatric ward'.[23]

The rearranged British Council tour of South Africa, now extended to take in Ethiopia, Malawi, Zambia, Kenya and Uganda as well, was scheduled to run from 24 April to 11 June 1971. But it turned out to be such a disaster that the British Council was obliged to put a stop to it well before the end of May.

The experience of Edge Semmens, who was the Council's man in Malawi, where Colin stayed for a week, may be taken as representative: Colin's behaviour followed the same pattern wherever he went.

His arrival in Malawi passed without incident, apart from his bizarre insistence on addressing the desk officials at the airport as 'Sir'. When he reached the hotel he said he needed a drink and, in the half-hour Semmens stayed with him there, proceeded to knock back three beers. By the time he arrived at the Semmens's house for a party in honour of Mrs Semmens's birthday 'he had obviously progressed well beyond the three bottle mark, and during the party he became extremely aggressive and rude.' The next afternoon, at a radio recording of a discussion with two young Malawian writers, he made it his business to put down the chairman, who was Provost of the University of Malawi; and in the evening, at another party, he managed to insult the Secretary for Education.[24]

The following morning he moved in on the Semmens's, who had invited him to stay before they realised what they were letting themselves in for. 'By noon six empty beer bottles lay around him, as he sat in an armchair flinging remarks, usually nice ones, at anyone who happened by. He smoked incessantly, coughed incessantly. After lunch he went to bed, snored loudly and talked to himself between bouts of coughing . . . Four more beers before leaving for the university . . .' Yet the lecture he gave

was pitched at the right level for a mixed audience, showed an excellent balance between information and humour, and evoked a large number of questions. Admittedly, the small part in which he surveyed the development of the novel was sketchy and controversial, but the delivery was flawless, and interest held throughout. The contrast with the lethargic, cantankerous, beer-sodden wreck of the previous days was quite incredible but, alas, temporary. At the drinks party afterwards he pontificated rudely, brushed comments and people aside, and made up for lost time with the beer . . .[25]

Colin's insomniac tendencies were evident to his hosts when they heard the clunk of the fridge door and the clink of bottles soon after 5 am. By breakfast at 7 am there were five empties waiting to be collected by their four-year-old son, whom Colin had enlisted to fetch and carry for him. Yet in contrast with his behaviour towards adults, Colin was quite natural and charming with this boy and with every other child he encountered on this tour – probably, Semmens reckons, because 'they represented no threat'.[26]

After a break of two days during which he visited Lake Malawi (and spent the entire time in a darkened rondavel drinking beer), Colin returned to the Semmens's for yet another party in which he offended everybody: 'When the first guests rose to leave there was near panic to be clear of the place . . . Nobody was willing to be left with him.' And on the following evening (his last in Malawi), when he was Edge Semmens's guest at a party at the Indian High Commission, 'he said some nice but horribly insincere things to the Indian High Commissioner, and some silly things to others. Q. "Where are you going after Malawi?" A. "What do you want to know for? Are you from Interpol or something?" Q. "Will you be visiting Durban?" A. "Where's that? In South America?" '[27]

Colin aptly described himself as a 'beer-junkie':

Before the third beer of the day he was morose, depressive. Between his third and his seventh he was charming, grateful for all that people were doing for him. After his seventh he began to get stroppy, and by his twelfth he was virtually intolerable . . . His favourite ploy concerned question and statement. If a person asked a question, Colin MacInnes accused him of making a statement rather than asking a question. If he asked an outright question, Colin MacInnes refused to be interrogated. What right had the interlocuter to probe? He resented being interrupted but himself shouted down anyone he disagreed with. The university staff were so incensed with his behaviour that they made an official complaint.[28]

Semmens missed Colin's departure from Malawi as he had other matters to attend to. But someone described to him afterwards the spectacle of 'this white-haired clown skipping and dancing his way out to the aircraft and everyone laughing at him.'[29]

Edge Semmens was mightily relieved to see the back of Colin MacInnes and he and his colleagues in Malawi had the idea of 'striking a Colin MacInnes Campaign Medal (with Bar)'. Yet he could not help but have

a sneaking sympathy for the man. This kind of person inevitably attracts the importunate, the superficial, the name-droppers. He seemed to regard it as his prerogative to prick the bubbles of pomposity, superficiality and importunity whenever these grew large enough to make a big pop. The great misfortune was that, in his cups, he was unable to distinguish adequately between those with a serious purpose and those without.[30]

From Malawi Colin flew on to Zambia (where his first words to the Council representative at Lusaka were that though he might begin by wondering what on earth he had got here, he would end up loving him as all the other representatives did; then he left his raincoat at the airport) and then to South Africa itself. By mid-May the British Council, acting on reports received from Edge Semmens and the other representatives, in Ethiopia and Zambia, had decided to do something. On 19 May telegrams were sent to East Africa to cancel the Kenyan and Ugandan sections of the tour; South Africa was left to decide for itself whether to allow MacInnes to continue lecturing there. On 20 May Colin himself wrote a remarkably cheerful 'mid-tour note' to the tour organiser in London. 'I think I can truthfully report that all is proceeding swimmingly. (Perhaps the kind & harassed representatives might say otherwise, yet I don't think so),' he wrote breezily – perhaps a trifle too breezily. '. . . No "incidents" in any country, so far, thank heaven – partly owing to everyone (even myself!) being on their best behaviour . . .'[31] His only complaint was that he was being pestered by local reporters whenever he got off a plane in a new country: he was probably thinking of a particular girl reporter in South Africa who had the temerity to ask him what he thought of apartheid.

'. . . True,' he continued, 'what is left of my brain has been battered into a pulp by penetrating student questions; my liver wrecked by the generous excesses of universal hospitality; and my natural modesty utterly corrupted by the "honoured guest" treatment of which I feel quite unworthy . . .'[32]

He gave three lectures in rotation: one on writing novels; another on his own current production, *Three Years to Play*, and his view of Shakespeare; and a third on bilingual culture, in which he expressed his delight at the vitality of African and Caribbean English as means of literary expression. These continued to interest his audiences – though his social behaviour got worse, if anything. For British Council representatives the tour had become nothing less than a nightmare; his rudeness became legendary. At a dinner party in South Africa, for example, one of the guests began to tell a story but got no further than 'I heard an interesting story . . .' when MacInnes interrupted him saying, 'Oh, don't tell me that one, I've heard it thirteen times.' At another dinner he was so appallingly rude that his host felt obliged to take him aside after the fish course and remonstrate with him; by the time they returned to the table all the other guests had vanished.[33]

It could not go on. When the British Council representative in Pretoria broke the news to him that the remainder of the tour was being cancelled, MacInnes indignantly demanded an explanation and threatened legal action. Later he relented to the extent of accepting official help in arranging his return journey to the UK, though he insisted on his right – as a free agent – to stop off in Nairobi.

On 19 June, after he had arrived back in Britain, he wrote to the tour organiser, threatening to publish his own account of the whole episode.[34] The reply he received pointed out that he had given offence to a number of people in various countries in a way which was damaging to the British Council's work: if he wished to discuss the matter further, he was welcome to come into the office to do so.[35] At which point he seems to have deemed it wisest to let the matter rest.

MacInnes was already a sick man before the tour began. At the end of 1970 he had gone to a Harley Street doctor for a chest x-ray: this may have been no more than a precaution following his unpleasant experience of *suffocación* in Peru. But later in 1971 he visited a succession of Harley Street doctors who, whatever else they did, were prompt in submitting their bills for professional services rendered. British Council representatives in the countries Colin visited were appalled at his sick appearance and 'graveyard cough'.[36] But even if he had not been sick, the conditions of a British Council tour, with flights from one capital city to another, endless social gatherings and the inevitable lionisation of the visiting celebrity, were guaranteed to bring out the very worst in him.

Between the time of his return from Africa and the end of 1971, MacInnes attended two Old Bailey trials of unusual social and political significance. Both were on pet subjects of his – the first, the *Oz* trial, on youth and obscenity; and the second, the Mangrove trial, on black-white relations.

By the beginning of the Seventies *Oz* had a paying readership in the region of 40,000 – such was the lure of the underground. There had been a number of special issues of the magazine, including a Women's Liberation (or 'Cunt-power') *Oz*, a Flying Saucer *Oz*, an Acid *Oz* and a Gay *Oz*. The Schoolkids *Oz*, No. 28, came about as a result of an invitation from the *Oz* editors – 'some of us at *Oz* are feeling old and boring' – to the under-eighteens among their readers to come forward and edit an issue of the magazine without adult interference. A point which Richard Neville made later was that though it was to be edited *by* schoolkids, *Oz* 28 was not intended *for* them.[37]

But the resulting combination of sexual explicitness and jokiness – summed up perhaps in the cartoon image of a cuddly Rupert Bear endowed with an enormous phallus – was too much for the authorities; and Neville and his co-editors, Jim Anderson and Felix Dennis, rather than the schoolkids involved, found themselves in the dock of the Old Bailey eleven years after the *Lady Chatterley* trial had seemed to clear the way for freer sexual expression. The earlier case – *cause célèbre* though it was – lasted only six days; this one went on for six weeks.[38]

MacInnes's loyalty to *Oz* was part-sentimental, part-ideological, but it did not blind him to its faults and excesses. 'It is a curiosity of literary obscenity trials,' he wrote, 'that "a case" is usually made over the less successful specimens; thus Lawrence was judged (in spirit) on *Lady Chatterley*, and the *Oz* editors on No. 28, one of their less brilliant productions.' But the crucial question was, did the text and images of the Schoolkids *Oz* tend to corrupt and deprave the young? The defence said no; the prosecution – and the judge – yes. 'It is surprising (by which I of course mean it is not) that no prosecution witness and, in particular, no juvenile, was called upon to declare himself corrupted by *Oz* 28.'[39]

MacInnes makes the point that obscenity trials are almost invariably political trials.

For while prosecutions of 'pure' pornography do occasionally occur, the favourite target is precisely some publication that takes sex seriously and thinks it matters. Thus, in its way, our Directorate of Public Prosecutions is an able literary and social critic; and the cases it brings to court are a tribute by conventional morality to the alarm aroused by artists trying to rediscover what social and moral precepts are really relevant to our present lives.

He saw this particular trial as 'one manifestation among many of the new morality of the "silent majority" – whose chief characteristic, both here and in the United States, is its vociferous clamour to deny.'[40]

Historically, the trial was the last backlash of an exhausted puritanism, effective in the short term perhaps – the defendants were convicted, though not of the gravest charge, that of conspiracy; and even the obscenity charges were quashed on appeal – but self-defeating in the long run:

By younger generations the trial will be seen as yet another proof of their elders' mistrust and dislike of them, which they will increasingly reciprocate. Nor do I believe many schoolkids will alter their life-styles because of the trial – rather the contrary. Nor yet do I think that these legal fingers stuck in a shaky dyke to withhold the flood of what the old call 'permissiveness', and the young call living, will hold back the rising waters.[41]

MacInnes succeeds brilliantly in evoking the Gilbert and Sullivan scene inside Court No. 2 at the Old Bailey, with its long-haired and colourfully attired defendants, its trendy advocates and solicitors, its star reporters in the press box, its celebrity spectators and interested schoolkids and, 'surmounting these, a judge in the weirdest fancy-dress of all, who was to tell the court, among so many other things, that the trial which invoked this spectacle was not political.'[42]

By comparison, his description of the Mangrove trial, later in the year, was low-key. A confrontation between young and old, even where the young defendants are convicted, may be exhilarating in the sense that, as MacInnes recognised, the young must be the ultimate victors come what may – the old 'will soon be asking the young to pay our pensions, and maybe even defend us'.[43] No such certainty of ultimate poetic justice hangs over a race trial, even when the defendants are acquitted as they were – by and large – in the trial of the 'Mangrove Nine'.

The trial was occasioned by a demonstration by blacks against the police, which turned into a confrontation in Portnall Road, London w9. The protesters' idea had been to undertake a peaceful march on the three police stations responsible for policing that part of West London, make speeches outside each one of them and then disperse. Initially it went according to plan. But then the pressure of numbers built up to such an extent that skirmishes broke out between police and marchers, each side blaming the other for provocation. As is generally the case with such incidents, there was an instant search for scapegoats.

In a letter to *The Times* shortly after the demonstration MacInnes wrote:

It is now said that 'outside influences', Black Power and so forth, have moved in to exacerbate a hitherto peaceful situation. So far as 'outside influences' go, it must be understood that any provocation of blacks in London anywhere, is known almost instantly to those in other regions, who react just as I hope I would if living, say, in one suburb of Montevideo, I learned that compatriots were being assaulted in another. As for Black Power intervention, I would ask: had the Mangrove been left alone to pursue its peaceful and legal ways, would Black Power have had any pretext, or practical possibility of intervening?[44]

In fact, the police had taken a special interest in the Mangrove restaurant ever since Frank Critchlow had opened it in 1968 – there were two abortive drug raids on the premises in the first half of 1969, after the second of which Critchlow lost his late-night licence. Things came to a head in the Spring of 1970 when, following another police raid, Critchlow was charged with serving food after 11 pm. When Colin MacInnes, who had been invited by Scotland Yard to make suggestions on how relations between police and public might be improved – a new department having just been formed for precisely that purpose – heard of the

attempt to ensure the Mangrove closed at midnight, he tele-
phoned the Yard

and pointed out that this move, if successful, might result in many who
were peacefully eating chicken and peas in the Mangrove at 1 a.m.,
finding other activities, less socially desirable, outside it. For no one
denies that villains might visit this restaurant: just as they do countless
white night-spots I could name. But the point was that, while at the
Mangrove, their villainy, strictly prohibited by the management, was in
abeyance.[45]

The midnight closure was enforced, however, and the 'over-
policing of black people', as one of the Mangrove Nine put it at
the trial, continued. It was in response to this situation that the
August demonstration was organised. The arrests followed some
weeks later, when the police rounded up the nine people they
regarded as ringleaders and charged them with inciting a riot.

The trial, which was one of the longest ever held at the Old
Bailey, was in a way a continuation of the demonstration: street
theatre became courtroom drama, but both were forms of
political confrontation despite the judge's routine denial of
political implications.

During the trial, Colin appeared as a character witness for
Frank Critchlow. Critchlow was amazed at his behaviour in court:
'He put on this different personality – he's not rude! He behaved
like a perfect gentleman.'[46] To Frank's girlfriend at the time,
Sheila Sage, Colin wrote: 'That horrible, horrible stupid trial! My
chief feeling about it was that the "Nine" were really heroic,
sitting it out there week after week listening to all those lies and
rubbish. Anyway, it's nice the goodies won for once in a while – it
so often seems to be the baddies who do.'[47]

When he came to summarise what he owed most to West
Indians, MacInnes listed three things:

1. Patience, tolerance and kindness beyond words.
2. A vision, through them, of what a society looks like when you've none of
the privileges and most of the handicaps.
3. How to write English . . . I have borrowed shamelessly from African
and West Indian English – neither of which are 'broken English' but
fresh, re-created English languages of their own.[48]

This was, so to speak, the official version; but there was another
side to it. In an article on hustlers, MacInnes does not specifically
say that he is thinking primarily of West Indians – indeed, when

he mentions nationalities at all, he confines himself to Europe where, he writes, 'the palm goes to the Italians, since they throw in dollops of utterly spurious charm, with the Greeks as runners-up, because splendidly unscrupulous: not for nothing was Odysseus the legendary hustler of all time.' But the example he gives of a 'perfect specimen' is unmistakably Caribbean: 'Emmanuel Deedes (alas, a pseudonym) . . . lives in that paradise of hustlers – where once a weekly was published actually called *The Hustler* – the Grove, London, W11.'[49]

Mr Deedes's virtues are that he is

unfailingly pleased to see you, at whatever hour, in whatever company and whatever, momentarily, your state of fortune. If he has anything to offer, his hospitality is without stint. He never seems ill-humoured or, though a terrible gossip, argumentative. His chief defect, hustle-wise, is that he is totally unreliable: not through ill-will, or fraudulence, but because he believes his promises, yet has never learned the mechanics of how to keep them . . .

No proposition astounds him in the least, and on only two kinds does he impose an instant veto: on anything that is flagrantly illegal, or deplorably conventional . . . if you asked him to organise for you an orgy of one-legged shoe-fetishists, he would give this serious consideration.

Remarking that he should have lived in imperial Rome, I asked him once what he got out of it all. He sighed, smiled, and said, 'Well, you see, this life, it is a *style*.'[50]

Sometimes during a visit, MacInnes remarks, Mr Deedes will disappear with one of his stream of mysterious callers, 'leaving you, apparently without a qualm on his part, in full possession of his flat.'[51] Yet one possible original for Mr Deedes well remembers an occasion when Colin arrived at his flat in the early hours of the morning accompanied by a young man, and he turned them out as he was going to work; that day his colour television was stolen. He knew Colin was not responsible, but it was too much of a coincidence to be an accident. When he reported his loss to Colin, he got little sympathy. All Colin said was: 'You should've insured it.'[52]

Another possible model for Mr Deedes recalls Colin getting in touch with him and saying he wanted sex. They went to Ladbroke Grove, but there was nothing doing there – nobody wanted to know. So Colin turned to this Mr Deedes, whom he had known for nearly twenty years, and said it would have to be him. But where could they go? Colin was no longer living in London and

'Mr Deedes' by now had a wife and four children. Fortunately, he also had a bisexual friend living in the flat above his who left him his keys when he was away. So they went there, had sex (and it was *sex* – he might curl up in bed beside Mr Deedes and say something loving, but there was no pretence of love) and came downstairs in time to meet Mr Deedes's daughters on their return from school. Colin was soon chatting and playing with these girls . . .[53]

'On reflection,' MacInnes writes,

I have come to think the reason why so many seek out hustlers is not so much that they couldn't make it on their own, as that they like the idea of an intermediary, with whom they can discuss the other prospect both before and after they have met. And the fact that such retrospective chats are so often stories of disaster, doesn't seem to prevent the victims coming back for more.[54]

He himself, he cheerfully admitted, was

a born and perpetual sucker for the hustler: they can spot me coming, anywhere, from a mile off. This is not only due to lust or solitude, but because, however bad or silly they may be, I find their company frequently delightful. Truth to tell, I rather admire them, despite every disillusionment; for their lives have a sort of desperate courage, and isn't their fragile independence, in our structured societies, rather admirable?[55]

Colin's love affair with the hustler-figure sometimes backfired, however. When he was drunk he would pick up, or allow himself to be picked up by, almost anybody; and occasionally he chose the wrong people and got beaten up. Frank Critchlow remembers that once Colin had a rib broken and had to go to hospital.[56] But Colin courted danger semi-deliberately. He could, of course, be extremely provocative. He was forever mimicking West Indian accents, pretending to be a Jamaican, or a Barbadian, or a Trinidadian. Critchlow's friend Sheila Sage cannot even recall what his normal voice was like. 'When he wasn't drunk and offensive,' she says, 'he was imitating people.' He would turn up at their flat in the middle of the night clutching a bottle of whisky and Frank would groan: 'Oh no, not Colin. Tell him I'm not here.' But Colin knew perfectly well he was there; putting on a West Indian accent, he would barge straight past Sheila.[57]

When Horace Ové first met Colin, at Michael X's house in the mid-Sixties, he was suspicious and wondered what 'this white man, so tall and aristocratic looking, was doing in the ghetto'.[58]

Colin succeeded in gaining Ové's respect, but his habit of turning up at 3 a.m. with a bottle of malt whisky, waking up the household and settling down to talk till 6 or 7 a.m. did not endear him to everyone. Ové's first wife hated these nocturnal visitations and would ask Horace why he allowed them. On occasion Colin would arrive with his face battered and bruised after some set-to, which Ové found sad – not because he was queer, but because of the type of people he sometimes went with. Ové ascribes it to 'white man's guilt': 'He wanted to get whipped as black people had been by whites. Whites had to pay for it; and blacks had to be violent.'[59]

West Indian friends were amazingly tolerant of Colin's eccentric behaviour; he presumed on their good nature in a way he could have done with precious few of his white friends. Indeed, when he tried it on Kenny Graham, turning up in the middle of the night with his taxi driver in tow, Graham (who had to be up for work at 7 a.m.) would not let him into the house. The driver was so embarrassed that he held back as far as he could to dissociate himself from Colin, who said, 'You want me to cut out?' 'No,' Kenny Graham replied, 'I want you to fuck off.'[60] That was the last he saw of Colin. But West Indians appreciated that, as Horace Ové puts it, 'in identifying with the black world he was trying to find a new family. He found more love in the West Indian family. Got love, too. West Indian emotions are very honest and open, not shrouded in polite forms or suppressed in the English manner.'[61]

In his role of artistic promoter Colin once took Ové, who was a photographer before he turned to film-making, to lunch with an executive from Time-Life. But being Colin he had to put Ové down at the same time as he tried to help him – only on this occasion Ové had the last word. When Ové ordered steak, sauté potatoes and a salad, Colin observed sneeringly, 'It's interesting that, coming from a poor background, you should've ordered basic foods – very interesting.' Colin himself was having avocado vinaigrette. So Horace explained that in Trinidad avocados grow on trees: 'We eat some and feed the rest to the hogs.'[62]

But Colin was a pioneer:

He stands out because he was out there alone. Later everybody freaked out . . . But Colin didn't freak out and move on to the next fashion; he stayed there till he died. He was bitter-sweet. There were lots of nice things about him, but he was no saint. People hated him because he was rude! He would bring round his little lover, show you off to him: 'If you want to know something about photography . . .' But if the boy ventured an opinion, he really caught it: 'Shut up, you ignoramus, what do you know about photography?'[63]

Dispassionate whites may observe, from a comfortable distance, that Colin's behaviour towards blacks was reprehensible and patronising, if not hypocritical and, in the sexual arena, downright exploitative. But few blacks would agree. They were not unaware of his faults but in their view these were far outweighed by his virtues and his commitment. He was, says Horace Ové,

the first white to speak honestly to blacks, as an equal. He didn't mind his Ps and Qs – it might have been better (for him) if he had. He was not patronising – is it patronising to be prepared to help at any hour of the day or night, to go to courts to bail people out? . . . He had a tough personality but he was a gentle man. If you needed help, money, whatever, Colin would be there.[64]

Horace Ové introduced Colin to Calvin Hernton, the black American author of *Sex and Racism*. Typically, Colin at first resisted the idea of meeting Hernton; but when he read his book he was instantly converted and offered to help find him an English publisher.

They met in Soho, at the French pub. Hernton was twenty minutes late. He recognised Colin instantly, standing at the far end of the bar carrying on three different conversations simultaneously. They started drinking. Colin said how much he liked the book, then 'proceeded to harass me with important questions'. It was a kind of intellectual quiz (one question that Hernton still remembers – because he impressed Colin by getting the answer right – from this, or from some other night, was: who was the American general whose name epitomised what was going on in Vietnam? The answer was West[wants]moreland). They drank, talked and argued all evening – but not about the book. When the pub closed they went to an off-licence to buy a bottle of whisky. Colin fell into conversation with someone else and Hernton, who was disappointed that they had not even discussed the English publication of his book, walked out and took a taxi home. When he told Horace Ové what he had done, how he had probably 'blown it' with Colin, Ové was delighted. 'That was ego territory,' he said and he told Hernton that it was the best thing he could have done. Hernton and Colin became firm friends.[65]

One day when Colin got a cheque for £500 he invited Hernton to go round with him while he paid off some debts. The visiting American was amazed at the range of Colin's acquaintance.

First we went to a rich man's house with pictures on the walls, and just stood up, had a drink and left. Next we went to a house in Notting Hill which was falling down and Colin owed the man £2. The man wasn't there, but Colin talked to his family and left the £2 for him . . . We went to people's houses, pubs and off-licences. By the end of the evening he'd paid out about half of the £500 – we ended up at this woman's who'd first helped him to get published and he'd never forgotten [Nancy Shepherd-son] and there he was quite different: he'd make a joke or two but he was respectful.[66]

Hernton thinks there were three or four things involved in Colin's negrophilia: 'the sex, the quasi-masochism of letting himself be ripped off, and the politics – also the renegadeness from his family'. Had he been an American, his writing and his behaviour would have earned him far more of a reputation than he had in Britain. He would have been another Norman Mailer.[67]

13
Cancer Ward

Objectively one may chart a man's life – the early promise, the mature achievement, the later decline. But this is not, of course, how a life is lived. Whereas the biographer may be tempted to equate decline with unhappiness, the truth will inevitably be more complex. For example, was Colin whistling to keep up his spirits when he wrote, early in 1972, to Hudson Smith, '. . . I'm sorry to have to admit that, of each decade of my existence hitherto, I've liked the present one more than the last one. Of course, that depends entirely on health, but given that . . .'?[1] Or was that how he truly felt?

Three months later, in a typed memo to the same recipient on the subject of 'The career literary,' he strikes a more elegiac note:

As time rolls by, silver threads appear among the gold, calendars assume a sinister aspect, and so forth, there is something reassuring in getting some books behind one . . . 1950-this, 1960-that, and 1970-now, become not just vanished epochs, but a past dotted with handsome memorial columns, which are the published books. Especially in later life, I think doing these gives a certain shape to one's existence, which is reassuring. Admittedly, there's not much reassuring about growing older: possibly nothing, really, if one were entirely realistic about it. However, the illusion of permanence is powerful.

By this I do not mean anything as vainglorious as assuming one's word will last forever, and so on. Simpler than that, really: a feeling of having halted time a bit in one's own favour.[2]

Although he assured Hudson Smith there was no particular virtue in being a writer, that it was not an ideal life at all – 'Just living is probably more enjoyable, and does less harm'[3] – in reality he never ceased to take a childish pride and delight in the fact that he had succeeded in making a living, however precarious, out of writing.

'Yet the novelist's life is, in so many ways, a happy one,' he writes in the upbeat conclusion to *'No Novel Reader'*:

for provided he has a resolute and resilient publisher, the health of an Olympic runner, total belief in what he is doing, and an absolute refusal to admit defeat, he enjoys the immense privilege, rare indeed in our institutionalized society, of being monarch of his own tiny kingdom. For as everyone is sucked into offices and factories, who is so 'self-employed' as he? Who other can produce a saleable product, with no raw material save his life, his talent, a felt pen and a foolscap pad?[4]

The novelist, as he grew older, might enjoy a sense of independence and accomplishment; but the man who desired other men had no such consolation. As he writes in a posthumously published essay on Rimbaud,

All love affairs between older and younger human beings are perilous, and those of homosexuals especially so. The older man offers experience, encouragement, admiration, and often material help; the younger, really, offers nothing but his love – yet what a 'nothing' that can be! Most usually, and sadly, the younger takes all the older can give and teach him, and then moves on; and unless the older man is wise enough freely to turn the younger loose in time, what could have become a lasting affection, is apt to end in bitterness and regret.[5]

Colin tried to protect himself from such regrets by being determinedly promiscuous. In his disappointing long essay on bisexuality, *Loving Them Both* (1973) – disappointing because it hides its disingenuousness under a cloak of impersonality – he writes that

even when a male bisexual may incline more towards men so far as numbers of individual relationships go, I think his more serious, if less frequent affairs, are likely to be with women. Thus, a pattern one often finds is that of a man whose emotional-sexual relationship is with a wife (or mistress, or both), while his promiscuous-sexual activity is directed towards men. The bisexual might thus be seen to get the best of both worlds, if one believes that all men are instinctively promiscuous, and that homosexual relationships are essentially transitory.[6]

At first glance, this brave new world may seem to have attractive possibilities; but on closer examination it turns out to be the old, familiar double standard in a new, updated guise.

'Colin once made a very unqueer remark,' Paul Potts recalls: ' "When it's love, it's a girl; when it's pleasure, a boy." '[7] (MacInnes wanted to dedicate *Loving Them Both* to Potts, but the latter told the publisher, Tim O'Keeffe, he did not want that. Colin said to him later, 'You can't stop me thinking of you when I look at it, though', which Potts considered a nicely turned compliment.)[8] In this sense he was the opposite of the stereotype repressed Englishman who *loves* other men – though usually asexually – and only has *sex* with women. Francis Wyndham noticed that Colin would pinch the bottoms of the black mini-cab drivers he dragged around with him and generally treat them 'like chorus girls – with disdain'.[9]

But a bisexual, according to his definition, 'is one who is equally attracted by individuals of both sexes';[10] and with regard to women, MacInnes seems to have been more pursued than pursuing. Mayou Iserentant kept in touch with him by letter (though even she came to regard him in later life as *un ours* – a bear);[11] but apart from her there was no woman in his life with whom, to use his own phrase, he could have a 'serious . . . emotional–sexual relationship',[12] though there was more than one with whom he could have a serious emotional, *non*sexual relationship. In his writings MacInnes might strive to transcend the male chauvinism that came naturally to him; nevertheless he remained something of a misogynist. Indeed, while living at Hythe, he told Peggy Little and her son Marcus that he intended to write a book on misogyny.[13]

A more honest guide to his feelings than *Loving Them Both* is an essay he wrote in the last year of his life called 'Growing Old Gayfully'. In this he admits that 'some gays do feel a hostility or indifference to the other sex.' This is regrettable in that it prevents them from getting to know half of humanity, and they should at least remember that 'even if you don't like persons of the opposite sex, they at any rate collaborate in producing offspring of the sex you do like.'[14]

This article appeared in *Gay News*, the fortnightly newspaper started in 1972 which, like the Gay Liberation Front that preceded it by two years, was part of the change of homosexual identity 'from oppressed sub-group ('queers') to a legitimate minority ("gays")' as a result of the Sexual Offences Act of 1967.[15] A decade after Wolfenden, the Act legitimised homosexual activity so long as it was in private and between 'consenting adults'. It also enabled an individual like Colin MacInnes to identify himself publicly as a gay without fear of repercussions. 'As for heterosexual pals,' he writes, 'I think the more a gay makes the better, provided they unreservedly accept *us* as we are'[16] (my italics).

This remark comes towards the end of a passage of considerable autobiographical interest:

Some gays are alienated from their families (often not by their own fault), and some don't care to move among heterosexual groups at all. If possible, one should try to overcome these obstacles; for a family is a natural group in which to start building relationships with younger people, and even if one's 'closest' relatives may be hostile, there are often nephews, nieces or cousins with whom one can be friends . . .[17]

No doubt Colin had in mind his relationship with his own half-brother, Lance, Lance's wife Kate and their children – a relationship which was often strained. Kate Thirkell remembers how 'he would ring up from a telephone kiosk, saying he would be round in five minutes, then arrive three hours later, dead drunk.'[18] Sometimes he would bring a black boy, whom he patronised horribly, and – whether or not he was accompanied – he would then boast obscenely of his sexual conquests. Between him and Lance, too, there was an element of fraternal rivalry: Colin envied Lance his family; and Lance's aspirations to be a writer (which Colin had encouraged) had perforce to take second place to his career with the BBC. Lance recognised that Colin battened on to his family because he had no family of his own; recognised too that he was good with the children, at least when they were young, inventing stories and playing games with them. Colin's residual influence, though, he sees as malign.[19]

Two of Lance's children, Serena and Robert, have been deeply influenced by Colin. By his example, Serena says, Colin encouraged you 'to go your own way, do your thing, be an individual'. She found his freedom from middle-class conventionality and his anti-establishment attitudes liberating; he gave her the courage to do as she wanted without feeling that she was some kind of freak: 'If you like, he legitimised my revolt.'[20]

In Peggy Little and her son Marcus at Hythe, Colin acquired another family – and home, though he was loath to admit as much, even to himself. He never used the word 'home', not just of Hythe, but of anywhere he had ever lived: it was always 'the house in Melbourne' or wherever. But once, when he phoned Peggy from London, he slipped up and said, 'I'll be ho . . . at such and such a time' – and then punished her for the next three weeks for having, as it were, caught him out.[21]

Yet despite this, and despite the article he wrote on the joys of living outside London, he never entirely accepted his exile, and up to the end of 1972 at least he kept a foothold in the metropolis.

For over a year he had a room in West Hampstead, in addition to which, for part of this time, he also had an address in neighbouring Kilburn. He wrote an article about West Hampstead, praising its village atmosphere;[22] and his last novel, *Out of the Garden*, is partly set in Kilburn.

This novel, at first sight, represents a welcome return by Mac-Innes to the contemporary scene. Captain Rattler, an early retired army officer, recruits his old sergeant, Adams, and Adams's family to help him run a ruin of a stately home for profit. But under the cover of this relatively innocent venture he pursues a dangerous political career involving gun-running to Northern Ireland and plans for a military takeover of the UK (in the early Seventies there were rumblings of discontent among the officer caste and newspaper stories raised the spectre of a military coup). Unfortunately this promising theme is swamped in allegory. The 'Garden' of the title refers to Eden; Rattler is another name for the serpent; Adams is Adam with an 's'; his wife is called Evie, her father Angell . . . but the biblical echoes are strongest of all in the denouement, in which Adams's teenage sons, named Kik and Mas after the Kikuyu and Masai tribes of Kenya, reenact the story of Cain and Abel.

The stately ruin, it seems, represents both the Garden of Eden and the condition of England – 'Imperialism ends where it begins: the last natives are the native-born'; 'Poor England is desolate, and licking its sad wounds. Rattler's intention is to heal them and revive it'; 'the last battles of a decaying imperialism are likely, if not certain, to be fought at its very point of origin.'[23] So this is a cautionary tale, with the family squabble ending in fratricide – a gloomy prognosis which is made no more palatable by the relentless facetiousness of the dialogue (and the novel consists almost entirely of dialogue) between the old Etonian Rattler and the titled heiress known as Aspen who is his ward (if that's the word for a relationship which is deliberately left highly ambivalent: part daughter, part mistress). Let us draw a veil . . .

At Hythe, Colin had settled into a life of comparative domesticity. He did his share of the household chores; he emptied the dustbin, cleaned the kitchen and looked after the pocket-handkerchief sized garden between the house and the sea-front (he dusted the tamarisk tree and cut the tiny patch of lawn with nail-scissors). He was responsible for carrying the weekly grocery order up the steps at the back of the house and into the kitchen; but there he left it. He did not put the things away. He did all his own washing and made his own meals when Peggy was out, but not when she was there. On Sundays, he would take her breakfast in bed, and then pester her with demands to know if it was all right and how she was getting on. He drank endless cups of tea and Peggy's son Marcus remembers that he was always changing his tea habit: sometimes he claimed to like it strong and black; at other times, he preferred it weak and milky. Generally speaking, he was 'light in his own requirements'.[24]

If Peggy went away on holiday, on her return she would find the house spotless. Colin hated things to be changed. When new chair covers of a sulphurous yellow were fitted, Peggy came back from work to find Colin waiting for her on the doorstep, shredding his handkerchief in agitation. He wanted to warn her that the effect of these bright new yellow covers *en masse* was lurid. In time, of course, the colour would fade . . . They had big dramas over little things.

Money, for instance. There was no formal rent-paying arrangement but, Peggy writes, 'If [he] found [me] in hysterical heap on floor clutching huge bill Colin would *leap* into *hired car* & go all the way to London & back to "raise the wind" in the early days, as he didn't like me to be worried or "vexed" – his favourite word for my tantrums.'[25]

He loved to organise treats, though they seldom went smoothly. He shared Peggy's love of donkeys and they would go together to the annual donkey show. He took her to Lords' once to watch cricket, but was happy to leave when she complained that it was easier to see what was happening on television. Sometimes they went out to restaurants, where his behaviour was as uncertain as ever.

He read vastly. There was a library ticket for everyone who had ever so much as stayed a night in the house, so that he could get out quantities of books. His room was on the first floor, overlooking the sea, and he had arranged his desk by the window. Each morning he would sit at his desk and write, but only for two hours; the rest of the day he read.

In these years he wrote innumerable book reviews, as well as articles, for a number of journals. But the writing that gave him most pleasure was the series he did for *Gay News* entitled 'Captain Jockstrap's Diary'.

Captain Jockstrap is the archetypal male chauvinist pig, a peppery old buffer, prurient to a degree. 'You've all met the Captain, in one form or another,' MacInnes tells *Gay News* readers by way of introduction. 'Some think his antipathy to gays is due to fears of his own latent homosexuality; some, that his aggression towards women is explained by doubts about his own virility. But whatever his psychological motivation, there's no doubt Captain Jockstrap is a nasty piece of work . . .'[26]

His crusade against homosexuals lands the Captain in a variety of compromising situations, from massage parlours to drag shows, which MacInnes exploits for all they are worth – and sometimes a bit more. There were seven episodes in all; and after only three, Colin was discussing with the editor of *Gay News*, Denis Lemon, the 'notion of a possible Jockstrap pamphlet . . . to be targeted, sales-wise, at hetero as well as gay readers . . .'[27] Nothing came of the idea, but Colin's enthusiasm reflects his pride in his creation.

Sadly, though, when read in bulk, the 'continuing misadventures of the Dorking desperado' soon become tedious: the irony is too laboured and obvious, the situations too contrived to carry conviction, even as satire. This is not to say that Colin did not have insight into the Captain Jockstrap personality. In his disapproval of camp behaviour, as well as in his misogyny, Captain Jockstrap resembles his creator far more closely than the latter could ever have admitted *in propria persona*. But therapeutic though the series may have been for the writer, the reader merely feels assaulted, if not insulted, by so blatant a caricature. Captain Jockstrap is a Frankenstein's monster of self-hatred.

Colin himself, of course, was something of a monster, and his increasingly eccentric behaviour alienated some erstwhile friends. When Victor Musgrave phoned him at Hythe, for instance, the conversation went thus:

VM: Colin, it's Victor.
CM: Oh, is it?
VM: How are you?
CM: How I am is that I don't like answering the phone to people and that's why I'm in the country. (*End of conversation*.)[28]

Colin's friendship with Robert Waller had long since lapsed, but he was godfather to Waller's two children and when one of them was killed in a car accident he came to the funeral drunk and embarrassed everyone there. Waller met him again at another funeral – of an old friend from pre-war days in Belgium, a gentle accountant called Bobby Hayne, 'who adored him but whom he callously neglected; he seemed to be very sick; as it turned out he was . . .' Waller's daughter Anne was also at Hayne's funeral: 'So Colin was polite and friendly at first to her; then in the car on the way to Bobby Hayne's sister (who had invited us all to drinks, etc) he shouted, "Why am I going to see this silly old woman?", stopped the car and leapt out – the last I ever saw of him.'[29]

Colin *was* ill. For several months he had been having difficulty in swallowing; but by switching to less solid foods he was able to carry on with no apparent ill effects other than a loss of weight. When Bryan Robertson wrote to him in October 1975 suggesting that he see a famous heart surgeon, Colin ignored the letter.[30]

'The reason I didn't go at once to see the doctors,' he wrote later,

was twofold. First, I believe you can rid yourself of many ailments if you trust nature, both consciously and subconsciously – and indeed, many ominous aches I've had at various times have gone as mysteriously as they came by following this method. On the other hand, I must admit that on two prior occasions, and now this one, my 'system' has failed and I went to the doctors in the nick of time.

In view of this, it may seem rank ingratitude to declare that, save in the rarest cases of one physician or surgeon in a thousand, I profoundly mistrust the medical profession . . .[31]

Eventually he did go and see 'the only doctor I have ever known whom I trust completely.' This was Maurice Marcus, who had a practice in Stepney for half a century and became an East End legend in his lifetime (sadly he died soon after Colin). Dr Marcus saw at once that the swollen feet Colin complained of were merely a symptom. He asked Colin if he would be willing to go into hospital for tests: '. . . Only for tests, I said, with no action until I'd heard the results and – if the proposed cure involved surgery – had the opportunity of refusing. Well, said the sage, since I'd be seeing only physicians for the tests, and they don't operate anyway, my options would still be open. So in I went to a London teaching hospital for ten days' tests.'[32]

Before he went into University College Hospital, however, he stayed with Bryan Robertson. By now he could not tolerate the slightest cold or draught, so the central heating had to be full on. In addition, he was a 'total insomniac' and probably had not had a proper night's sleep in twenty years. He took cat naps during the day and kept Bryan up till 1 or 2 a.m. every night and then, if Bryan was obliged to get up in the night, called out to him and started up again where he had left off. 'It nearly killed me,' Robertson recalls.[33]

In hospital Colin learned he had cancer.

My reaction, on discovering what was wrong, was one of resentment even more than terror . . . I was convinced cancer was one I wouldn't get, both because it's in neither of my families, and I didn't think I was the psychological type. The medical snob in me (we're all this about diseases, I believe) was outraged too. 'In his early sixties, he contracted cancer . . .' What a drearily conventional addition to my *curriculum vitae*! And what a foul infliction like leprosy – so different from the classy tropical disease that nearly killed me 20 years ago, but which was such a lovely one to name-drop.[34]

Colin had cancer of the oesophagus, or gullet. The hospital recommended an immediate operation but Colin stalled for a while – ' I truly believe this wasn't due to cowardice, or a subconscious suicidal urge, but rather to a combination of quite rational factors.' He claimed not to trust the diagnosis – perversely because the doctors seemed *too* sure of it. Further, he questioned whether his body would be able to withstand the impact of a major operation: 'And if there's one place I didn't want to die, it was in a hospital and, in particular, on an operating table.'[35] So he wanted time to think it over.

He went to stay with Bryan Robertson again and discussed it with him – he even talked of taking his own life. Bryan persuaded him to agree to the operation because he felt it would give him a chance.[36] But the clinching argument was put by Dr Marcus in Stepney: when Colin asked him what he should do, the good doctor said, oh no, he must decide, but pointed out that 'suppose I decided to soldier on solo, then changed my mind, I might find I'd become too weak for surgery.'[37]

Fiona Green, who was then married to the publisher Martin Green (the 'Martin' of Martin Brian & O'Keeffe), thinks that part of his reluctance to return to hospital stemmed from his experience in UCH, his horror of the old men's ward: 'There were these men, many of them perhaps no older than he was, but they were so apathetic and he was so alive.'[38]

Fiona had known Colin for many years, but to begin with she had been no more to him than 'an annoyance at Martin's elbow'. The breakthrough came when she returned from a party (where, she now reckons, she must have drunk more than she realised) to the pub where Colin and her husband were drinking and said: 'Oh Colin, you're so gorgeous – you're such a handsome man!' After that his attitude to her changed completely. They developed a fantasy relationship in which they were lovers; and part of the fantasy was that they would consummate the affair in Paris. It was a tender relationship but it was strictly a fantasy (when Colin once proposed *mariage blanc* to another young woman, she is said to have replied, 'Oh Colin, why *blanc*?')[39]

While Colin was undergoing tests at UCH, Fiona assumed the role of go-between on his behalf with Dr Marcus, who gave her pain-killing drugs to smuggle in to him. Her doctor friends warned her that she was running a risk, but Dr Marcus told her he would share the responsibility.[40]

The notebook Colin kept at this time records in detail the stages of his long-running battle with the hospital authorities over pain-killers:

Mon. 22.XI [1975]: Bad night – not having been given any pills; but reinforcements from the Mafia have arrived.

Tues. 23.XI: . . . Constipation fuck-up for specimen. Ask for stronger (& refused) pills . . . New depth-charge for constipation useless. Generous (!) with pain/sleep rubbish, but now careless.

Wed. 24.XI: Must contact MM[arcus] as pain situation hopeless . . .

Thurs. 25.XI: Tried enema: failed. 11.00 M. Marcus rings. I ring back. He will send pills today for ? Sat ? Mon c/o F. Green. 15.40 Fiona. Enema works. Nurse says 1 FORTRAL in 4 hrs.

Fri. 26.XI: Surface 3/4 a.m. Night nurse FORTRAL. Tantrums. Phone M. Marcus & Fiona for U.S. Cavalry . . . 12.40 During lunch Dr McLellan arrives, No real news. Prescribes DF 118 for pain. We shall see! 14.00ish Fiona makes connection. After tea – run temperature, autodose, steady by late p.m. DF 118 n.b.g: acquiesce.

Sat. 27.XI: . . . 'BDHO' (2) is offered as same as 'OF O', which is O ADOX 118. We shall see. Also 3 yellow, small 'sleep' pills – we shall also see.

Sun. 28.XI: Drama! [the nurses] imagine they have discovered galaxies of good old NHS pills, introduced by MacInnes's craft and guile into the hospital. Steps are taken immediately & accordingly much more vigilance

& organisation are called for; or else more guile & eccentricity, not losing one's cool . . .'[41]

In his article, 'Cancer Ward', MacInnes describes how, when he was discovered with his own supply of drugs that night, 'I was subjected to a third degree by a house doctor and sister, demanding that I hand them over. This I absolutely refused to do, and they let the matter drop for the moment, though labelling me a trouble-maker; whereas' – he adds, perhaps a trifle disingenuously – 'my chief aim in any institutional situation is to preserve as low a profile as possible.'[42]

The medical profession's attitude to pain was, Colin believed, its gravest defect. 'In hospitals abroad,' he writes,

I have had morphia injections, and though their effect is of short duration, the boost to morale is prodigious; for pain, if persistent and believed to be avoidable, can be demoralising, and surely unhelpful in the total cure. The English medical establishment has always taken the hardest line at international gatherings, and tried to get addictive drugs banned in hospitals altogether.[43]

What made Colin particularly angry was that, though he had been promised he would be spared unnecessary pain after the operation (which was performed at St Pancras Hospital at the end of January 1976), when the time came,

during the 48 really hairy hours the best I got (administered by a nurse, not doctor, or at least sister – always a sign of a minor medical manoeuvre) was an injection which made me dozy, and didn't affect the pain at all. When I reproached [the doctors] for refusing me . . . substitute morphia, they told me a tale of my blood pressure having fallen slightly – which I regret to say I don't believe, or believe to be relevant.[44]

His own explanation goes beyond purely medical considerations:

England is, after all, the land where children are beaten, wives and babies bashed, football hooligans crunch, and Miss Whip and Miss Lash ply their trade as nowhere else in the western world. Despite our belief [that] we are a 'gentle' people we have, in reality, a cruel and callous streak in our sweet natures, reinforced by a decadent puritan strain which makes some of us believe that suffering, whether useful or not, is a fit scourge to the wanton soul.[45]

How is it, he goes on to ask, that 'the stalwart Briton, so independent, so insistent on his rights, puts up with this? Either, I'd guess, because in his heart of hearts he shares this masochistic view; or through superstitious respect for authority – "doctor knows best", as the nurses love to tell you . . .'[46]

Colin's own bravery in hospital consisted not in a convention-ally stoical response to pain, but in transcending this mealy-mouthed attitude of obeisance before the great medical panjan-drum. He never lacked moral courage, and there is an element of heroism in his lonely stand against 'the spirit of the charity ward', as there is, too, in the way he faced up to the reality of his post-operative condition:

From the surgeons themselves, plus blow-by-blow accounts from friendly students, I learned exactly what happened. As to the location of the growth, the physicians' diagnosis was entirely accurate; but not as to the nature of the particular fungus. They had guessed it to be one that grows in a single clump, so that once this was cut out, and the stomach itself possibly reduced a bit in size, I could then be fed intravenously while recovering. But when they opened me up, what they did find was a nasty variety of fungus that spreads itself everywhere in tiny patches. They consequently decided to remove the oesophagus altogether and replace it by a plastic one (thereby making it impossible, henceforth, for me to speak ill of this unpleasant substance), and to clean up the stomach as best they could – for to remove all the growth from it would have left me with no serviceable stomach at all.[47]

In other words, he was not cured and he knew it. Yet he was determined to live. After the operation he went to stay with Bryan Robertson for a further three weeks; his behaviour was 'pretty manic'. He was 'still a monster and a clever chap', even though he was sick. 'Suffering,' Robertson concludes, 'is not ennobling.'[48]

Colin was very demanding. He would not drink ordinary water, it had to be Vichy water; and he drank a little port for his health. Bryan Robertson gave him the confidence to travel by telling him he would be able to have a wheelchair at airports, and in the last months of his life he went, first, to Amsterdam and then to Paris – whence he made a last sentimental journey to visit Mayou Iserentant (who was herself unwell and died not long after him).[49]

When he returned to Hythe, it was not to rest but to work. In early April he accepted an invitation from the Runnymede Trust to lead a discussion on 'Futurology: blacks and other minorities in evolving Britain' on 22 June for the modest fee of £20.[50] On 13 April Irving Kristol wrote from New York to say how sorry he was to hear of Colin's operation, how he wished he might help him in some way but that there were not many magazines in America of the sort he might write for . . .[51] And the *Sunday Times, The Times Educational Supplement, New Society* and *Gay News* all published recently written articles by MacInnes after his death. In addition, at the time of his death he was learning both Gaelic and Japanese. He still read voraciously and he was quite prepared to tackle a new subject – be it the Islamic world or Chinese civilisation. Less than four months before his death he wrote a review for *The Times Educational Supplement* entitled 'Discovering Cathay' in which he urged on the reader Joseph Needham's massive three-volume *Science and Civilisation in China*, which was not the work under review but was 'perhaps the most astounding twentieth-century book written by any Englishman about anything.'[52] His intellectual curiosity remained undiminished to the very end.

He died at 11 pm. on 23 April of a massive haemorrhage. He was sixty-one.

He was, according to his wish, buried at sea: the date, Friday 30 April; the venue, the Fish Market at Folkestone.

'The funeral was rather sparsely attended, about 20 people turned up, maybe a few more or less,' Frank Norman reported to Francis Wyndham a day or two later.

Actually it turned out to be a rare and memorable experience. The undertaker's men carried the coffin from the hearse and put it on the deck of a rusty old fishing boat. It was not the usual sort of coffin, the bottom half was wood, but there was no lid. The top was covered with blue nylon material and tacked around the edges with brass studs. They covered the coffin with a tatty length of red velvet and a few bunches of daffodils. A very young curate, from the local parish church, I think, conducted a touching little ceremony at the quay-side – amid the hustle and bustle of fishermen coming and going with baskets of fish and the voice of the auctioneer selling off the catch in a nearby shed.

When the curate had finished his incantations, about a dozen of us clambered aboard and the skipper set out to sea. It put me in mind of the old bucket on which Humphrey Bogart and Katherine Hepburn once took a cruise. The skipper, a friend of Colin's, had bright gold rings in his ears and tattoos on his arms. A bottle of Teacher's was passed around from mouth to mouth, the sun shone far too brightly and a party atmosphere prevailed.

At the three-mile marker buoy the skipper cut the engine and the curate read the bit about the sea giving up its dead, and Colin was pushed, feet first, over the side. For a few alarming moments the coffin floated, just a foot or two beneath the water.

'It ain't gonna sink!' cried the skipper. The undertaker cast a professional eye over the side and said: 'It'll sink – just as soon as the air gets out of it.' A moment or two later it upended and slowly disappeared from sight.[53]

Fiona Green felt that it was as if Colin 'had stage-managed the whole thing: as the boat's engine cut there was this bell on a buoy going "ding-ding-ding." They heaved the coffin overboard and it wouldn't sink! So the boat circled round it, leaving a ring of white water. And just then a seagull landed on the coffin and then flew off as if it were carrying his spirit – it was weird.'[54]

The undertaker, more prosaically, told Lance Thirkell, 'We always bury them under the buoy, so that it tolls for them'; he went on to say it was also to prevent the fishing trawlers getting coffins entangled in their nets.[55]

The reason the coffin took so long to sink – according to Mel Lasky, who was also on the boat – was that it was put into the water back to front: 'There's a hole that should have been at the front, and then it would have filled with water and sunk: but the hole was at the back, so it took longer.'[56] But the delay enabled the younger Thirkells to throw garlands of flowers, and the poet Eddie Linden to drop a copy of the magazine he edits, *Aquarius* – the Welsh issue, it was – on to the coffin. 'I threw it,' he recalls, 'and it landed on top of the coffin and the coffin sank. Down went the coffin and everyone laughed!'[57]

When the boat returned to shore, the funeral party adjourned to the nearest pub where, if they did not quite sing, 'Oh, didn't he ramble', they did recite poems . . .

The grotesquery of it all, Mel Lasky was not alone in thinking, would have appealed to the author of *Mr Love and Justice*. Colin himself was fond of telling the story of Chekhov's funeral: how when the dramatist's coffin arrived at a Moscow terminus it was muddled up with that of a general killed in the Russo-Japanese war and Chekhov's funeral procession was for a while (as William Gerhardie describes it) 'headed by a military policeman on a fat white horse and a military band and followed by General Müller's relatives.'[58]

There were, however, two anomalies in MacInnes's otherwise sympathetically bizarre funeral. One was the absence of any black friends. When the American Calvin Hernton visited London in the early summer of 1976, he did not even know Colin had died.

He had a drink in a pub in the Finchley Road one lunchtime and then went into a second-hand bookshop where he noticed a copy of the U.S. edition of MacInnes's London novels with an Introduction by Nat Hentoff. He thought to himself how good it was that Colin should get this American recognition; yet he felt funny about it and mentioned seeing the book to his friend Horace Ové. It was only then that he learned that Colin was dead.[59]

The other anomaly, which probably escaped the notice of everyone at the funeral except Lance Thirkell, was that Colin was buried in that same English Channel above which, seventy miles away in Rottingdean, his mother's ashes rested.[60] Even in death, it seems, 'Angela Thirkell's son' was not entirely free of his mother.

References

1 A Victorian Cultural Dynasty, pp 3–13

1 – A.W. Baldwin, *The Macdonald Sisters* (Peter Davies, 1960)
2 – *Ibid*
3 – *Ibid*
4 – Georgiana Burne-Jones, *Memorials of Edward Burne-Jones* (Macmillan, 1904)
5 – *Ibid*
6 – *Ibid*
7 – *Ibid*
8 – Penelope Fitzgerald, *Edward Burne-Jones: a Biography* (Michael Joseph, 1975). Angus Wilson, in *The Strange Ride of Rudyard Kipling* (Secker & Warburg, 1977) disputes the claim that Burne-Jones is the model for the lama in *Kim* and thinks it more likely that he is Puck in *Puck of Pook's Hill* and *Rewards and Fairies*
9 – A.W. Baldwin, *op.cit.*
10 – Georgiana Burne-Jones, *op.cit.*
11 – Colin MacInnes, 'A Tardy Revival', *Spectator*, 17 April 1976
12 – Angela Thirkell, *Three Houses* (Oxford, 1932)
13 – A.W. Baldwin, *op. cit.*
14 – Angela Thirkell, *op. cit.*
15 – *Ibid*
16 – Colin MacInnes, 'Edward Burne-Jones of Birmingham', BBC Midland Home Services, 2 December 1952
17 – W. Graham Robertson, cited in P. Fitzgerald, *op. cit.*
18 – Georgiana Burne-Jones, *op. cit.*
19 – Author's conversation with Lance Thirkell (6 November 1978)
20 – Angela Thirkell/Colin MacInnes, 'Mrs Thirkell Remembers', BBC Home Service, 14 December 1954
21 – Georgiana Burne-Jones, *op. cit.*
22 – Quoted in Margot Strickland, *Angela Thirkell: Portrait of a Lady Novelist* (Duckworth, 1977)
23 – Angela Thirkell/Colin MacInnes 'Mrs Thirkell Remembers'
24 – Cynthia Asquith, *Haply I May Remember* (Barrie, 1950)
25 – Colin MacInnes, 'A Pre-Raphaelite Memory', *Spectator*, October 1963
26 – Colin MacInnes, 'Born and Bred', *Times Educational Supplement*, 3 January 1975
27 – *Ibid*
28 – Private memo from Colin MacInnes to Reg Davis-Poynter, 3 February 1960

29 – Colin MacInnes, 'Born and Bred'
30 – Georgiana Burne-Jones, *op. cit.*
31 – Margaret Mackail's unpublished notebook
32 – Colin MacInnes, 'A Pre-Raphaelite Memory'
33 – Margot Strickland, *op. cit.*
34 – *Ibid*
35 – Angela Thirkell, *Peace Breaks Out* (Hamish Hamilton, 1946)

2   A Family at War, pp 14–23

1 – Private memo from Colin MacInnes to Reg Davis-Poynter, 3 February 1960
2 – Margot Strickland, *Angela Thirkell, Portrait of a Lady Novelist* (Duckworth, 1977)
3 – Letter from Colin MacInnes to Robert Waller, 14 November 1950
4 – G.M. Trevelyan, *Grey of Falloden* (1937), quoted in Graham McInnes, *Finding a Father* (Hamish Hamilton, 1967)
5 – Letter from Angela Thirkell to Barbara Parson, now in the possession of Mrs Pamela Sharpe
6 – Angela McInnes's diary 1915–19, now in the possession of Mrs Joan McInnes
7 – Lady Cynthia Asquith, *Diaries 1915–1918* (Hutchinson, 1968)
8 – Michael Roe, ' "Thirk": A Tragic Australian, 1891–1959', *Meanjin Quarterly*, December 1969
9 – Margot Strickland, *op. cit.*
10 – Letter from Queenie Campbell to Barbara Parson, 27 June 1917
11 – Margot Strickland, *op. cit.*
12 – Angela Thirkell, *O, These Men, These Men!*
13 – Letter from Angela Thirkell to Barbara Parson, 29 October 1917
14 – Angela McInnes's diary
15 – *Ibid*
16 – Letter from Margaret Mackail to Mrs Parson, 26 February 1918
17 – Angela Thirkell, *O, These Men, These Men!* (Hamish Hamilton, 1935)
18 – Angela McInnes's diary
19 – *Ibid*
20 – Colin MacInnes, *London, city of any dream* (Thames & Hudson, 1962)
21 – *Ibid*
22 – *Ibid*
23 – Letter to the author from Mrs Pamela Sharpe, 7 December 1978
24 – Colin MacInnes, *op. cit.*
25 – *Ibid*
26 – *Ibid*
27 – Letter from Margaret Mackail to Barbara Parson, 18 June 1919
28 – Letter from Georgiana Burne-Jones to Barbara Parson, 15 June 1919
29 – A.W. Baldwin, *The Macdonald Sisters* (Peter Davies, 1960)

3 Mother versus Australia, pp 24–47

1 – Graham McInnes, *The Road to Gundagai* (Hamish Hamilton, 1965)
2 – *Ibid*
3 – Colin MacInnes, 'Mum's the Word', *New Statesman*, 7 June 1963;
Angela Thirkell's pseudonym for *Trooper to the Southern Cross*
(Faber, 1934) was 'Leslie Parker'
4 – Graham McInnes, *Humping My Bluey* (Hamish Hamilton, 1966)
5 – Peter Porter, review of *Humping My Bluey, New Statesman*, 8 April
1966
6 – Graham McInnes, *The Road to Gundagai*
7 – Colin MacInnes, 'Through the Looking Glass to Adolescence', in
The World of Children, edited by Edward Blishen (Paul Hamlyn, 1966)
8 – Graham McInnes, *op. cit.*
9 – *Ibid*
10 – Asa Briggs, *Victorian Cities* (Odhams Press, 1963)
11 – *Ibid*
12 – Graham McInnes, *op. cit.*
13 – Colin MacInnes, *Australia and New Zealand* (Time-Life Books, 1964)
14 – Graham McInnes, *op. cit.*
15 – Author's conversation with Bryan Robertson (26 July 1978)
16 – Graham McInnes, *op. cit.*
17 – *Ibid*
18 – Colin MacInnes, 'Through the Looking Glass to Adolescence'
19 – Colin MacInnes, 'Mum's the Word'
20 – Angela Thirkell interviewed by Colin MacInnes, 'Mrs Thirkell
Remembers', BBC Home Service, 14 December 1954
21 – Colin MacInnes, 'Through the Looking Glass to Adolescence'
22 – Colin MacInnes, *'No Novel Reader'* (Martin Brian & O'Keeffe, 1975)
23 – Graham McInnes, *op. cit.*
24 – Colin MacInnes, *op. cit.*
25 – Graham McInnes, *op. cit.*
26 – *Ibid*
27 – Colin MacInnes, review in the Sydney *Bulletin*, 30 May 1964
28 – Graham McInnes, *op. cit.*
29 – Letter to the author from Sir Keith Waller, 22 August 1978
30 – Colin MacInnes, 'Through the Looking Glass to Adolescence'
31 – Author's conversation with Lance Thirkell (6 November 1978)
32 – Colin MacInnes, 'A Case in Favour', *New Society*, 21 July 1966
33 – Letter to the Author from Sir Keith Waller
34 – Colin MacInnes, *No Novel Reader*
35 – Colin MacInnes, 'Elderly Boys', *New Society*, 19 September 1968
36 – Graham McInnes, *op. cit.*
37 – *Ibid*
38 – Colin MacInnes, *op. cit.*
39 – *Ibid*
40 – Colin MacInnes, 'Chief Boy', *New Statesman*, 5 May 1961
41 – Colin MacInnes, 'Through the Looking Glass to Adolescence'

42 – *Ibid*
43 – Graham McInnes, *op. cit.*
44 – Colin MacInnes, *op. cit.*
45 – Graham McInnes, *op. cit.*
46 – Colin MacInnes, *op. cit.*
47 – *Ibid*
48 – Colin MacInnes, 'Finding a Family', BBC Home Service, 7 July 1952
49 – Colin MacInnes, 'Sidney Nolan: the Search for an Australian Myth', *England, Half English* (MacGibbon & Kee, 1961)
50 – Cited in Asa Briggs, *op. cit.*
51 – Colin MacInnes, *Australia and New Zealand*
52 – Graham McInnes, *op. cit.*
53 – *Ibid*
54 – *Ibid*
55 – *Ibid*
56 – *Ibid*
57 – Colin MacInnes, 'Sidney Nolan'
58 – Margaret Kiddle, *Men of Yesterday: a Social History of the Western District of Victoria 1834–1890* (Melbourne University Press, 1961)
59 – *Ibid*
60 – Colin MacInnes, *op. cit.*
61 – Colin MacInnes, *All Day Saturday* (MacGibbon & Kee, 1966)
62 – Graham McInnes, *op. cit*
63 – Angela Thirkell, *Ankle Deep* (Hamish Hamilton, 1933)
64 – *Ibid*
65 – Graham McInnes, *op. cit.*
66 – Graham McInnes, *Humping My Bluey*
67 – Graham McInnes, *The Road to Gundagai*
68 – Colin MacInnes, 'Through the Looking Glass to Adolescence'
69 – *Ibid*
70 – Colin MacInnes, 'Sidney Nolan'
71 – Graham McInnes, *op. cit.*
72 – Letter to the author from A.P. Fleming, 20 January 1978
73 – Letter to the author from Sir Keith Waller, 31 October 1978
74 – *Ibid*
75 – Colin MacInnes, 'Fighting Words', *Times Educational Supplement*, 21 September 1973
76 – Colin MacInnes, 'Through the Looking Glass to Adolescence'
77 – Graham McInnes, *Humping My Bluey*

4 Family Reunions, pp 48–69

1 – Letter to the author from Maurice Wasterlain, September 1979
2 – Colin MacInnes, *London, city of any dream* (Thames & Hudson, 1962)
3 – Colin MacInnes, 'Finding a Family', BBC Home Service, 7 July 1952
4 – *Ibid*
5 – *Ibid*, and Colin MacInnes, *London, city of any dream*; and Colin MacInnes, 'A Pre-Raphaelite Memory', *Spectator*, October 1963

References

6 – *Ibid*

7 – *Ibid*

8 – *Ibid*

9 – Colin MacInnes, 'Yvette', *New Statesman*, 22 April 1966

10 – Colin MacInnes, 'Aunt Trix', BBC Home Service, 14 September 1952; and 'Aunt Trix', *England, Half English* (MacGibbon & Kee, 1961)

11 – Colin MacInnes, 'A Pre-Raphaelite Memory'

12 – *Ibid*

13 – Colin MacInnes, 'Finding a Family'

14 – Colin MacInnes, 'Going into Business', *Spectator*, December 1965, reprinted in *Out of the Way: Later Essays* (Martin Brian & O'Keeffe, 1980)

15 – Colin MacInnes, review of Martin Turnell: *Jean Racine: Dramatist*, in the *Sunday Times*, 21 May 1972

16 – Colin MacInnes, 'Declaration', *Jewish Chronicle*, 22 January 1960

17 – Colin MacInnes, 'Going into Business'

18 – Author's conversations with Lance Thirkell (6 November 1978) and Joan McInnes (5 December 1978)

19 – Colin MacInnes, *op. cit.*.

20 – *Ibid*

21 – *Ibid*

22 – *Ibid*

23 – *Imperial Continental Gas Association, 1824–1974* (privately printed)

24 – Colin MacInnes, *op. cit.*.

25 – Author's conversation with Lance Thirkell

26 – Colin MacInnes, *op. cit.*

27 – Letter from Colin MacInnes to his mother, 27 March 1933

28 – Letter to the author from Maurice Wasterlain

29 – Colin MacInnes, *To the Victors the Spoils* (MacGibbon & Kee, 1950)

30 – Colin MacInnes, 'No Quiet Time', *Queen,* 5 July 1961

31 – *Ibid*

32 – *Ibid*

33 – *Ibid*

34 – *Ibid*

35 – *Ibid*

36 – Margot Strickland, *Angela Thirkell: Portrait of a Lady Novelist* (Duckworth, 1977)

37 – Angela Thirkell, *High Rising* (Hamish Hamilton, 1933) quoted in Strickland, *op. cit.*

38 – Colin MacInnes, 'Mum's the Word', *New Statesman*, 7 June 1963

39 – Letter from Colin MacInnes to his mother, 18 July 1933

40 – *Ibid*

41 – Graham McInnes, *Finding a Father* (Hamish Hamilton, 1967)

42 – *Ibid*

43 – Letter to the author from Ross Campbell, 8 June 1979

44 – Graham McInnes, *op. cit.*

45 – *Ibid*

46 – Graham McInnes, *Goodbye, Melbourne Town* (Hamish Hamilton, 1968)
47 – Graham McInnes, *Finding a Father*
48 – Kerrison Preston (editor), *Letters from W. Graham Robertson* (Hamish Hamilton, 1953)
49 – Colin MacInnes, 'Thoughts' notebook – author's translation (MS at University of Rochester)
50 – Graham McInnes, *op. cit.*
51 – *Ibid*
52 – *Ibid*
53 – Colin MacInnes, 'Going into Business
54 – Colin MacInnes, *London, city of any dream*
55 – Graham McInnes, *op. cit*; and author's conversation with Joan McInnes
56 – Colin MacInnes, Introduction to catalogue of Thelma Hulbert Retrospective at the Whitechapel Gallery, London, October 1962
57 – *Ibid*
58 – *Ibid*
59 – Author's conversation with Lance Thirkell
60 – Colin MacInnes, *op. cit.*
61 – *Ibid*
62 – Colin MacInnes, *London, city of any dream*
63 – Author's conversation with Sir William Coldstream (25 January 1979)
64 – Author's conversation with Thelma Hulbert (29 April 1979)
65 – Author's conversations with Thelma Hulbert, Sir William Coldstream, Rodrigo Moynihan (14 May 1979) and Elinor Bellingham Smith (November 1977)
66 – Letter from Graham Bell to Robert Waller, undated
67 – Lawrence Gowing, 'Rodrigo Moynihan', Introduction to catalogue, 3 June 1978
68 – Colin MacInnes, *op. cit.*
69 – *Ibid*
70 – Letter from Colin MacInnes to Robert Waller, 10 September 1943

5   In War and Peace, pp 70–86

1 – Colin MacInnes, 'Pacific Warrior', *New Society*, 30 June 1966
2 – Letter from Graham Bell to Robert Waller, undated
3 – Colin MacInnes, 'Stephen Tennant', *Encounter*, January 1957, reprinted in *Out of the Way: Later Essays* (Martin Brian & O'Keeffe, 1980)
4 – *Ibid*
5 – *Ibid*
6 – Letter to the author from James Foston, a wartime Intelligence Corps NCO and peacetime teacher, 6 November 1978
7 – Colin MacInnes, 'Now that I Find I Love My Mother', 16 November 1941

References

8 – Colin MacInnes, 'Farewell, for Charles Causley', *England, Half English* (MacGibbon & Kee, 1961)

9 – Quoted in letter to the author from R. Hudson Smith, 14 November 1978

10 – *Ibid*

11 – Colin MacInnes, 'Kim's Game', *New Statesman*, 27 September 1968

12 – Colin MacInnes, 'The Anarchists: Part II', *Queen*, 22 May 1962

13 – Author's conversation with Peggy Little (10 September 1978) and Colin MacInnes, *Angus Bard* (TS University of Rochester)

14 – Colin MacInnes, *To the Victors the Spoils* (MacGibbon & Kee, 1950)

15 – *Ibid*

16 – Author's conversation with Robert Waller (2 February 1979)

17 – *Ibid*

18 – Colin MacInnes, *op. cit.*

19 – Author's conversation with Robert Waller

20 – *Ibid*

21 – Colin MacInnes, *op. cit.*

22 – Colin MacInnes, 'Prison Governor by Chance', BBC Home Service, 21 June 1953

23 – *Ibid*

24 – *Ibid*

25 – Colin MacInnes, 'Pacific Warrior'

26 – Author's conversation with Robert Waller

27 – Margot Strickland, *Angela Thirkell: Portrait of a Lady Novelist* (Duckworth, 1977)

28 – Graham McInnes, *Goodbye, Melbourne Town* (Hamish Hamilton, 1968)

29 – Angela Thirkell, *Peace Breaks Out* (Hamish Hamilton, 1946)

30 – *Ibid*

31 – Colin MacInnes, 'An Unrewarded Virtue: Britain 1945–51', *Queen*, 25 September 1963

32 – Colin MacInnes, 'At the Galleries', *Observer*, 9 November 1947

33 – Ivor Brown, 'Burlington Arcady', *Observer*, 2 May 1948

34 – Colin MacInnes, 'Art Review', BBC Third Programme, 2 December 1947

35 – Author's conversation with George Melly (1 November 1977)

36 – Author's conversation with David Sylvester (24 January 1979)

37 – Colin MacInnes, 'Out of the Way', *New Society*, 27 December 1962

38 – Colin MacInnes, 'Thoughts' notebook (MS University of Rochester)

39 – *Ibid*

40 – Author's conversation with David Sylvester

41 – Letter from Colin MacInnes to Robert Waller, 5 January 1949

42 – Colin MacInnes, 'Thoughts' notebook

43 – *Ibid*

44 – *Ibid*

44 – *Ibid*

45 – Letter from Colin MacInnes to Robert Waller, 14 November 1950

46 – Quoted in letter from Colin MacInnes to Eric Dadson, 21 November 1950

47 – Author's conversation with Robert Waller
48 – Author's conversation with David Sylvester
49 – Private information
50 – Letter from Colin MacInnes to Robert Waller, 17 February 1952
51 – *Ibid*
52 – Colin MacInnes, *June in Her Spring* (MacGibbon & Kee, 1952)
53 – Colin MacInnes, 'Mum's the Word', *New Statesman*, 7 June 1963
54 – *Ibid*
55 – Colin MacInnes, 'Thoughts' notebook
56 – Colin MacInnes, 'Mum's the Word'
57 – Angela Thirkell/Colin MacInnes, 'Mrs Thirkell Remembers', BBC Home Service, 14 December 1954

6   City of Spades, pp 89–109

1 – All quotes at the start of this chapter are from Colin MacInnes, *Fancy Free* (unpublished typescript)
2 – Angela Thirkell, *Peace Breaks Out* (Hamish Hamilton, 1946)
3 – Angela Thirkell, *Ankle Deep* (Hamish Hamilton, 1933)
4 – Colin MacInnes, 'Mum's the Word', *New Statesman*, 7 June 1963
5 – Author's conversation with Robert Waller (2 February 1979)
6 – Author's conversation with Monty Haltrecht (26 October 1978)
7 – Author's conversation with Michael Law (18 May 1979)
8 – Author's conversation with Bryan Robertson (26 July 1978)
9 – Colin MacInnes, *City of Spades* (MacGibbon & Kee, 1957)
10 – Richard Buckle, *Katherine Dunham: and Her Dancers, Singers, Musicians* (Ballet Publications, London, undated)
11 – Letter from Colin MacInnes to Robert Waller, undated
12 – *Ibid*
13 – *Ibid*
14 – Colin MacInnes, 'Thoughts' book (MS University of Rochester)
15 – Colin MacInnes, MS links to *England, Half English* (University of Rochester)
16 – Colin MacInnes, 'England Queerdom', *Partisan Review*, January/February 1961
17 – Letter from Colin MacInnes to Robert Waller, 28 December 1952
18 – Ditto, 3 January 1953
19 – Ditto, 3 March 1953
20 – Ditto, 28 December 1952
21 – Ditto, 26 November 1952
22 – Letter from Colin MacInnes to Eric Dadson, 28 December 1952
23 – H. Montgomery Hyde, *The Other Love: an Historical and Contemporary Survey of Homosexuality in Britain* (Heinemann, 1970)
24 – *Ibid*
25 – *Ibid*
26 – *Ibid*
27 – Letter from Colin MacInnes to Robert Waller, undated
28 – Colin MacInnes, 'English Queerdom'

29 – Letter from Colin MacInnes to Robert Waller, 3 March 1953
30 – Author's conversation with Robert Waller
31 – Letter from Colin MacInnes to Robert Waller, 13 January 1954
32 – Ditto, 15 January 1954
33 – *Ibid*
34 – Letter to the author from Robert Waller, 6 November 1978
35 – Letter from Colin MacInnes to Robert Waller, 2 July 1954
36 – Author's conversation with Charles Causley (29 December 1968)
37 – Letter from Colin MacInnes to Eric Dadson, 9 September 1954
38 – Ditto, 20 January 1955
39 – Draft MS link to *England, Half English*
40 – 'The Critics', BBC Home Service, 14 November 1954
41 – 'William Walter', 'Look and Listen', *New Statesman*, 27 November 1954
42 – Letter to the author from Elspeth Huxley, 11 November 1979
43 – Letter from Colin MacInnes to Robert Waller, 7 September 1955
44 – Author's conversation with Lance Thirkell (6 November 1978)
45 – Colin MacInnes, 'East African Diary', *Twentieth Century*, August 1955
46 – *Ibid*
47 – *Ibid*
48 – Colin MacInnes, 'Nicked', *New Society*, 16 September 1965
49 – *Ibid*
50 – *Ibid*
51 – *Ibid*
52 – *Ibid*
53 – Author's conversation with Lance Thirkell; and Francis Wyndham, 'Lost in the Law', *Sunday Times* interview with Colin MacInnes (1967)
54 – Quoted in Margot Strickland, *Angela Thirkell* (Duckworth, 1977)
55 – Author's conversation with Joan McInnes (5 December 1978)
56 – Quoted in Strickland, *op. cit.*
57 – *Ibid*
58 – Author's conversation with Barney Greenman (17 December 1979)
59 – Colin MacInnes, 'Nicked'
60 – Francis Wyndham, *op. cit.*
61 – *Ibid*
62 – Letter from Colin MacInnes to Robert Waller, 16 November 1955
63 – Francis Wyndham, *op. cit.*
64 – *Ibid*
65 – Letter from Colin MacInnes to Robert Waller, undated
66 – Colin MacInnes, *City of Spades*
67 – *Ibid*
68 – Colin MacInnes, 'A Short Guide for Jumbles', *Twentieth Century*, March 1956, reprinted with postscript in *England, Half English* (1961)

7 Soho Bohemia, pp 110–122

1 – Colin MacInnes, *Absolute Beginners* (MacGibbon & Kee, 1959)
2 – Colin MacInnes, *London, city of any dream* (Thames & Hudson, 1962)

3 – *Ibid*
4 – Colin MacInnes, 'Victor Musgrave' (unpublished TS, undated)
5 – *Ibid*
6 – Author's conversation with Victor Musgrave (30 November 1978)
7 – Colin MacInnes, *op. cit*.
8 – Author's conversation with Victor Musgrave
9 – Colin MacInnes, *op. cit*.
10 – Author's conversation with David Sylvester (24 January 1979)
11 – Author's conversation with Kenny Graham (22 May 1979)
12 – Author's conversation with Bryan Robertson (26 July 1978)
13 – Letter from Colin MacInnes to Hugh Stevenson, undated
14 – Author's conversation with Alexander Weatherson (13 November 1978)
15 – *Ibid*
16 – *Ibid*
17 – Author's conversation with Terry Taylor (22 March 1979)
18 – Terry Taylor's letter to the author, undated
19 – *Ibid*
20 – Colin MacInnes, 'City after Dark', *Twentieth Century*, December 1957
21 – *Ibid*
22 – Author's conversation with Terry Taylor
23 – *Ibid*
24 – *Ibid*
25 – *Ibid*
26 – Colin MacInnes, 'See You at Mabel's', *Encounter*, March 1957 (reprinted in *England, Half English*)
27 – *Ibid*
28 – *Ibid*
29 – Letter from Colin MacInnes to Francis Wyndham, 25 February 1956
30 – Author's conversation with Francis Wyndham (12 October 1978)
31 – Letter from Colin MacInnes to Francis Wyndham, 25 February 1956
32 – Author's conversation with Francis Wyndham
33 – Author's conversation with Patrick Harvey (9 March 1979)
34 – *Ibid*
35 – Draft MS link to *England, Half English* (University of Rochester)
36 – Colin MacInnes, 'The Music Hall World', *Nimbus* Vol 3 No. 2, undated
37 – Colin MacInnes, *Sweet Saturday Night* (MacGibbon & Kee, 1967)
38 – *Ibid*
39 – Author's conversation with Patrick Harvey
40 – Author's conversation with Alfred Maron (30 October 1978)
41 – Author's conversation with Bernard and Erica Kops (16 October 1979)
42 – BBC internal memo, 12 December 1956
43 – BBC internal memo, 23 January 1957
44 – Colin MacInnes, in 'Expectation and Realisation', BBC Home Service, 20 March 1957
45 – Colin MacInnes, 'Britain's Mixed Half-Million', *Africa South in Exile*

Vol 5 No. 2, January–March 1961
46 – *Ibid*
47 – Author's conversation with Kenny Graham
48 – Colin MacInnes, *op. cit.*
49 – Pamela Hansford Johnson, review of *City of Spades*, *New Statesman*, 21 September 1957
50 – Colin MacInnes, in *World of Books*, BBC Home Service, 26 October 1957
51 – Letter from Colin MacInnes to Roy Edwards, 31 August 1957
52 – Author's conversation with Francis Wyndham
53 – Letter to the author from Roy Kerridge, 7 March 1979

8   The Road to Notting Hill, pp 123–145

1 – Colin MacInnes, 'The Anarchists II', *Queen*, 22 May 1962
2 – Peter Lewis, *The Fifties* (Heinemann, 1978)
3 – Colin MacInnes, *Absolute Beginners* (MacGibbon & Kee, 1959)
4 – Ray Gosling, *Personal Copy* (Faber, 1980)
5 – George Melly, *Revolt into Style* (Allen Lane, 1970)
6 – Ray Gosling, *op. cit.*
7 – George Melly, *op. cit.*
8 – *Ibid*
9 – George Melly, *Owning-Up* (Weidenfeld & Nicolson, 1965)
10 – George Melly, *Revolt into Style*
11 – Ray Gosling, *op. cit.*
12 – Colin MacInnes, 'Young England, Half English', *Encounter*, December 1957 (reprinted in *English, Half English*, 1961)
13 – *Ibid*
14 – Colin MacInnes, 'Pop Songs and Teenagers', *Twentieth Century*, February 1958 (reprinted in *England, Half English*)
15 – *Ibid*
16 – *Ibid*
17 – Colin MacInnes, *Absolute Beginners*
18 – Colin MacInnes, 'National Health Lottery', *New Society*, 5 May 1966
19 – Author's conversation with David Sylvester (24 January 1979)
20 – Colin MacInnes, draft MS link to *England, Half English*
21 – Letter from Colin MacInnes to Francis Wyndham, 19 March 1958
22 – Colin MacInnes, 'National Health Lottery'
23 – *Ibid*
24 – *Ibid*
25 – Colin MacInnes, 'Out of the Way', *New Society*, 4 October 1962
26 – *Ibid*
27 – *Ibid*
28 – Author's conversation with Francis Wyndham (12 October 1978)
29 – Colin MacInnes, 'Thoughts' book (University of Rochester)
30 – Author's conversation with Bryan Robertson (26 July 1978)
31 – Colin MacInnes, *Absolute Beginners*

32 – Author's conversation with Serena Thirkell (17 November 1978)
33 – Colin MacInnes, *op. cit.*
34 – Dan Jacobson, 'After Notting Hill', *Encounter*, December 1958 and Ruth Glass, *Newcomers: the West Indians in London* (Allen & Unwin, 1960)
35 – Dan Jacobson, *op. cit.*
36 – Colin MacInnes, 'Pop Songs and Teenagers'
37 – Colin MacInnes, *Absolute Beginners*
38 – Memo from Colin MacInnes to Reg Davis-Poynter, 5 September 1958
39 – *Ibid*
40 – Ruth Glass, *op. cit.*
41 – Colin MacInnes, *Absolute Beginners*
42 – Ruth Glass, *op. cit.*
43 – Colin MacInnes, *op. cit.*
44 – Letter from Colin MacInnes to Peggy Barker, BBC, 28 August 1958
45 – Colin MacInnes, 'Thoughts' book
46 – Colin MacInnes, *Absolute Beginners*
47 – *Ibid*
48 – Author's conversation with Eric Hobsbawm (12 June 1979)
49 – Author's conversation with Victor Musgrave (30 November 1978)
50 – Author's conversation with Max Jones (5 June 1979)
51 – *The Kensington News*, 30 October 1959, quoted in Ruth Glass, *op. cit.*
52 – Ruth Glass, *op. cit.*
53 – Letter from Colin MacInnes to Terence Cooper, BBC, 20 May 1959
54 – Colin MacInnes, 'Declaration', *The Jewish Chronicle*, 22 January 1960
55 – Colin MacInnes, 'Living in Spitalfields', *Jewish Chronicle*, 25 November 1960
56 – Author's conversation with Bernard and Erica Kops (16 October 1979)
57 – *Ibid*
58 – *Ibid*
59 – *Ibid*
60 – Author's conversation with Kenny Graham (22 May 1979)
61 – *Ibid*
62 – Colin MacInnes, 'Cream for Kittens: jazz in two scenes' (unpublished, January 1960)
63 – Author's conversation with Kenny Graham
64 – Letter from Colin MacInnes to Francis Wyndham, 19 September 1958
65 – Author's conversation with Richard Wollheim (25 January 1979)
66 – Richard Wollheim, 'Babylon, *Babylone*', *Encounter*, May 1962
67 – *Ibid*
68 – *Ibid*
69 – Letter from Colin MacInnes to David Sylvester, 23 September 1959
70 – Richard Wollheim, *op. cit.*
71 – *Ibid*
72 – *Ibid*

73 – Colin MacInnes, *Absolute Beginners*
74 – Richard Wollheim, *op. cit.*
75 – *Ibid*
76 – Letter to the author from Roy Kerridge, 7 March 1979
77 – *Ibid*
78 – *Ibid*
79 – *Ibid*
80 – Letter from Colin MacInnes to Eric Dadson, 23 September 1959

9   Success and Failure, pp 146–166

1 – Memo from Colin MacInnes to Reg Davis-Poynter, 22 January 1960
2 – Letter from Colin MacInnes to Barbara Parson, 1 December 1959
3 – Colin MacInnes, *London: city of any dream* (Thames & Hudson, 1962)
4 – Author's conversation with Joan McInnes (5 December 1978)
5 – Letter from Colin MacInnes to R. Hudson Smith, 1 January 1960
6 – Colin MacInnes, 'Out of the Way', *New Society*, 14 March 1963
7 – Letter from Colin MacInnes to Lance Thirkell, 11 July 1959
8 – Author's conversations with Richard Wollheim, George Melly, Nancy Shepherdson, Bryan Robertson *et al.*
9 – Colin MacInnes, memo 'on Writers and Publishers', 6 February 1960
10 – Colin MacInnes, 'A Wild Glance at the Book Trade', 15 February 1960 (and *Encounter*, January 1962)
11 – Memo from Colin MacInnes to Reg Davis-Poynter, 22 January 1960
12 – Colin MacInnes, 'The Englishness of Dr Pevsner', *Twentieth Century*, January 1960 (reprinted in *England, Half English*, MacGibbon & Kee, 1961)
13 – Colin MacInnes, *England, Half English*
14 – Memo from Colin MacInnes to Reg Davis-Poynter, 22 January 1960
15 – Author's conversation with Victor Musgrave (30 November 1978)
16 – Author's conversation with Elaine Bromwich (15 January 1979)
17 – Author's conversation with Alexander Weatherson (13 November 1978)
18 – Colin MacInnes, 'A Kind of Religion', *Spectator*, February 1963
19 – Colin MacInnes, *Mr Love and Justice* (MacGibbon & Kee, 1960)
20 – Colin MacInnes, 'Thoughts' book (University of Rochester)
21 – Colin MacInnes, *England, Half English*
22 – Colin MacInnes, 'Welcome, Beauty Walk', *Encounter*, October 1960 (reprinted in *England, Half English*)
23 – *Ibid*
24 – *Ibid*
25 – Colin MacInnes, *City of Spades* (MacGibbon & Kee, 1957)
26 – Colin MacInnes, 'Welcome, Beauty Walk'
27 – *Ibid*
28 – *Ibid*
29 – *Ibid*
30 – *Ibid*
31 – *Ibid*

32 – Letter from Colin MacInnes to Francis Wyndham, 14 September 1960
33 – Elspeth Huxley, 'What Future for Africa?' *Encounter*, June 1961
34 – *Ibid*
35 – Letter from Colin MacInnes to Elspeth Huxley, 19 May 1961
36 – Letter from Elspeth Huxley to Colin MacInnes, 27 May 1961
37 – Letter from Colin MacInnes to Elspeth Huxley, 29 May 1961
38 – Letter from Elspeth Huxley to Colin MacInnes, 27 May 1961
39 – Ditto, 6 June 1961
40 – Author's conversation with Richard Wollheim (25 January 1981)
41 – Letter from Elspeth Huxley to Colin MacInnes, 6 June 1961
42 – Letter from Colin MacInnes, to Elaine Bromwich, 16 December 1965
43 – Margot Strickland, *Angela Thirkell* (Duckworth, 1977)
44 – Author's conversation with Lance Thirkell (6 November 1978)
45 – Letter from Colin MacInnes to Lance Thirkell, 15 February 1961
46 – Author's conversation with Geoffrey Lawson (28 May 1979)
47 – Ditto and author's conversation with Kenny Graham (22 May 1979)
48 – Author's conversation with Joan McInnes
49 – Author's conversation with Iain Campbell (8 February 1979)
50 – Letter from Colin MacInnes to Lance Thirkell, 27 July 1961
51 – Letter from Colin MacInnes to Hudson Smith, undated (1961)
52 – Letter from Colin MacInnes to Eric Dadson, 11 May 1961
53 – Colin MacInnes, 'Mum's the Word', *New Statesman*, 7 June 1963
54 – *Ibid*
55 – Letter from Colin MacInnes to Kenny Graham, 10 May 1961
56 – Letter from Reg Davis-Poynter to Colin MacInnes, 12 May 1961
57 – Letter from Colin MacInnes to Reg Davis-Poynter, 26 May 1961
58 – Letter from his accountant to Colin MacInnes, 5 December 1960
59 – Letter from Colin MacInnes to Eric Dadson, 5 June 1961
60 – Letter from Eric Dadson to Colin MacInnes, 5 June 1961
61 – Letter from Colin MacInnes to Eric Dadson, 11 June 1961
62 – Author's conversation with Kenny Graham
63 – *Ibid*
64 – V.S. Naipaul, review of *England, Half English*, *Listener*, 7 September 1961
65 – Colin MacInnes, review of *A House for Mr Biswas*, *Observer*, 1 October 1961
66 – Letter from Colin MacInnes to Francis Wyndham, 19 September 1961
67 – Letter from Robert Graves to Colin MacInnes, 29 June 1957
68 – Ditto, undated
69 – Letter from Colin MacInnes to Kenny Graham, 3 November 1961
70 – Author's conversation with Richard Wollheim
71 – Author's conversation with Charles Causley (29 December 1978)
72 – Author's conversation with David Sylvester (24 January 1979)
73 – Max Beerbohm, *And Even Now* (Heinemann, 1920)
74 – Author's conversation with Bryan Robertson (26 July 1978)

75 – Max Beerbohm, *op. cit*.
76 – Private tape-recording by Tony Parker sent to the author, 25 November 1978
77 – Colin MacInnes's interview with Norman Mailer, 'A Cruel Soil for Talent', BBC Third Programme, 18 November 1961
78 – Norman Mailer, 'The White Negro' (1957), reprinted in *Advertisements for Myself* (André Deutsch, 1961)
79 – Author's conversation with Philip French (18 November 1979)
80 – Norman Mailer, *op. cit*.
81 – Colin MacInnes, 'A Kind of Religion'
82 – *Ibid*
83 – Letter from Colin MacInnes to Roy Kerridge, 13 July 1966

10 Anarchist Sympathiser, pp 167–186

1 – Colin MacInnes, 'In the World as it is Today', *Freedom*, 2 December 1961
2 – Colin MacInnes, 'The Anarchists', *Queen*, 15 and 22 May 1962
3 – Nicolas Walter, 'Colin MacInnes', *Freedom*, 15 May 1976
4 – Author's conversation with Bernard Kops (16 October 1979)
5 – Colin MacInnes, 'Experts on Trial', *Encounter*, March 1962
6 – Colin MacInnes, 'Out of the Way', *New Society*, 8 November 1962
7 – *Ibid*
8 – Author's conversation with Kenny Graham (22 May 1979)
9 – Author's conversation with Paul Potts (25 May 1979)
10 – Colin MacInnes, 'Pop Heroes', *New Left Review*, 1960
11 – Colin MacInnes, 'Socialist Impresarios', *New Statesman*, 15 June 1962
12 – George Melly, 'Death of a Rebel', *Observer*, 25 April 1976
13 – Colin MacInnes, *op. cit*.
14 – Colin MacInnes, 'The Writings of Brendan Behan', *London Magazine*, August 1962
15 – Colin MacInnes, review of *Tropic of Cancer, Spectator*, 5 April 1963
16 – Author's conversation with Norman Mailer (November 1979)
17 – Author's conversation with James Campbell (8 April 1979)
18 – *Ibid*
19 – Colin MacInnes, 'Out of the Way', *New Society*, 6 December 1962
20 – *Ibid*
21 – *Ibid*
22 – Author's conversation with Monty Haltrecht (26 October 1978)
23 – *Ibid*
24 – Ray Gosling, Foreword to *Out of the Way* (Martin, Brian & O'Keeffe, 1979)
25 – Author's conversation with Ray Gosling (25 September 1978)
26 – Ray Gosling, *op. cit*.
27 – Colin MacInnes, *England, Half English* (MacGibbon & Kee, 1961)
28 – Colin MacInnes, 'The Parthenon Marbles', *New Society*, 28 February 1963
29 – *Ibid*

30 – Author's conversation with Monty Haltrecht
31 – Ray Gosling, *op. cit.*
32 – Colin MacInnes, MS of *Children of Eve* (University of Rochester)
33 – Colin MacInnes, 'The New British', *Spectator*, June 1963 (reprinted in *Out of the Way*)
34 – *Ibid*
35 – *Ibid*
36 – Author's conversation with Richard Keen
37 – Colin MacInnes, 'Out of the Way', 13 December 1962
38 – Colin MacInnes, 'Second Test, fifth day', *New Society*, 4 July 1963 (reprinted in *Out of the Way*)
39 – *Ibid*
40 – *Ibid*
41 – *Ibid*
42 – C.L.R. James, *Beyond a Boundary* (Stanley Paul, 1963)
43 – Colin MacInnes, 'Dark Angel', *Encounter*, August 1963 (reprinted in *Out of the Way*)
44 – *Ibid*
45 – *Ibid*
46 – Author's conversation with Philip French (18 November 1979). ('An Unrewarded Virtue' Britain 1945–51, *Queen*, 25 September 1963)
47 – Colin MacInnes, 'Letter from London', *Partisan Review*, September 1963
48 – Wayland Young, *The Profumo Affair* (Penguin, 1963)
49 – V. Bogdanor and R. Skidelsky (eds), *The Age of Affluence 1951–1964* (Macmillan, 1970)
50 – Colin MacInnes, 'Sterilities (and Virilities)', *Encounter, November* 1963 (reprinted in *Out of the Way*)
51 – Colin MacInnes, *Australia and New Zealand* (Time-Life Books, 1964)
52 – Letter to the author from Ross Campbell, 8 June 1979
53 – Colin MacInnes, 'The Disinherited', dated December 1965
54 – Colin MacInnes, 'A Peculiar Neighbourhood', *New Society*, 12 November 1964
55 – *Ibid*
56 – Colin MacInnes, 'Life with Time', *New Statesman*, 24 December 1965
57 – *Ibid*
58 – Frank Norman, 'Colin MacInnes, 1914–1976', *New Statesman*, 30 April 1976
59 – Ray Gosling, *op. cit.*

11   Michael X's Pale Pink Friend, pp 187–201

1 – Colin MacInnes, 'Las Vegas – London', *New Society*, 17 March 1966
2 – Author's conversation with Frank Norman (10 November 1978)
3 – Colin MacInnes, *All Day Saturday* (MacGibbon & Kee, 1966)
4 – *Ibid*
5 – Colin MacInnes and the Editors of *Life, Australia and New Zealand* (Time-Life Books, 1964)

References

6 – Colin MacInnes, *All Day Saturday*

7 – D.A.N. Jones, review of *All Day Saturday*, *New Statesman*, 19 August 1966

8 – Graham McInnes, *Humping My Bluey* (Hamish Hamilton, 1966)

9 – Quoted in Rex and Tomlinson, *Colonial Immigrants in a British City* (Routledge & Kegan Paul, 1979)

10 – Derek Humphry and David Tindall, *False Messiah* (Hart-Davis, MacGibbon, 1977)

11 – Colin MacInnes, 'Michael and the Cloak of Colour', *Encounter*, December 1965

12 – Colin MacInnes, 'Through a Glass, Darkly', *New Statesman*, 18 August 1967

13 – Author's conversation with Horace Ové (26 November 1978)

14 – Humphry and Tindall, *op. cit.*

15 – *Ibid*

16 – Author's conversations with Frank Critchlow (6/9 December 1978, 7 April 1979)

17 – *Ibid*

18 – *Ibid*

19 – *Ibid*

20 – *Ibid*

21 – Author's conversation with Horace Ové

22 – Author's conversation with Frank Critchlow

23 – Colin MacInnes, 'Mr Chairman!' *New Society*, 10 November 1966

24 – Colin MacInnes, 'Through a Glass, Darkly'

25 – Colin MacInnes, 'Michael and the Cloak of Colour'

26 – Author's conversation with Frank Critchlow

27 – Author's conversation with Horace Ové

28 – Humphry and Tindall, *op. cit.*; and V.S. Naipaul, 'The Killings in Trinidad' (reprinted in *The Return of Eva Perón*, André Deutsch, 1980)

29 – Letter to the author from Roy Kerridge, 7 March 1979

30 – Colin MacInnes, 'Weekend in White', *New Society*, 17 November 1966

31 – Colin MacInnes, 'Wizard', *New Society*, 26 January 1967

32 – Author's conversation with Richard Wollheim (25 January 1979)

33 – Author's conversation with Melvin Lasky (4 June 1979)

34 – Author's conversation with Frank Kermode (13 May 1980)

35 – Author's conversation with Melvin Lasky

36 – Letter from Colin MacInnes to the Editor of *The Times*, 9 May 1967

12 Travels Abroad and Trials at Home, pp 202–221

1 – Colin MacInnes, *'No Novel Reader'* (Martin, Brian & O'Keeffe, 1975)

2 – Robert Kiely, review of *Westward to Laughter*, *New York Times*, 18 January 1970

3 – Colin MacInnes, letter to *The Times*, 1 February 1973

4 – Colin MacInnes, *Three Years to Play* (MacGibbon & Kee, 1970)

5 – Author's conversation with Iain Campbell (8 February 1979)

6 – *Ibid*
7 – *Ibid*
8 – *Ibid*
9 – *Ibid*
10 – *Ibid*
11 – Letter from Second Secretary, Peruvian Embassy to Colin MacInnes, 28 November 1969
12 – Author's conversation with Joan McInnes (5 December 1978)
13 – Letter from Colin MacInnes to British Council, 16 June 1970
14 – Letter from Colin MacInnes to R. Hudson and Margaret Smith, 24 January 1971
15 – Colin MacInnes, 'The Breathless Railroad', *Sunday Times* Magazine, 20 December 1970
16 – *Ibid*
17 – Letter from Colin MacInnes to Charles Causley, 21 January 1971
18 – Letter from Colin MacInnes to the Hudson Smiths.
19 – Letter from Colin MacInnes to Charles Causley
20 – *Ibid*
21 – Colin MacInnes, 'Exile's Delight', *Encounter*, June 1971
22 – Author's conversation with Bryan Robertson (26 July 1978)
23 – Colin MacInnes, *op. cit.*
24 – Author's conversation with Edge Semmens (10 October 1979)
25 – *Ibid*
26 – *Ibid*
27 – *Ibid*
28 – *Ibid*
29 – *Ibid*
30 – *Ibid*
31 – Letter from Colin MacInnes to British Council, 20 May 1971
32 – *Ibid*
33 – Author's conversation with Edge Semmens
34 – Letter from Colin MacInnes to British Council, 19 June 1971
35 – Letter from British Council to Colin MacInnes, 24 June 1971
36 – Author's conversation with Edge Semmens
37 – Francis Wheen, *The Sixties* (Century, 1982) and J.A. Sutherland, *Offensive Literature* (Junction Books, 1982)
38 – *Ibid*
39 – Colin MacInnes, 'Trial of a Trial', *New Society*, 5 August 1971
40 – *Ibid*
41 – *Ibid*
42 – *Ibid*
43 – *Ibid*
44 – Colin MacInnes, Letter to *The Times*, 25 August 1970
45 – *Ibid*
46 – Author's conversations with Frank Critchlow (6/9 December 1978, 7 April 1979)
47 – Letter from Colin MacInnes, to Sheila Sage, 12 April 1972
48 – Colin MacInnes, 'Calypso Lament', *New Society*, 6 April 1972

49 – Colin MacInnes, 'Hustler', *New Society*, 19 August 1971
50 – *Ibid*
51 – *Ibid*
52 – Author's conversation with a 'Mr Deedes' (25 January 1979)
53 – Author's conversation with another 'Mr Deedes' (31 May 1979)
54 – Colin MacInnes, *op. cit.*
55 – *Ibid*
56 – Author's conversation with Frank Critchlow
57 – Author's conversation with Sheila Sage (9 December 1978)
58 – Author's conversation with Horace Ové (26 November 1978)
59 – *Ibid*
60 – Author's conversation with Kenny Graham (22 May 1979)
61– 64 – Author's conversation with Horace Ové
65 – Author's conversation with Calvin Hernton (25 June 1979)
66 – *Ibid*
67 – *Ibid*

13 Cancer Ward, pp 223–236

1 – Letter from Colin MacInnes to R. Hudson Smith, 22 February 1972
2 – *Ibid*, 17 May 1972
3 – *Ibid*
4 – Colin MacInnes, *'No Novel Reader'* (Martin, Brian & O'Keeffe, 1975)
5 – Colin MacInnes, 'Fallen Angel', *Gay News* No. 95, 20 May–2 June 1976 (reprinted in *Out of the Way: Later Essays*, Martin Brian & O'Keeffe, 1979)
6 – Colin MacInnes, *Loving Them Both* (Martin, Brian & O'Keeffe, 1973)
7 – Author's conversation with Paul Potts (25 May 1979)
8 – *Ibid*
9 – Author's conversation with Francis Wyndham (12 October 1978)
10 – Colin MacInnes, *op. cit.*
11 – Author's conversation with Joan McInnes, (5 December 1978)
12 – Colin MacInnes, *op. cit.*
13 – Author's conversation with Peggy and Marcus Little (10 September 1978)
14 – Colin MacInnes, 'Growing Old Gayfully', *Gay News* No. 82, 1975
15 – J.A. Sutherland, *Offensive Literature* (Junction Books, 1982)
16 – Colin MacInnes, *op. cit.*
17 – *Ibid*
18 – Author's conversation with Lance and Kate Thirkell (6 November 1978)
19 – *Ibid*
20 – Author's conversation with Serena Thirkell (17 November 1978)
21 – Author's conversation with Peggy Little
22 – Colin MacInnes, 'Urban Village', *New Society*, 8 June 1972
23 – Colin MacInnes, *Out of the Garden* (Hart-Davis, MacGibbon, 1974)
24 – Author's conversation with Peggy and Marcus Little
25 – *Ibid*

26 – Colin MacInnes, 'Learning from Gays', *Gay News* No. 72, 1975
27 – Memo from Colin MacInnes to Denis Lemon, 5 August 1975
28 – Author's conversation with Victor Musgrave (30 November 1978)
29 – Letter to the author from Robert Waller, 6 November 1978
30 – Author's conversation with Bryan Robertson (26 July 1978)
31 – Colin MacInnes, 'Cancer Ward', *New Society*, 29 April 1976 (reprinted in *Out of the Way*)
32 – *Ibid*
33 – Author's conversation with Bryan Robertson
34 – Colin MacInnes, *op. cit.*
35 – *Ibid*
36 – Author's conversation with Bryan Robertson
37 – Colin MacInnes, *op. cit.*
38 – Author's conversation with Fiona Green (19 October 1978)
39 – *Ibid*
40 – *Ibid*
41 – Colin MacInnes, medical notebooks (University of Rochester archive)
42 – Colin MacInnes, 'Cancer Ward'
43 – *Ibid*
44 – *Ibid*
45 – *Ibid*
46 – *Ibid*
47 – *Ibid*
48 – Author's conversation with Bryan Robertson
49 – *Ibid*
50 – Letter from Tom Rees to Colin MacInnes, 5 April 1976
51 – Letter from Irving Kristol to Colin MacInnes, 13 April 1976
52 – Colin MacInnes, 'Discovering Cathay', *The Times Educational Supplement*, 2 January 1976
53 – Letter from Frank Norman to Francis Wyndham, 2 May 1976
54 – Author's conversation with Fiona Green
55 – Author's conversation with Lance Thirkell
56 – Author's conversation with Mel Lasky (4 June 1979)
57 – Author's conversation with Eddie Linden (14 November 1978)
58 – William Gerhardie, *God's Fifth Column*, edited by Michael Holroyd and Robert Skidelsky (Hodder & Stoughton, 1980)
59 – Author's conversation with Calvin Hernton (25 June 1979)
60 – Author's conversation with Lance Thirkell

Index

Index

MORE ABOUT PENGUINS, PELICANS, PEREGRINES AND PUFFINS

For further information about books available from Penguins please write to Dept EP, Penguin Books Ltd, Harmondsworth, Middlesex UB7 0DA.

In the U.S.A.: For a complete list of books available from Penguins in the United States write to Dept DG, Penguin Books, 299 Murray Hill Parkway, East Rutherford, New Jersey 07073.

In Canada: For a complete list of books available from Penguins in Canada write to Penguin Books Canada Ltd, 2801 John Street, Markham, Ontario L3R 1B4.

In Australia: For a complete list of books available from Penguins in Australia write to the Marketing Department, Penguin Books Australia Ltd, P.O. Box 257, Ringwood, Victoria 3134.

In New Zealand: For a complete list of books available from Penguins in New Zealand write to the Marketing Department, Penguin Books (N.Z.) Ltd, Private Bag, Takapuna, Auckland 9.

In India: For a complete list of books available from Penguins in India write to Penguin Overseas Ltd, 706 Eros Apartments, 56 Nehru Place, New Delhi 110019.